Funeral Service Law
In the United States

A Guide for Funeral Service Students

Larry J. Cleveland

Funeral Service Instructor and Educator
Licensed Funeral Director

~ Second Edition ~

Second edition, June 2022

ISBN 978-1-736-6101-1-4

Published by Hudson Valley Professional Services
Queensbury, New York 12804
www.HudsonPros.com

Printed by Lightning Press
Totowa, New Jersey 07512
www.Lightning-Press.com

Disclaimer - The author of this book is not licensed to practice law and is not an attorney. The material provided herein has been developed from several sources, including: state and federal statutory, administrative, and case law; government agency advisory opinions, bulletins, and administrative orders; knowledgeable instructors and practitioners in the funeral service; and information available to the general public in various communication mediums. The content of this book is believed to be accurate and true; however, practitioners should always consult an attorney for legal advice on any question of law in funeral service matters.

Front cover photo - *The Apex Building*, Headquarters of the Federal Trade Commission in Washington, DC. The building was completed in 1938 at a cost of $125 million. Photo from the Carol M. Highsmith collection; November 6, 2005. Retrieved online at Wikimedia Commons, October 2019.

Back cover photo - *Man Controlling Trade*. One of two monumental equestrian statues created by Michael Lantz for the Federal Trade Commission Building in Washington, DC. Photo by Einar E. Kvaran, circa 1985. Retrieved online at Wikimedia Commons, October 2019.

Table of Contents

    Purpose and intent
    The Funeral Rule
    Definitions, notes, forms, and documents
    Use of the terms: requirement and regulation
    Sources
    Generic nature of state material
    Disclaimer

    Overview
    Chapter definitions
    Introduction
    Constitutions
    Legislation (statutory law)
    Case law
    Common law
    Administrative law
    Bodies of law of special interest

PART 2: LIABILITY EXPOSURES

    Overview
    Chapter definitions
    The dead human body
    Property and possession rights in a dead human body
    Final disposition
    Right to control final disposition
        1: Surviving spouse
        2: Next-of-kin
        3: Decedent's guardian
        4: Volunteer
    Survivor disputes
    Liability for funeral expenses
        1: Contracts
        2: Decedent estates
        3: Volunteer
        4: Public authorities

PART 3: FUNERAL ESTABLISHMENTS

PART 4: PREFUNDED PRENEEDS

Other funding strategies
Portability of preneed contracts

Overview
Chapter definitions
Regulatory compliance
Preneed arrangement conferences
The FTC and preneeds
Changes to prefunded preneeds
Other legal considerations
Supplemental Security Income (SSI) and Medicaid programs

PART 5: METHODS OF FINAL DISPOSITION

Overview
Chapter definitions
Final disposition by interment (burial)
Final disposition by entombment
Final disposition by natural (green) burial
Final disposition by burial at sea

Overview
Chapter definitions
Final disposition by cremation
Final disposition by body donation
Final disposition by alkaline hydrolysis
Final disposition by natural organic reduction (NOR)

PART 6: ESTATES AND PROBATE PROCEEDINGS

Overview
Chapter definitions
Last will and testament
Special wills
Revocation and amendments
Distribution issues
Intestacy

Overview
Chapter definitions
Probate court
Appointment of personal representative

Duties of personal representative
Payment of claims
Estate asset distribution
Other estate and health care documents

PART 7: STATE LAWS, RULES, AND REGULATIONS

Overview
Chapter definitions
Use of titles: funeral director, undertaker, and mortician
Funeral director qualifications
Reciprocity and dual licensure
Duties and responsibilities
Regulatory compliance related to vital statistics
Regulatory compliance for transportation of human remains

Overview
Chapter definitions
State oversight
Regulatory agency procedures
Criminal and civil actions

PART 8: FEDERAL TRADE COMMISSION FUNERAL RULE

Overview
Chapter definitions
Mission and goals of the FTC
History of the FTC and the Funeral Rule
Consumer rights
Who must comply?
Preneeds and the Funeral Rule
Enforcement

Overview
Chapter definitions
Requirement for a general price list
Providing a general price list
Information required on a general price list
The 16 items and six disclosures

Overview
Chapter definitions

Other price lists
The casket price list
Casket price list requirements
The outer burial container price list
Outer burial container price list requirements
Statement of funeral goods and services selected
Required disclosures on a statement
    1: Legal requirements disclosure
    2: Embalming disclosure
    3: Cash advance items disclosure

Overview
Chapter definitions
Approval for embalming
    1: Law requires embalming
    2: Prior approval required
    3: No one available to give approval
Telephone price disclosures
Alternative price lists for special groups
Misrepresentations prohibited by the Funeral Rule
    1: Embalming requirements
    2: Casket for direct cremation
    3: Legal and cemetery requirements
    4: Outer burial container
    5: Preservative and protective value claims
    6: Cash advance items
What consumers cannot be required to purchase
Third-party merchandise
Recordkeeping
Comprehension of disclosures
State exemption provisions

PART 9: OTHER FEDERAL LAWS

Overview
Fair Labor Standards Act
Civil Rights Act - Title VII
Family and Medical Leave Act
Age Discrimination in Employment Act
Americans with Disabilities Act

Overview
FTC Credit Practices Rule
Federal Truth-in-Lending Act

Gramm-Leach-Bliley Act
Fair Credit Reporting Act
Fair Debt Collection Practices Act
Magnuson-Moss Warranty Act
FTC Cooling-off Rule

PART 10: FORMS AND GUIDES

<u>Forms</u>

<u>Guides</u>

Preface

Funeral service academic institutions across the United States provide students with the skills and knowledge they need to enter the workforce and successfully pursue their chosen profession. A significant portion of the material they study will deal with issues of regulatory compliance, as virtually every funeral event they encounter – from embalming human remains to meeting with families – will involve some level of compliance with federal, state, and/or local laws.

Regulatory compliance questions on the two-part National Board Examination (NBE) are developed from *specific* federal funeral service laws and *generic* state funeral service laws. There are no questions on the exam specific to a particular state or local government. Therefore, this book reviews in detail the federal statutes and their relationship to the funeral service industry, while also offering an overview and broad discussion of the more frequent and common requirements found across the nation in state and local statutes.

The content of this book has been identified by the American Board of Funeral Service Education (ABFSE) as being important in educating students about funeral service law, and this same ABFSE material is the foundation for the development of regulatory compliance questions on the NBE. This textbook provides both instructors and students with an up-to-date source of material designed to complement and enhance ABFSE educational mandates related to funeral service law in general and the Federal Trade Commission Funeral Rule in particular. The material is current, accurate, and essential to not only preparing future funeral directors for taking the NBE but for understanding regulatory compliance fundamentals they will be expected to follow throughout their careers as professional funeral service practitioners.

Larry Cleveland

Other Hudson Valley Professional Services Publications

Funeral Service Marketing & Merchandise 1E1R
ISBN: 978-0-998-2571-2-9
Cleveland - January 2021

Funeral Directing in the United States 2E
ISBN: 978-1-736-6101-2-1
Cleveland - June 2022

Funeral Service Rites and Customs 2E
ISBN: 978-1-736-6101-3-8
Cleveland - June 2022

Cremation in the United States 1E
ISBN: 978-0-998-2571-7-4
Cleveland - June 2021

Funeral Service Business Law 1E
ISBN: 978-1-736-6101-0-7
Mevec/Cleveland - June 2022

Funeral Service Law in New York 2E
ISBN: 978-0-998-2571-9-8
Cleveland - January 2022

Chapter 1: Book Introduction

Purpose and Intent
Purpose - The purpose of this textbook is to assist and promote funeral service students as they pursue a career in the funeral service industry, as well as to provide support to the college-level faculty and staff members serving as student mentors and classroom instructors. It has been developed by integrating the educational material identified by the American Board of Funeral Service Education (ABFSE) as being of importance to the subject of funeral service law.

Intent - The intent of this textbook is to serve as a shared, common link between student and instructor; a link designed to serve both groups by presenting pertinent and relevant material in a consistent and organized style conducive to the learning environment. Integrating the information in this textbook with the skills and knowledge of the educator in the classroom is the formula to effectively preparing for and passing the two-part National Board Examination (NBE) at the conclusion of collegiate academic studies.

The Funeral Rule
Title 16 of the Code of Federal Regulations includes a section titled, *Federal Regulation Rule for Funeral Industry Practices*. It is a regulatory statute enforced by the U.S. Federal Trade Commission and commonly referred to as the FTC Funeral Rule, or just Funeral Rule, by both the funeral service industry and government agencies. The FTC periodically issues a guidebook titled, *Complying with the Funeral Rule*. This guide is specifically written for funeral directors and is referenced in this book as 'FTC Guide.' The most recent edition of this guide was released in April 2019 and may be found on the FTC website.

Definitions, Notes, Forms and Documents
Definitions - Where convenient for the reader, definitions are provided in the chapters and thereafter highlighted within the text with bold print. These definitions may also be repeated in subsequent chapters to provide prompt, easy access when of importance to the material being presented. All of the terms and definitions are compiled in a comprehensive glossary located in the back of this book, with each term cross-referenced to the chapters in which they appear.

The terms, with the exceptions noted below, are the definitions provided for use in funeral service law courses and represent a potential source for test questions on the NBE.

Exception #1 - Terms in the FTC guidelines titled, *Complying with the Funeral Rule*, are identified in brackets following the definition, e.g., [FTC, pg. 21].

Exception #2 - Terms in the U.S. Code of Federal Regulations (CFR) are identified in brackets following the definition, e.g., [16 CFR §453.1(b)].

Exception #3 - ABFSE terms in other textbooks are identified in brackets following the definition, e.g., [FD term] is a term in the textbook titled, *Funeral Directing in the United States*.

Exception #4 - Other terms of importance have been defined by the author and are identified in brackets, e.g., [by Author].

Notes - Notes are used within the text of chapters to draw attention to material of specific interest or importance, or to provide additional clarification to a particular topic or subject of discussion. They are styled in the narrative as Note: with the additional information following immediately after the colon.

Use of the Terms: Requirement and Regulation

There are numerous federal and state laws, rules, regulations, and codes found in funeral service statutes and legislation; however, the different terms are of no major importance when viewed from the perspective of regulatory compliance. In the interest of maintaining simplicity, the terms *requirement* and *regulation* are generally used to identify laws, rules, regulations, and codes at all levels of all governments. When important to bring context to a specific topic, a note is provided within the chapter text to further identify a legal source.

Sources

Sources of information are provided throughout the book and may be found in captions, annotations, or attribution in the narrative. Each source includes the information or reference needed to quickly find it in the Sources Consulted section, where additional details and URLs (when available) are provided.

Generic Nature of State Material

Students should bear in mind the regulatory compliance questions on the two-part National Board Exam are developed from *specific* federal funeral service laws and *generic* state funeral service laws. There are no questions on the exam specific to a particular state or local government. Therefore, this book reviews in detail the federal statutes and their relationship to the funeral service industry, while also offering an overview and broad discussion of the more frequent and common requirements found across the nation in state and local statutes.

Unless otherwise noted, regulations and laws in this book are not specific to any particular state. Funeral service professionals are cautioned to always research the law in the states where they practice, and consult with an attorney for legal advice on funeral service matters.

Disclaimer

The author of this book is not licensed to practice law and is not an attorney. The material provided herein has been developed from several sources, including: federal and state statutory, administrative, and case law; government agency advisory opinions, bulletins, and administrative orders; knowledgeable instructors and practitioners in the funeral service industry; and information available to the general public in various communication mediums. The content of this book is believed to be accurate and true; however, practitioners should always consult an attorney for legal advice on any question of law in funeral service matters.

Chapter 2: Sources of Funeral Service Law

Overview
The information in this book is by design presented in a simplified format, free of complex narratives, stifling legal language, and administrative minutia. However, it is important for funeral service students and professionals alike to have a basic understanding of how laws, rules, and regulations are created and structured. Therefore, this chapter reviews sources of funeral service law and provides basic guidance on the structure and dynamics of funeral service law in the U.S.

Chapter Definitions
Administrative agency - a governmental body created by legislation empowered to make and enforce rules and regulations.

Administrative law - the rules and regulations created by Federal and State administrative agencies (e.g., OSHA, FTC, state board rules and regulations).

Case law - appellate court decisions based on custom and usage and prior decisions.

Constitution - the fundamental law that establishes the government; limits what government can and cannot do; and states the underlying principles to which the government will conform.

Contract - a legally enforceable agreement.

Funeral service law (*mortuary law/mortuary jurisprudence*) - that branch of law which relates to matters concerned with the disposal of the dead and regulation of funeral directors, embalmers, and funeral establishments.

Law - those rules of conduct commanding what is right and prohibiting what is wrong.

Ordinance - a law passed by a local municipal governing body (e.g., zoning, building, safety, etc.).

Police power - the inherent power of a government to make reasonable laws to protect the safety, health, morals, and general welfare of its citizens.

Rules and regulations - laws created by an administrative agency within its jurisdiction.

Stare decisis - a policy of courts to stand by a decision and apply it to future cases where the facts are substantially the same.

Statute - a law enacted by a legislative body.

Introduction
Laws are those rules of conduct commanding what is right and prohibiting what is wrong. **Funeral service law** is that branch of law which relates to matters concerned with the disposal of the dead and the regulation of funeral directors, embalmers, and funeral establishments.

Sources of funeral service law include:

Federal and state constitutions	Federal and state statutory laws	Municipal ordinances and local laws
Administrative law	Case law	Common law

Constitutions

A **constitution** is the fundamental law that establishes the government; limits what government can and cannot do; and states the underlying principles to which the government will conform.

Federal - The powers contained in the Constitution of the United States and granted to the three branches of federal government are the foundation upon which individual federal codes, laws, rules, and regulations are developed and promulgated. The U.S. Constitution also provides checks and balances by and between the three branches by ensuring each has a defining role to play in writing, further defining, enforcing and, thereafter, interpreting these laws. The laws found in the U.S. Constitution are superior to all other sources in both federal and state regulations and may only be superseded by amendment to the constitution, a process that would require the collective agreement of the government branches, as well as the express approval of the people.

State - Similar to the federal government, individual states have their own constitutions that provide the basis for *state* laws, rules, and regulations. Laws identified in a state constitution are superior to all other sources within the same state and may only be superseded by the Constitution of the United States.

Legislation (Statutory Law)

A **statute** is defined as a law enacted by a legislative body.

Constitution → Legislative Branch → Legislature → Writes Statutory Law

Federal - The legislative body in the United States is the U.S. Congress, as represented by two houses of government: the U.S. Senate and U.S. House of Representatives. Members of congress are elected by the citizens of their home state and sent to the government seat in Washington, D.C. to represent them. While in office, they carry out the duties afforded to them under the U.S. Constitution, including writing federal statutory laws, initially known as bills.

Bills may undergo numerous iterations and changes as the two houses of Congress attempt to reconcile differences of opinion and strive to include provisions that best serve their constituents needs. Bills passed by Congress are sent to the President of the United States (a part of the executive branch of government) for approval or veto. If approved, they become statutory law, known as a United States Code (USC); if vetoed, they may never become law, or may become law if Congress can muster the necessary number of votes to override the veto. This process is all part of the checks and balances provided under the U.S. Constitution to ensure no one branch of government becomes excessively powerful.

A *statutory law*, written and passed by Congress, grants the Federal Trade Commission the authority to oversee government efforts to prevent unfair methods of competition. As will be explored in the administrative law section, this legislation was the genesis from which the Funeral Rule was born; this being the single, most important federal legislation to ever affect the funeral service industry in the United States.

State - State governments derive their authority to write laws based on the 10th Amendment to the U.S. Constitution. This amendment grants state governments **police power**, defined as the inherent power of a government to make reasonable laws to protect the safety, health, morals, and general welfare of its citizens. State statutes may regulate such areas as the licensing of professionals; defining the parameters for owning and operating a business; setting minimum workplace standards for employees; establishing business practices to provide for consumer protections; and creating minimum standards that govern the health care community.

Using the police power granted to them by the U.S. Constitution, the legislatures of the 50 states write and pass statutory law in a fashion similar to the federal government, although the names of the legislative bodies and the procedures they follow vary from one state to the next. State laws that affect funeral directing activities, such as contract laws and probate laws, are in addition to those existing in federal statutes, but are of equal importance to the funeral service professional.

Note: A state legislative body is called a legislature or state legislature in 27 states; a general assembly in 19 states; a general court in Massachusetts and New Hampshire; and a legislative assembly in North Dakota and Oregon.

Municipal - Government municipalities – such as counties, cities, towns, and villages – may write laws specific to their communities. This is usually accomplished through a municipal board, council, or legislature. The laws they pass may be known as **ordinances**, defined as laws passed by a local municipal governing body (e.g., zoning, building, safety, etc.). They may also be known as local laws in certain states. For example, a town government may pass a local zoning *ordinance* that lists the building and construction zones where a funeral establishment may be erected and operated; while a county government may pass a *local law* to regulate the duties and activities of a county coroner or medical examiner.

Case Law
Understanding legislative branches of government write statutory law, the focus now shifts to the role played by the judicial branches of government, the branches tasked with *interpreting* those laws. Appellate courts in the judicial branch are responsible for hearing appeals from cases that have already been heard in trial (lower) courts. The decisions they render become **case law**, defined as appellate court decisions based on custom and usage and prior decisions.

Decision making - When questions of law come before a court for interpretation, the court gathers information from a wide range of sources and applies legal principles to assist them in the decision-making process, including:

➢ written briefs (narratives and summaries) from the parties involved;

➢ sworn testimony of relevance to the issue under consideration;

➢ legislative records, which often contain insight on the intent and purpose of lawmakers that prompted them to write the relevant statutory law under review;

➢ administrative agency records, which often contain background information on the reasoning and motive behind any rules and regulations under review;

➢ prior rulings and decisions of a higher court on similar matters that serve as an example to resolve future similar cases (known as case precedents);

➢ adhering to the principle of **stare decisis**, which provides for a court to stand by a decision and apply it to future cases where the facts are substantially the same; and

➢ existing common law rulings, decisions, and opinions.

Federal courts - The federal court system has three levels: district courts (the trial courts); circuit courts (the first level of appeal); and the Supreme Court of the United States, the highest level of appeal in the federal system. There are 94 district courts and 13 circuit courts throughout the country, with the U.S. Supreme Court located in Washington DC.

State courts - State court structures vary slightly but generally follow a pattern similar to the federal court system. They have one or more levels of trial courts, where cases originate; and one or more levels of appellate courts, where decisions rendered by the trial courts may be appealed by the parties involved.

With two exceptions, the highest court in each of the 50 states is named a Supreme Court. The two exceptions – New York and Maryland – name their highest a Court of Appeals. Whenever the highest court in a state renders a decision, the ruling becomes the superior authority (law of the land) on all of the inferior courts in the home state, subordinate only to any decisions and case laws of the United States Supreme Court on the same issue.

Common Law
Unlike a statutory law, with its origin easily traced to the legislative branch of a government, common law finds its roots in the judicial branch. The law is derived from the court review of custom, practice, judicial rulings and decisions, and established case law. Because of this close affiliation with the judicial branch, it is often called judge-made law. Common law may be encountered by funeral service practitioners, especially when making a determination on who has a priority right to control the final disposition of human remains.

As an example, a man wants to make funeral arrangements for his deceased wife. He and his wife were together for 46 years; have four children and nine grandchildren; owned a home together; and shared all of the common attributes of a husband and wife. The problem is they were never actually married in a civil proceeding, and the state statute says a 'spouse' has the priority right to control the funeral.

In similar cases, judges have consistently viewed this from the perspective of long-standing custom and practice, which would demonstrate – but for the lack of a civil wedding – the couple were in a common law marriage and equally entitled to the rights and privileges bestowed on a civilly married husband and wife. The wife would be considered – for all practical purposes – the spouse. There may be no statutory law that directly supports this position, but by exercising the power and authority of the court, common law has been established to support this position.

Note: Many states have proactively addressed the issue presented in the example above and changed statutory law to provide for a 'domestic partner' to have the next priority right to control a disposition following a 'spouse,' when no spouse exists.

Administrative Law

As provided earlier, all three government branches – legislative, executive, and judicial – play a role in writing, further defining, enforcing, and interpreting laws. Discussion to this point has focused on the power of the legislative branch to write statutory law and the judicial branch to interpret statutory law. The discussion now turns to contributions made by the executive branch.

The executive branch of government exercises authority through **administrative agencies** – such as commissions, departments, divisions, bureaus, and offices – by giving them rule-making power and authority. These administrative agencies *further define and reinforce* statutory laws by writing **rules and regulations** and issuing opinions, orders, and decisions. Administrative agencies are also charged with the enforcement of administrative laws, rules, and regulations, with all of these activities coming under the heading of **administrative law**.

Federal - In order to ensure statutory law meets the intended purpose of Congress, federal administrative agencies routinely undertake a wide range of activities to further define and reinforce statutory law. These actions, and the written rules and regulations they develop, create the federal administrative laws they are then charged with enforcing.

As an example, the *Prevention of Unfair Methods of Competition* statute, written by Congress and found in USC Title 15, gave the Federal Trade Commission (an administrative agency) the power and authority to issue a rule to regulate Funeral Industry Practices. This rule, now known informally as the Funeral Rule, may be found in the Code of Federal Rules (CFR).

In addition to formal rules, administrative agencies often issue guidelines, opinions, and decisions. In the case of the Federal Trade Commission and the Funeral Rule, the agency has issued several advisory opinions on the purchase, delivery, and use of so-called third-party caskets; caskets purchased from an entity other than the funeral establishment of record that is providing all of the other goods and services for a funeral. These opinions are only advisory in nature but often become a part of the rule when next revised. The issue of third-party caskets is addressed further in following chapters.

State - All 50 states have administrative agencies that create and actively enforce administrative laws, rules, and regulations to further define and reinforce state statutes. The title of the official compilations of state administrative laws vary state to state but are usually readily recognizable.

As examples:

Regulations of **Connecticut** State Agencies	Rules and Regulations of the State of **Georgia**	**New York** Codes, Rules and Regulations
Code of **Rhode Island** Rules	Code of **Colorado** Regulations	**Texas** Administrative Code

In most states, there is a bureau or office under the umbrella of a health department that oversees the funeral service industry in the state. These agencies write rules to provide for such things as the licensure of funeral service professionals; ownership and operation of funeral service establishments; and acceptable practices in funeral service – such as the removal, transfer, and transportation of human remains within the state.

Bodies of Law of Special Interest
Contract law - A **contract** is a legally enforceable agreement. The four elements to a contract are:

1. An offer, defined as a proposal to make a contract.

2. An acceptance, defined as an agreement to an offer resulting in a contract.

3. Consideration, defined as the bargained-for exchange in a contract.

4. Contractual capacity, defined as the legal ability to enter into a contract.

An offer and acceptance are often called mutual assent or a 'meeting of the minds' between the parties. Mutual assent – together with the valid consideration and contractual capacity elements – meet the requirements for a legally binding agreement.

If the terms of a contract are broken (breached), an aggrieved party may file a civil claim to seek restitution and compensation for any damages or loss. As a business entity, funeral establishments work with contracts on a continual basis, including contracts with families to provide funeral services and contracts with vendors to purchase funeral goods for resale. Information on the use of contracts for specific purposes are provided in several of the chapters that follow.

Probate law - Probate law deals with the administration and settlement of estates, and funeral directors are often called upon to consult with estate representatives to provide for the payment of funeral expenses on behalf of the estate of a deceased person. An in-depth discussion on probate law is provided in the chapter titled, *Estate Administration*.

Chapter 3: Human Remains

Overview
When a death occurs, there are a number of questions that need to be answered to facilitate the process of caring for the remains. Chief among them will be the need to know how to determine who has the legal right to control the final disposition, and the duties imposed on that person by the government that require them to provide a decent and proper disposition. The answers to these and other similar questions are the focus of this chapter.

Chapter Definitions
Actual custody - the physical possession of the dead human body or other property.

Brain death - total and irreversible cessation of brain function as indicated by a flat EEG reading.

Cadaver - a dead human body intended solely for scientific study and dissection.

Constructive custody - the situation whereby one party has a right to acquire actual custody and possession of the dead body although another party has actual physical possession.

Contract - a legally enforceable agreement.

Corpse (dead human body) - the body of a dead human being, deprived of life, but not yet entirely disintegrated.

Custodian - status associated with funeral service practitioner and funeral establishment who becomes legal protector of dead human body from time of removal until final disposition.

Death - the cessation of life; permanent cessations of all vital functions and signs.

Degree of kindred - relationship of decedent to blood relatives.

Estate - the property and debts of a deceased person, both real and/or personal.

Estrangement - the physical and/or emotional separation for a period of time showing the lack of affection, trust, and regard.

Funeral director (funeral service practitioner) - a person properly licensed, engaged in, or conducting, or holding himself/herself out as being engaged in preparing, other than by embalming, for the burial or disposition of dead human bodies.

Guardian - person appointed by the court to administer the affairs of another person who is incompetent by virtue of age or legal disability.

Kin - one's relatives collectively; referring to blood relationship (legally, the surviving spouse is not a kin).

Liability - responsibility for actions and/or other debts; the quality or state of being legally obligated or accountable.

Police power - the inherent power of a government to make reasonable laws to protect the safety, health, morals, and general welfare of its citizens.

Preferred claim - a claim which is accorded a priority, advantage, or privilege.

Prefunded funeral arrangements - funeral arrangements made in advance of need that include provisions for funding or prepayment.

Pre-planned funeral arrangements - funeral arrangements made in advance of need that do not include provisions for funding or prepayment.

Priority - the order in which claims will be paid when there are insufficient assets to pay all of the claims, or the order in which certain classes of people have the right to make decisions concerning the disposition of the dead body.

Quasi contract - a fictional contract created or implied by a court for a person who is unable to contract for himself (e.g., medical care, death); an obligation which law creates in the absence of agreement; is invoked by courts where there is unjust enrichment.

Quasi-property theory - the accepted theory of the legal status of a dead human body; rights associated with the body are as if it were property for the purpose of disposition only.

Secured claim - a debt which is supported by a pledge, mortgage or lien on assets belonging to the debtor.

Unsecured claim - a claim which is not supported by a pledge, mortgage, or lien on other assets.

Will - an instrument executed with required formality, by persons making disposition of their property to take effect upon their death.

The Dead Human Body

Death is defined as the cessation of life, including the permanent cessation of all vital functions and signs. Up until the mid-20th century, *clinical death* was largely the standard used to determine the death of a human being. If no signs of respirations or breathing could be heard or observed, and no signs of a pulse or circulation of blood could be detected, it was accepted that clinical death had taken place and life was extinct.

While this standard remains, it has been expanded to accommodate advancements in medical technology that provide medical practitioners with the ability to maintain circulatory and respiratory systems mechanically when not being supported naturally by the human body. This expansion gave rise to the **brain death** standard, which is the total and irreversible cessation of brain function and activity (life) as indicated by a flat EEG reading. Brain death is the accepted medical standard to conclude life has been lost and may not be restored, even when machines are still providing circulation and respiration within the body. Brain death plays an important role in the medical community if there is any uncertainty that life has ceased.

Note: An EEG (electroencephalogram) is a sophisticated instrument used to measure electrical activity in the brain.

Individual state laws, rules, and regulations address how the process of confirming death is to be handled in the funeral service industry. These statutes often require **funeral directors** to perform specific tests for signs of life and, in the absence of these signs, determine life is extinct. Such tests may include activities to verify pulsation has ceased in the arteries and, upon careful examination, heart and respiratory sounds are not heard.

Funeral directors must therefore familiarize themselves with the requirements in the states and municipalities where they practice, and exercise due diligence in making certain a human being is in fact deceased before removing, embalming, cremating, or burying the body.

A **corpse** is the body of a dead human being, deprived of life but not yet entirely disintegrated. The dust of a long dead body and the bones of a skeleton are not classified as a body. In addition, with the rapidly increasing number of cremation cases, several states have undertaken to define a clear distinction between human remains and cremated remains. The purpose is to ensure compliance with rules and regulations that are dependent on the type of remains and the activity taking place. As an example, some states require *human* remains be transported to a place for cremation by a licensed professional but have no such requirement for picking up and transporting *cremated* remains back to a funeral establishment or other location for disposition.

> **Mississippi Man Found Alive in Body Bag at Funeral Establishment**
>
> A Mississippi man has been found literally alive and kicking in a body bag at a funeral home after being declared dead.
>
> Workers at Porter and Sons Funeral Home were preparing to embalm ▉▉▉▉▉▉ on Thursday when he moved.
>
> A coroner pronounced the 78-year-old dead after finding no pulse when he was called to Mr ▉▉▉▉ home in the city of Lexington on the previous evening.
>
> It is thought that his pacemaker may have temporarily stopped working.
>
> Holmes County coroner Dexter Howard told the BBC he was called to Mr ▉▉▉▉ home by a hospice nurse, who said the man had passed away.
>
> Mr Howard said he went through the "normal procedure" of checking for Mr ▉▉▉▉ vital signs, but found none.
>
> Source: BBC News

The three criteria necessary to define a corpse are the remains must:

1. Be human (identified or unidentified).

2. Be deprived of life.

3. Not be entirely disintegrated.

A corpse may be referred to as a dead human body or – when intended solely for scientific study and dissection – as a **cadaver**.

Property and Possession Rights in a Dead Human Body

Property and possession rights of a corpse have been debated, argued, and advanced over a period of centuries. Broadly, property is anything owned by a person or entity. *Real property* is land (real estate) and any improvements made on it, such as a building or structure. *Personal property* is everything that is not real property. Early English common law and subsequent court opinions have clearly established a corpse is *not real or personal property* in the traditional or commercial sense. This is called the no-property theory as it relates to human remains.

Notwithstanding the established no-property theory, courts have recognized there is a qualified public interest in mandating a duty to provide for the decent and proper disposition of human remains for the purposes of preserving public health and safety. Consequently, if there is a duty to provide for the disposition of human remains, there must also be a mechanism for others to take legal possession and control over the remains to carry out that duty. The courts provided the mechanism to do so by adopting the **quasi-property theory**. This theory provides an exception following death for human remains to be treated as if they are property for the purpose of *disposition only,* while still maintaining the no-property theory associated with a human body.

> **Cases on Point**
>
> There is no right of property as such in body of dead person, even though quasi-property right to its possession is recognized for limited purpose of determining who shall have its custody for burial. Cohen v. Groman Mortuary, Inc. (App. 2 Dist. 1964) 41 Cal.Rptr. 481, 231 Cal.App.2d 1.
>
> Dead bodies are quasi property and right to bury corpse and preserve remains is a legal right of those entitled to body, which will be enforced by courts in an action at law. Diebler v. American Radiator & Standard Sanitary Corp., 1949, 196 Misc. 618, 92 N.Y.S.2d 356.

West's Encyclopedia of American Law provides the following on the property and possession rights of a corpse:

> In the ordinary use of the term, *a property right does not exist in a corpse.* For the purpose of burial, however, the corpse of a human being is considered to be property or quasi-property, the rights to which are held by the surviving spouse or next of kin. This right cannot be conveyed and does not exist while the decedent is living. Following burial, *the body is considered part of the ground in which it is placed.* Articles of personal property that have been buried with the body, such as jewelry, may be taken by their rightful owner as determined by traditional property rules or laws relating to descent and distribution or wills, as they are material objects independent of the body.
>
> *A corpse may not be retained* by an undertaker as security *for unpaid funeral expenses,* particularly if a body was kept without authorization and payment was demanded as a condition precedent to its release.
>
> At times, the need to perform an autopsy or postmortem examination gives the local coroner a superior right to possess the corpse until such an examination is performed. The general rule is that such examinations should be performed with discretion and not routinely. Some state statutes regulate the times when an

autopsy may be performed, which may require the procurement of a court order and written permission of a designated person, usually the one with property rights in the corpse.

Today, states have legislated a mandatory duty and responsibility to ensure all deceased persons are afforded a decent and proper final disposition, broadly defined to include the care, disposal, transportation, burial, cremation, or embalming of the body of a deceased person and any associated measures.

Final Disposition

In the mid-1800s, the late Sir William Gladstone, four-time Prime Minister of Great Britain and widely known for his eloquent oratory, declared, *"Show me the manner in which a nation cares for its dead and I will measure with mathematical exactness the tender mercies of its people, their respect for the laws of the land, and their loyalty to high ideals."*

In 1875, a court stated, *"The decent burial of the dead is a matter in which the public has concern, and it is against the public health if it does not take place at all, and against a proper public sentiment, that it should not take place with decency."* (Patterson v. Patterson, 1875, 59 N.Y. 574.)

In 1917, in Finley v. Atlantic Transport, a court recognized, *"At common law it is the duty of an individual under whose roof a poor person dies to carry the body decently covered to the place of burial and to refrain from doing anything which prevents in anyway a suitable burial. The body cannot be cast out so as to expose the same to violation, or to offend the feelings or injure the health of the living."* (Finley v. Atlantic Transport Co., 1917, 220 N.Y. 249, 115 N.E. 715.)

The United States has a long history of legally and morally supporting the inherent public duty and need to provide for the decent and proper disposition of human remains. To accomplish this lofty goal, states have exercised their **police power**, defined as the inherent power of a government to make reasonable laws to protect the safety, health, morals, and general welfare of its citizens. Through this power, states have codified the duties and responsibilities of providing for the proper disposition of human remains.

The requirements for a decent final disposition are developed from four sources:

1. The standard of care expected in the funeral service profession and affiliated groups serving the funeral service industry.

2. Community standards, which may include local, regional, and national values, morals, ethics, rites, and customs.

3. Considerations, including the wishes of the decedent; the wishes of the survivors; and the need to protect the public interest.

4. Statutes and ordinances that require the decent and proper final disposition of human remains. States have taken the responsibility to provide laws that directly address this

requirement at a core level, while local governments have taken a lesser role, such as regulating the location and construction of funeral establishments.

Funeral Director Arrested on 2 Counts of Abuse of Corpse Following Excavation of Graves

PRICHARD, Ala. (WALA) -- Funeral director ▮▮▮▮▮▮▮▮ has been arrested on two counts of abuse of corpse following excavation of graves at Heritage Memorial Gardens cemetery in Prichard.

Capt. Paul Burch with the Mobile County Sheriff's Office said officials found burial vaults that were not properly sealed -- with standing water in the vaults and water in the caskets. They found vaults covered with less than eight inches of dirt rather than the industry standard of two feet, he said.

"What we are going to be dealing with is more so industry standard rather than law," Burch said at the cemetery Wednesday morning. "There is not a law governing some of these procedures. But I think we are on good solid ground using industry standards."

Source: Kirby

Right to Control Final Disposition

The right to control the final disposition of human remains follows a priority list. The **priority** is the order in which certain classes of people have the right to make decisions concerning the disposition of human remains.

The order of these lists is not exactly the same in all the states, but they do have common elements, including the four classes listed below from highest to lowest priority:

1: Surviving Spouse

When defining a spouse, the law may require consideration be given to factors that would materially alter the relationship and thereby potentially affect a priority right, such as a divorce; a court sanctioned legal separation; or an **estrangement**, defined as a physical and/or emotional separation for a period of time showing a lack of affection, trust, and regard.

2: Next of Kin

The **kin** of a decedent are those family members with a biological blood relationship, such as a mother, son, or sister. Kin, with one exception (see note), does not include anyone that has no blood relationship, such as a spouse, an in-law, or a step-child. The **degree of kindred** is the relationship level of the decedent to blood relatives. The majority of states provide separate line items on a priority list to identify the closest degrees of kindred.

For example, state laws may list different classes or degrees of kindred in an order similar to this:

A. Surviving children, 18 years or older

B. Surviving parents

C. Surviving siblings, 18 years or older

Note: A legally adopted person will in most cases have equal rights to a biological person of the same class and degree of kindred. For example, if a woman is survived by three biological children and one adopted child, all four would be in the same class of kinship (children) and, upon her death, would have an equal right to control the final disposition of her human remains.

3: Decedent's Guardian

A guardian is a person appointed by a court to administer the affairs of another person who is incompetent by virtue of age or legal disability. Each state has laws specific to making a determination of incompetence that may necessitate the appointment of a legal guardian, and priority right statutes frequently list guardians as a specific class on a priority list.

4: Volunteer

Generally found near the bottom of a priority list, a volunteer may be granted the right to control the disposition of human remains when all other classes preceding them are – for one reason or another – eliminated.

Other priority list influences - State priority lists are usually expanded well beyond the four common classes described above. Probably the most significant developments are state statutes that recognize the right of an individual while still living to select the person they wish to provide for the disposition of their remains following death. The methods chosen to accomplish this task vary but may include such avenues as the execution of **pre-planned** or **prefunded funeral arrangements**, wherein there is an option for the purchaser or beneficiary to name the person they want to have the priority right to provide for the final disposition of their remains.

Another method used in some states provides for an individual to appoint an agent or representative for the sole purpose of providing for the disposition of their remains after death. These documents may be called declarations, designations, appointments, or other similar titles, and usually have a required format that must be followed to be legally binding. In other cases, the last **will** and testament of the decedent may be given consideration.

The level to which any of these documents will be controlling is dependent on the language found in the specific statute. For example, some states provide a designated agent document, properly executed pursuant to specified state requirements, will have the number one position on a priority list and supersede all other classes; while another state may provide disposition instructions in a last will and testament are only considered reflective of the intent of the decedent, not necessarily absolute or binding.

In addition to pre-arrangements and written documentation, some states allow consideration be given to oral declarations or statements made by an individual in the presence of witnesses. The weight these statements may be given is very fluid, as in some cases it may be difficult to sufficiently resolve any conflicts among those who heard the statements. In other cases, the intent may be clear and convincing, as evidenced by such things as being witnessed by several people over a period of time or the status and diversity of the persons present to hear the declaration.

Another factor that may affect the general priority rule is a special relationship between the decedent and another person. The most common of these are domestic partnerships and common law marriages. In either case, a certain amount of due diligence is required to be undertaken by a funeral director to support a decision to afford a surviving partner the right to control a final disposition over the right of any next of kin. The determination may be as simple as being a party to a domestic partnership legally recognized or sanctioned by a state; or as complicated as gathering enough evidence to base the decision on the totality of the circumstances. Circumstances might include such matters as shared expenses, joint ownership of property, children in common, signs of an intent to marry, and the length of the personal relationship.

Note: As of this writing, there are no more than ten states that recognize common law marriages, with another half a dozen states that only recognize such marriages that existed prior to state legislation that now prohibits them.

A final factor that may affect the general priority rule is the waiver of an individual within a class to exercise a priority right. For example, a very elderly parent living in Europe may waive the right to control the final disposition of an adult daughter that has died in the United States, and thereby allow her other children (the decedent's siblings) to have the priority right.

When there is an exception, persons with an equal priority in the same class are next to have the right to control the disposition, followed by persons of the next succeeding priority class until someone is identified and accepts the responsibility.

Statutory exceptions affecting the general priority list - In addition to the factors provided above, there may be certain statutory exceptions that will also affect a priority list. As examples, when a person has the priority right to control a final disposition pursuant to a statutory priority list, they may lose that right if, at the time of death, they were:

➢ the subject of a court order or other similar legal directive protecting the decedent;

➢ under arrest or charged with a crime related to the death of the decedent, such as a homicide or manslaughter;

➢ not reasonably available to serve;

➢ unwilling to serve; or

➢ legally not competent to serve.

Not all states include all of the exceptions listed, and there may be other exceptions in select state laws that are not listed. Funeral directors must therefore familiarize themselves with exceptions that exist in the states and municipalities they serve.

Secondary priority right - If a general priority list is exhausted, with no one in the various classes identified to control a final disposition, a secondary right is usually included within the same statute to provide for a state or local government to not only have a right but a duty to provide for a decent and proper disposition. A state, county, or local government official may be identified by title on a secondary right list. For example, governments may name such officials as a state commissioner of public health, a county administrator, or a municipal director of social services, as having the right, duty, and responsibility to ensure all deceased persons are afforded a decent and proper final disposition. In addition, these statutes usually mandate the responsible government pay any expenses related to carrying out these duties.

Rights of those having priority to control disposition - Once it has been established an individual (such as a child of suitable age), or in some states a class of individuals (such as all children of suitable age), have a priority right to control the disposition of human remains, they are afforded certain legal rights to accomplish the necessary tasks to provide for the disposition, including:

1. Custody of the human remains. This may include **actual custody**, defined as the physical possession of a dead human body or other property; and **constructive custody**, where one party has a right to acquire actual custody and possession of the dead body, although another party has actual physical possession.

2. The right and ability to convey actual custody to a funeral service practitioner.

3. The right to control, manage, and arrange for themselves or others to provide for the care, preparation, transportation, funeral, and final disposition of the remains.

Custodian is the status associated with the funeral service practitioner and funeral establishment who become the legal protector of human remains from the time of removal until final disposition.

Survivor Disputes

Inevitably, there will at times be disputes among the parties over who has the priority right to control the final disposition of human remains or some component of the final disposition. Given this fact, priority right statutes usually identify the means and avenues to resolve a dispute. These avenues may include varying levels of negotiation, mediation, or civil litigation.

The parties to a dispute are the individuals that cannot agree on who has the priority right to control the disposition. The funeral director is *not* a party to these disputes. They may assist in trying to reach an agreement but have no authority to unilaterally make any decisions on behalf of any of the parties to the dispute. When there is a dispute that cannot be settled, it must be resolved by the parties themselves or a court of law.

Until a funeral director receives a court order or other form of notification agreed to by all of the parties, they will not be in a position to provide any goods and services beyond safeguarding the human remains. Many state statutes specify funeral directors cannot be held liable for refusing to provide any services when the matter of who has the right to make decisions about a funeral is in question. This issue of dispute resolution differs from state to state, and funeral directors must always acquaint themselves with the law in the communities they serve and not hesitate to seek legal counsel when there is any question or doubt.

Liability for Funeral Expenses

Determining who has the responsibility (**liability**) to pay for a funeral is of course an important consideration when entering into an agreement to provide funeral services. Like any other business, the owner of a funeral establishment must have procedures and protocols in place to address financial manners with consumers. Discussions about payment for funeral services is an integral part of the arrangement conference, and the responsibility of the funeral director at that time is to determine who is going to be legally responsible for payment.

There are generally four sources through which the identity of who is legally responsible for making payment may be established:

1: Contracts - A **contract** is a legally enforceable agreement and the generally accepted means to establish a legally binding promise to pay. In many states, a contractual agreement to pay for a funeral is included on the FTC Statement of Funeral Goods and Services Selected that must be provided to a family at the conclusion of an arrangement conference.

Express contracts - These are contracts in which the parties have clearly and plainly set out and agreed to the terms of the agreement. Each service or item of the contract is specifically described and stated, and the purchaser offers an express promise to pay when they sign the contract. Both at-need contracts and prefunded funeral agreements are express contracts that itemize the intangible services and tangible goods funeral directors agree to provide in exchange for compensation (payment).

Express contracts may be oral or written but are almost always written agreements when making funeral arrangements for the purchase of funeral goods and services; and some states have identified certain contracts that must be in writing to be valid and enforceable.

Implied contracts - These contractual agreements are legally binding on the parties by virtue of the actions, acts, or conduct of at least one of the parties. An implied contract is one that is assumed to exist; it does not need to be confirmed in writing or orally. For example, a contract is implied when a party knowingly accepts a benefit from another party in circumstances where the benefit cannot be considered a gift. Therefore, the party accepting the benefit is under a legal obligation to give fair value for the benefit received. Such would be the case if you were to get your vehicle stuck in a snow bank and call a tow truck. When the towing company pulls your vehicle out of the snow (a benefit to you) there is an implied contract that they are doing so with the intention of being paid (pulling you out would not be considered a gift).

The most common example of an implied contract is an implied warranty. Caskets are purchased for the purpose of holding and safeguarding human remains and should therefore be capable of doing so. If the casket does not fulfill this purpose, the manufacturer has failed to meet the terms of an implied warranty and therefore an implied contract.

Quasi-contracts - This type of contract is created or implied by a court where there is unjust enrichment. Unjust enrichment takes place when an individual receives a material gain at the expense of another person that the law sees as unjust. The function of a **quasi-contract** is to raise an obligation in law where, in fact, the parties made no promises. An example of a quasi-contract would be when an automobile accident victim needs immediate medical attention but may not be conscious or is otherwise unable to consent for themselves to be treated. Under these circumstances, the law does so on their behalf and creates a legal obligation for the injured party to pay for the medical expenses.

2: Decedent estates - The property (assets) and debts of a deceased person make up their **estate.** The funeral bill is a debt owed by the estate of a decedent, not the decedent individually, and the estate has the primary obligation to pay the funeral expenses when there is no contract or other statutory provision to the contrary.

Limitations on claims for payment under insolvency - ~~Insolvency is the position of being unable to pay money owed to others.~~ When the estate of a decedent is insolvent (there are insufficient assets to pay all of the debts), there may be limitations and priorities placed on the order in which claims will be paid.

These limitations may be based or calculated on any of the following:

➤ Size of the estate - The amount of the funeral expenses to be paid may be limited by the amount of the assets in the estate.

➤ Status in life of the deceased - A funeral that coincides with the decedent's lifestyle and social status will be considered appropriate for the individual. For example: A $10,000 cast bronze casket for a decedent that lived week-to-week on a minimum wage would not be considered 'appropriate.'

➤ Reasonableness of the charges - In determining reasonableness, courts may look at a number of different factors, including the size and solvency of the estate; right of creditors; local and contemporary custom; and religious faith.

➤ The funeral director's knowledge of decedent's financial condition - This limitation is one the courts may review toward a determination of reasonableness. A funeral director cannot justify a funeral expense disproportionate to the size of the estate when they have prior knowledge of estate assets.

➤ Local or ethnic customs - Arrangements may be made based on a close relationship to a particular local, ethnic, religious, or fraternal custom. The cost, even if higher than services without such arrangements, may be considered by the court as valid and reasonable under the circumstances.

Certain items deemed necessary - The estate may recognize certain goods and services as necessary based upon customs and community standards, religion, fraternal requirements, legal requirements, and cemetery or crematory requirements. As an example, a cemetery requirement to have an outer burial container is something that may be deemed a necessary and acceptable expense against the estate.

Claims against the estate for funeral services - Claims against an estate may include, at a minimum, the goods and services shown in this table:

Embalming	Clothing	Cemetery fees	Transportation
Flowers	Grave marker	Professional services	Newspaper notices
Facilities	Casket	Outer burial container	Cremation fees

Priority of claims on estate assets - Claims made against an estate for payment are prioritized, with claims for funeral expenses generally receiving preferred status over most other debts of the estate.

> ➤ A **preferred claim** is one which is accorded a priority, advantage, or privilege over others.

> ➤ A **secured claim** is a debt which is supported by a pledge, mortgage, or lien on assets belonging to the debtor. As an example, a car loan is a secured claim, meaning the loan (the debt owed) is supported (secured) by a lien placed on the car (the asset) to ensure payment. If payment is not made, the car may be subject to repossession by the person who provided the loan.

> ➤ An **unsecured claim** is one which is not supported by a pledge, mortgage, or lien on other assets.

When there are insufficient assets to pay all of the claims against an estate, they will be paid in their order of **priority**.

3: Volunteer - Anyone may volunteer to pay for the funeral expenses of another person. These situations usually present themselves upon the death of an infant or child where the death is viewed as accidental or tragic, and the family does not have the funds to pay for a funeral. Employers, charitable organizations, religious entities, and anonymous donors are just a few of the potential sources where a volunteer may come forward and offer to pay for a funeral.

4: Public authorities - With an inherent duty to provide for the public health and safety of their communities, as well as the duty to provide for the decent and proper disposition of human remains, public authorities pay limited expenses to provide basic funeral services for the indigent and needy.

Chapter 4: Funeral Service Practitioners and Staff

Overview

Liability exposures in the funeral service industry are most often associated with either the personal actions and conduct of the owner and staff, or the operation, care, and maintenance of the funeral establishment as a business entity. This chapter reviews potential exposures related to practitioners and staff, while the next succeeding chapter reviews those related to the ownership and operation of a funeral establishment facility.

Chapter Definitions

Aftercare - those appropriate and helpful acts of counseling, personal and/or written contact that come after the funeral.

Autopsy (post-mortem examination) - An examination of a human body, organ, or other body part following death to determine the cause and manner of death [by Author].

Cause of death - diseases, injuries, or complications that resulted in death [by Author].

Coroner - a public officer whose duty it is to investigate the cause of death when the question of accident, suicide, or homicide may be evident or where there was no doctor in attendance.

Due diligence - the attention reasonably expected from, and ordinarily exercised by, a person who seeks to satisfy a legal requirement or to discharge an obligation.

Gross negligent act - the intentional failure or the reckless disregard of the consequences with respect to conduct affecting the life or property of another.

Layperson - an ordinary person; one without special training in a profession or occupation [by Author].

Lien - a claim or charge against real or personal property for payment of some debt (there can be no lien against a dead human body for it is not property).

Malpractice - failure to perform a professional service with the ability and care generally exercised by others in the profession.

Manner of death - the mode of death, such as accident, homicide, natural, or suicide [by Author].

Medical examiner - a forensically-trained physician whose duty it is to investigate questionable or unattended deaths (has replaced the coroner in many states).

Mental anguish - a condition which may result from an outrageous intentional or grossly negligent act and may be accompanied by physical injury.

Mutilation - any altering or change made to a dead human body from the time of death, other than by natural causes.

Negligence - failure to exercise care.

Outrageous act - an act with complete disregard for proper conduct which transcends the bounds of common decency.

Replevin - an action to recover possession of wrongfully withheld personal property.

Tort - a private or civil wrong against a person or his or her property, other than by breach of contract, for which there may be action for damages.

Due Diligence
Due diligence is defined as the attention reasonably expected from – and ordinarily exercised by – a person who seeks to satisfy a legal requirement or to discharge an obligation. In meeting the standards of due diligence in the funeral service industry, practitioners must be thoughtful, genuine, and determined in exercising fore-thought, good judgment, care, and prudence in providing funeral goods and services to families.

There are four key components establishing due diligence that can, when consistently applied, reduce the liability exposure of funeral directors:

1: Reasonable and Prudent Actions
The ordinary conduct of the practitioner must be such that no reasonable person would:

> ➤ have an objection;

> ➤ find such conduct to be overbearing; or

> ➤ perceive the conduct to be anything less than satisfactory and acceptable under the circumstances.

2: Establish and Follow Standards of Care
A funeral establishment business has an inherent duty to provide for the safeguarding, care, preparation, and final disposition of human remains. Therefore, the level and quality of suitable care to be taken when carrying out these duties must be clearly identified by management. Thereafter, to ensure an acceptable and satisfactory outcome, these standards of care must be communicated to funeral staff members charged with the responsibility for carrying out the duties.

3: Training and Communications
Proper training and open lines of communication are two common means to strengthen due diligence efforts in the areas of regulatory compliance and risk management.

The importance of *training and education* programs in regulatory compliance is underscored by the fact many states require continuing education on legal updates for licensed staff members. The goal of this training is to provide practitioners with the information they need to comply with government laws, rules, and regulations. It is also important to routinely meet with staff to review matters of compliance, thereby providing an opportunity to discuss new or updated laws and regulations, and verify the staff understands the application of current law in the workplace.

The importance of *risk management* is strengthened by the fact many insurance companies require and actively monitor risk management programs in the organizations they insure. These programs identify exposures in the work environment and then require proactive steps be taken to diminish the potential for these known risks to cause any injury or loss. Initiating a risk management program can reduce the possibility of a costly lawsuit or legal claim against the establishment.

For example, a funeral establishment owner may identify 'slip and fall' incidents in the facility restrooms as a potential risk to those who visit the establishment. To manage this known risk, the owner could implement a policy that requires staff members to inspect all restrooms on a scheduled basis for any hazardous condition during those times when visitation or funerals are taking place. This policy would then need to be personally communicated to all staff members, with supervisors being held responsible for verifying compliance on a case-by-case basis.

4: Documentation
When performing duties and tasks that demonstrate and support due diligence efforts, it is important all related records and documentation associated with the actions and activities undertaken by staff members are properly maintained. While creating and preserving documentation cannot prevent the filing of a claim, it may serve to mitigate (lessen) any damage awards when defending a civil claim in court.

Using the 'slip and fall' example, if a visitor were to fall on a wet floor in a restroom and injury themselves, it would be very beneficial to be able to submit documentation that supports the efforts taken by the funeral establishment to prevent just such an incident. This may include the risk management plan; proof of implementation; proof of staff training; and records specific to the claim. The records may also include a log of the rest room inspections performed by staff on the day of the incident.

Many establishments require an 'incident report' be completed whenever any unusual activity takes place, such as a person suffering an injury inside the facility. These reports are also used to demonstrate due diligence, as well as being reviewed by the owner to identify future risks and take steps to manage them.

At a minimum, funeral establishments should maintain documentation related to:

Body tracking	Facility inspections	Facility maintenance	Staff training
Authorizations and releases	Personal property inventory	Custom merchandise orders	Applications for survivor benefits
Vehicle maintenance	Embalming case reports		Crematory inspections

Torts
A **tort** is a private or civil wrong against a person or his or her property, other than by breach of contract, for which there may be action for damages. The Cornell Law School Legal Information Institute defines a tort as:

... an act or omission that gives rise to injury or harm to another and amounts to a civil wrong for which courts impose liability. In the context of torts, injury describes the invasion of any legal right, whereas harm describes a loss or detriment in fact that an individual suffers.

There are three basic types of torts:

1. *Intentional* - Exists when an individual knowingly and intentionally engages in conduct with the intended result that another will suffer some form of damage or loss.

2. *Negligent* - Exists when an individual carelessly or negligently engages in – or fails to engage in – conduct that results in an unintentional damage or loss to another. This type of tort has many potential sources, including failure to exercise due care (**negligence**), dereliction of duty, failure to perform a required or promised duty, carelessness, and inattentiveness.

3. *Strict liability* - Provides an individual or entity may be held liable for their conduct without the need to prove the act was either intentional or negligent. This type of tort is often associated with product liability, such as when a consumer purchases a product that is later determined to be defective or faulty in design.

Tort claims - The filing of a tort claim is an action taken by one party to pursue compensation for an injury or loss they believe was the result of an act or omission by another party. Tort claims are filed in civil courts, as opposed to criminal courts.

In addition to having the duty to provide for the safeguarding, care, preparation, and final disposition of human remains, funeral establishment owners must also be vigilant to the needs of the public in providing for the proper disposition of human remains, while maintaining and preserving public health and safety.

Similar to all other business operations, the owner of a funeral establishment must operate and maintain facilities and grounds in conformity with regulatory requirements to provide a safe environment for consumers, visitors, and employees. This would include compliance with any government regulations specific to the facility and the operations taking place therein.

As an example, owners have a duty and responsibility to comply with the Americans with Disabilities Act by providing for handicapped access to the facilities. Another example is the duty and obligation of an owner to comply with OSHA standards to provide a safe work environment for employees performing tasks in a preparation room or morgue facility. All of these duties, responsibilities, and obligations come with potential civil liability exposures, especially as related to activities that deal directly with the care and preparation of human remains.

Invasion of Rights

A tort claim against a funeral director or a funeral establishment may allege an invasion of some right, and these rights take many different forms.

Embalming rights - The Federal Trade Commission Funeral Rule identifies three circumstances under which a funeral establishment may charge a family for embalming:

1. State or local law requires embalming under the particular circumstances, regardless of any wishes the family might have.

2. The funeral director has obtained prior approval for embalming from a family member or other authorized person.

3. The funeral director is unable to contact a family member or other authorized person after exercising due diligence; has no reason to believe the family does not want embalming performed; and, after embalming the body, obtains subsequent approval from the family for the embalming.

Therefore, with very limited exceptions, the FTC Funeral Rule mandates obtaining permission prior to the embalming of human remains. If a funeral establishment embalms without first receiving permission from the person with the priority right to control the disposition – or fails to exercise due diligence in attempts to reach someone and ask for permission to embalm – it may face a civil tort claim.

Conversely, some states have identified specific cases or circumstances for which human remains must *by law* be embalmed, such as when a contagious disease is the cause of death or when remains will not be buried for an extended period of time. And virtually all common carriers require human remains be embalmed before they will be accepted for transportation. Any failure to embalm under these circumstances could subject funeral establishment staff to not only civil tort claims but also a criminal investigation if public health or safety is compromised.

Right of non-interference (right of sepulcher) - Common law and various courts have affirmed the right of a family to provide for a decent and proper funeral without any unreasonable interference from others. This would include the right to plan, execute, and attend common activities, such as the visitation period, funeral ceremony, and a cemetery burial. If a funeral director unreasonably denies the family these rights, such as going forward with a funeral event without the next-of-kin being present, they may by subject to a civil claim for damages based on interference.

The family also has the right to put forth personal requests, such as having the funeral procession pass by the decedent's home or business while proceeding to the cemetery.

> **Interesting Case**
>
> Allegations that funeral establishment's limousine driver drove decedent's family down freeway at 90 miles per hour, weaving in and out of traffic and tailgating while eating grapes and spitting seeds out window stated cause of action for breach of implied covenant to provide appropriate and dignified burial service.
>
> Wilson v. Houston Funeral establishment (App. 2 Dist. 1996) 50 Cal.Rptr.2d 169, 42 Cal.App.4th 1124.

Assuming the requests are reasonable and legal, they should be granted, as any denial or rejection may be deemed an interference in the right of the family to provide a decent and proper funeral and final disposition.

Errors in final disposition can also interfere with the right of a family to provide a decent and proper funeral. This may involve an error resulting in the wrong body being interred, cremated, or embalmed; placing the remains in the wrong cemetery plot, casket, vault, or other container; or shipping the body to a wrong location. Errors and mistakes such as these most often result in civil tort actions filed against the funeral director and the funeral establishment, as well as the operators and representatives of the cemetery or crematory, if any, where the error took place.

Cremation and interment disposition methods – and any other disposition methods used in those states where permitted – must be performed in compliance with state laws and standards applicable to both funeral establishments and the operators of cemeteries and crematories. A quick google search brings up dozens of cases where expected standards of care were not met, thereby violating the family right to non-interference. ➲

Many of these mistakes involve confusion about which remains were supposed to be cremated versus those that actually got cremated. As a result – with cremation now surpassing earth burial as the most popular disposition in the United States – many states have been proactive in requiring funeral establishments have a reliable system in place to tag human remains for identification, and thereafter track the remains until final disposition has taken place.

> **2018 Headlines**
> ✓ Grief-Stricken Siblings Sue Funeral Home Over Ashes Mix-up
> ✓ Woman Sues Funeral Home for $50 Million After Body Mistakenly Cremated
> ✓ A Funeral Home Mixed Up 3 Bodies and Accidentally Cremated the Wrong One
> ✓ Family Sues After Funeral Home Switches Corpses and Cremates Wrong Man
> ✓ Detroit Police Find Wrong Bodies Buried in Cemetery

A right of non-interference may be referred to as a *right of sepulcher*, a common law term that is most often used in legal proceedings. In 2019, Francois A. Rivera, a New York State Supreme Court Judge in Kings County, rendered a decision about non-interference rights and included this passage in reference to sepulcher:

> *The ancient right of sepulcher originated and developed long before the passage of the laws. It is rooted in pre-Christian civilization where reverence for the dead was a common practice among a variety of religious faiths and societies. Accordingly, the Courts recognize that the common-law right of sepulcher "gives the next of kin the absolute right to the immediate possession of a decedent's body for preservation and burial, and ... damages will be awarded against any person who unlawfully interferes with that right or improperly deals with the decedent's body."*
>
> *This right is less a quasi-property right and more the legal right of the surviving next of kin to find 'solace and comfort' in the ritual of burial. Damages are limited to the emotional suffering, mental anguish and psychological injuries and physical consequences thereof experienced by the next of kin as a result of the interference with the right of sepulcher. In order to recover for such emotional injuries, it must*

be shown that the injuries were the natural and proximate consequence of some wrongful act or neglect on the part of the one sought to be charged.

To establish a cause of action for interference with the right of sepulcher, a plaintiff must demonstrate that: (1) plaintiff is the decedent's next of kin; (2) plaintiff had a right to possession of the remains; (3) defendant interfered with plaintiff's right to immediate possession of the decedent's body; (4) the interference was unauthorized; (5) plaintiff was aware of the interference; and (6) the interference caused plaintiff mental anguish. A cause of action does not accrue until interference with the right directly impacts on the 'solace and comfort' of the next of kin, that is, until interference causes mental anguish for the next of kin.

Gutnick v. Hebrew Free Burial Soc'y for the Poor Brooklyn, 2019 N.Y. Slip Op. 51133 (N.Y. Sup. Ct. 2019)

Note: Quotes and citations identifying material from other sources have been deleted from this passage to provide for increased clarity and readability.

Interference may come from sources outside a funeral establishment, such as a hospital or health care institution misidentifying human remains, or a government official withholding the release of a body for the purposes of pursuing a criminal investigation. Funeral directors following the direction of these individuals cannot usually be held liable for the delay or interference, although the individuals themselves may be exposed to a claim if they did not act reasonably and in good faith, or with the proper authority. When confronted with a question of reasonableness, courts will question whether the omission or act that took place would be one a reasonably prudent person would exercise under similar circumstances.

It is important for funeral directors to follow through on agreements or promises made to the family and, when confronted with an inability to fulfill an agreement, to immediately notify them. Acting reasonably and in good faith goes a long way in a court of law toward mitigating any negative impact associated with the failure or unexpected inability to perform a specific duty or fulfill an obligation.

Right to privacy/confidentiality - An unwarranted invasion of personal privacy or disclosure of confidential information will almost certainly expose a funeral director to a tort claim for damages. As such, all personal information must be protected from public review or scrutiny. This includes personal communications between the parties; the state and condition of the human remains; the cause and manner of death; the health history of the decedent; and any family or pedigree information that would be considered personal. There should be no discussion with others about any of these details. To do otherwise would be considered a breach of confidentiality and could be cause for filing a liability claim.

Taking photos or videography of the decedent without permission from the person with the priority right to control a disposition could also be a violation of privacy and confidentiality. If a funeral director should want to maintain a visual record in a specific case, such as to document extensive restoration work performed on the decedent, they should seek *prior* permission, preferably in writing from the person with the right to control the final disposition.

When it comes to privacy, public officials may have qualified immunity, a legal condition that protects government officials from being sued for discretionary actions; as well as implied immunity, for acting in the performance of their official duty. For example, a law enforcement officer taking photographs of a deceased person for the purpose of conducting a criminal investigation and gathering evidence would have implied immunity, as the acts being performed are part of his or her official duty and would not require permission from the person with the right to control the final disposition. However, if a public official exceeds the bounds of their immunity, they may be subject to a civil tort claim.

Mutilation

The right to possession of human remains implies receiving the body in the same condition as at time of death, and **mutilation** is defined as any altering or change made to a dead human body from the time of death, other than by natural causes. Any deliberate change to the condition from when it was first received requires permission and authorization. Some of the more common activities and issues that could potentially be the source of a claim based on mutilation include embalming and other preparation of remains.

Embalming - Embalming without permission could expose a funeral service practitioner to a civil tort action, and that action may extend to a claim for the negligent mutilation of the body. Embalming is by definition a mutilation because it includes *altering or changing the body*. There is of course minimal intrusion to a body in performing the embalming process, and the mutilation is implicitly sanctioned by the permission to embalm given to a funeral director by the person with the right to control the final disposition.

Regardless, any unauthorized or negligent embalming or restorative procedures performed on human remains may expose the funeral director to a claim for mutilation.

Other preparation of the remains - In addition to embalming, an allegation of mutilation might be encountered following:

> the unauthorized removal of a moustache, beard, or facial hair;

> the removal of tissue, organs, or other body parts; or

> performing procedures other than required for embalming.

In any of these circumstances, the family should be consulted and requested to give their express permission before any procedure is performed. Additionally, in the case of removing tissue, organs, or body parts, the funeral establishment must comply with applicable state laws that regulate anatomical donation and gift programs.

Autopsies (post-mortem examinations) - An **autopsy** is defined as an examination of a human body, organ, or other body part following death to determine the cause and manner of death, and includes the retrieval of tissue samples and other dissections. **Cause of death** means the diseases, injuries, or complications that resulted in death; **manner of death** means the mode of death, such as accident, homicide, natural, or suicide.

If not *ordered by* an authorized public official acting pursuant to their duties and responsibilities, or *consented to* by the person with the right to control the final disposition, an autopsy could be the basis for a civil claim based on mutilation.

Public officials with the authority to order an autopsy may include:

> **coroners**, defined as a public officer whose duty it is to investigate the cause of death when a question of accident, suicide, or homicide may be evident or where there was no doctor in attendance;

> **medical examiners**, defined as a forensically-trained physician whose duty it is to investigate questionable or unattended deaths; and

> in a limited number of jurisdictions, other designated health or public official given specific authority to order an autopsy.

Note: There are no consistent definitions for these titles among the various state laws, but broadly speaking a coroner is usually a **layperson**, elected to their position and performing tasks under the supervision of a physician; and medical examiners are physicians that unilaterally perform their tasks with no direct oversight or supervision.

An exception to an autopsy by order or consent might include a contractual relationship in which an autopsy may be required, such as a life insurance policy. There are insurance policies that provide for a double indemnity benefit when the manner of death is accidental or the result of a homicide, while others may decline benefit payments pursuant to the terms of the insurance policy if the manner of death is suicide. From the perspective of the insurance carrier, the definitive cause and manner of death is therefore of significant importance.

Other unauthorized procedures - These may include unauthorized acts or procedures performed on a dead human body, such as piercing ears, adding tattoos, removing prosthetic devices, or practicing suturing.

Wrongful Withholding
As stated in the previous chapter, early English common law and subsequent court opinions have clearly established a corpse is not real or personal property in the traditional or commercial sense. Instead, the courts have adopted the quasi-property theory that provides an exception following death for human remains to be treated as if it were property for the purpose of disposition only, while still maintaining the general no-property theory associated with a human body. As such, human remains do not constitute property that may be withheld from a family. This includes cremated remains and any personal property that may be with the human or cremated remains.

A **lien** is defined as a claim or charge against real or personal property for payment of some debt; however, there can be no lien against a dead human body because a body is not real or personal property. Any refusal to surrender human remains upon demand of the person with the priority right to control the final disposition would almost certainly subject the person perpetrating the wrongful withholding to a civil tort claim.

Replevin is defined as an action to recover possession of wrongfully withheld personal property but, again, human remains are not real or personal property and therefore not subject to replevin.

To summarize and be clear, no person, including a funeral director, may withhold human remains or cremated remains in an attempt to:

> ➢ receive payment for any goods or services;

> ➢ extract payment for any debt;

> ➢ seek compensation or material gain; or

> ➢ exercise control over another for any purpose.

A family or individual with the right to control a final disposition has an absolute right to the

possession of the body, and any attempt to withhold it would – in virtually all cases and circumstances – result in an actionable tort claim with potentially severe consequences and sanctions levied against the offender.

Mental Anguish

Mental anguish is defined as a condition which may result from an outrageous intentional or grossly negligent act and may be accompanied by physical injury. Several of the rights described in this chapter, when violated, could result in mental anguish.

Mental anguish claims may arise from:

> ➢ the intentional infliction of emotional stress;

> ➢ an **outrageous act**, defined as an act with complete disregard for proper conduct which transcends the bounds of common decency; or

> ➢ a **gross negligent act**, defined as the intentional failure to perform a manifest duty, in reckless disregard of the consequences as affecting the life or property of another.

The definition for mental anguish states it *may* be accompanied by physical injury, but there has been a tendency for the courts to find liability for mental anguish may be based on the funeral service contract, with no requirement for physical injury or harm be proven to be successful in a civil claim. The courts have reasoned the unique personal nature of a funeral contract – and the fact that the contract puts the funeral director on notice that any breach would probably result in mental anguish – makes proof of a physical injury unnecessary. However, it should be noted this area of law is still in a state of change in the various states and not easily applied or uniformly held to any particular set of circumstances.

A 1964 case in California addressed the issue of the weight given to a contractual relationship between a funeral establishment and the family of a decedent. In summary, the court ruled:

> *Damages may be assessed against mortician for physical suffering and illness caused to contracting party by mental anguish and shock resulting from breach of contract to preserve and prepare body for burial on theory that contract relates to his comfort in manner in which body of deceased is prepared and laid to rest.*
>
> Cohen v. Groman Mortuary, Inc. (App. 2 Dist. 1964) 41 Cal.Rptr. 481, 231 Cal.App.2d 1.

To avoid the potential for a claim alleging mental anguish, funeral directors should bear in mind:

➢ The family has a right to all details and information (full disclosure) about a death case.

➢ Failure to provide accurate information, withholding information, or being deceitful (providing misinformation) are causes of mental distress and may result in a civil claim.

➢ Families have the right to exercise 'informed consent' for all procedures involving the handling of human remains and aspects of the funeral events being provided.

➢ Based on recent court decisions, a contract whereby a funeral director agrees to prepare a body for burial or other method of final disposition is one in which it is reasonably foreseeable that any breach of the contract may cause mental anguish and therefore a liability exposure.

➢ Public policy requires funeral directors adhere to a high standard of care in view of the potential for psychological devastation likely to result from any mistake.

Malpractice
Any failure to perform a professional service with the ability and care generally exercised by others in the profession is the definition of **malpractice**. It may also be known as professional negligence.

Malpractice claims typically are founded on allegations of negligence or incompetence on the part of professionals in the medical, legal, and financial communities, although other professions may also be subject to this level of scrutiny depending on the requirements of the employment position they hold. As there is no standard definition of a professional or a professional occupation, the question of who may be the subject of a malpractice claim is open to interpretation by the courts.

Aftercare Liability Exposures
One concept recently garnering considerable attention and support in the funeral service industry has been the offering of aftercare services to survivor families. **Aftercare**, defined as those appropriate and helpful acts of counseling, personal and/or written contact that come after the

funeral, may present potential liability exposures for the funeral establishment. These exposures are greatest when providing *indirect* aftercare services, such as:

- ➢ making professional referrals;

- ➢ sponsoring community educational programs;

- ➢ hosting support groups;

- ➢ hosting social events for seniors; and

- ➢ providing informational literature and media.

To help manage these risks, funeral directors should verify the organizations or individuals providing aftercare services have:

- ➢ the proper and appropriate training and credentials;

- ➢ adequate and suitable insurance to cover the facilities being used and the activities taking place therein; and

- ➢ required certifications, licenses, or approvals if programs are regulated by government authorities.

Chapter 5: Funeral Establishment Operations

Overview

Negligent tort acts or omissions have many potential sources, including failure to exercise due care, dereliction of duty, failure to perform a required or promised duty, carelessness, and inattentiveness. While the personal conduct and any perceived failure to exercise **due diligence** by owners and staff may open the door to a civil claim, so too may the establishments they own and operate in the funeral service business. The duties and responsibilities for owning and operating a funeral establishment and some of the associated liability exposures are the subject of this chapter.

Chapter Definitions

Agent driver - those drivers under the directions and control of the funeral establishment which is liable for the driver's negligent actions.

Bailee - a person who receives personal property from another as a bailment.

Bailment - a delivery of personal property by one person (the bailor) to another (the bailee) who holds the property for a certain purpose under an express or implied-in-fact contract.

Bailor - a person who delivers personal property to another as a bailment.

Building code - laws, ordinances, and government regulations setting forth requirements for construction, maintenance, operation, occupancy, use or appearance of buildings.

Cemetery - an area of ground set aside and dedicated for the final disposition of dead human bodies.

Crematory - the location of the retort/cremation chamber which will perform a cremation process.

Due diligence - the attention reasonably expected from, and ordinarily exercised by, a person who seeks to satisfy a legal requirement or to discharge an obligation.

Funeral establishment - a facility used in the care and preparation for the funeral and/or final disposition of dead human bodies.

Invitee - one who has been invited on the property by the landowner; persons coming to a funeral establishment for the purpose of attending funerals, viewing remains, or engaging the funeral director's services are some examples.

Livery - automotive equipment made available for hire.

Nuisance - a landowner's use of property which interferes with the public or another landowner's use of their property.

Nuisance in fact - acts, occupations or structures which are not nuisances per se, but may become nuisances by reason of the location or manner in which it is operated.

Nuisance per se - acts, occupations or structures which are nuisances at all times and under all circumstances; it may be prejudicial to public morals, dangerous to life, or injurious to public rights.

Ordinance - a law passed by a local municipal governing body (e.g., zoning, building, safety, etc.).

Restrictive covenant - provision in a deed limiting the use of real property and prohibiting certain uses.

Tort - a private or civil wrong against a person or his or her property, other than by breach of contract, for which there may be action for damages.

Trespasser - one who intentionally and without consent or privilege enters another's property.

Viewing - *(calling hours, visitation, visiting hours, wake)* time set aside for friends and relatives to pay respect for the deceased prior to the funeral service.

Volunteer driver - those drivers not under the control of the funeral director.

Zoning ordinance - a law passed by a local unit of government which regulates and prescribes land use planning.

Funeral Processions

Funeral directors often organize and supervise the formation of a funeral procession for the orderly transportation of the deceased, family members, and guests attending various funeral events. With this characteristic duty and responsibility comes exposure to liability for acts or omissions related to the funeral procession that others may allege caused them to suffer an injury or loss. The degree to which the funeral director and the **funeral establishment** may be held liable will be dependent on the specific circumstances as determined on a case-by-case basis.

Restrictions - Broadly speaking, drivers in a funeral procession do not have the right to disobey traffic laws or regulations of the road. They may not pass-through red signals, ignore stop signs, speed, pass stopped school buses, or disregard any other traffic law unless directed to do so by an authorized public official, such as a police officer, flag person, or traffic aide.

However, there are exceptions, as many states have statutory laws and administrative rules specific to regulating funeral processions on public highways. These exceptions may exempt procession vehicles from compliance with certain provisions of traffic laws; while others may impose additional requirements on *non-procession* vehicles when they encounter a funeral procession.

For example, a state may exempt the operators of funeral procession vehicles from being ticketed for 'following too close' or 'operating hazard lights (four-way flashers) when in motion.' Another state may prohibit vehicles from crossing between funeral procession cars when they are going through an intersection; cutting into a procession on a controlled access highway; or failing to yield to a procession when it is turning into a cemetery.

Drivers - Generally speaking, the driver of a motor vehicle will be held accountable for its safe and legal operation. Whether or not the funeral establishment will have any potential liability will depend on the connection the establishment has with the driver.

There are three potential relationships that may exist:

1. Livery drivers - **Livery** is defined as automotive equipment made available for hire. These for-hire vehicles include a driver, and these drivers are under the direct control of the funeral establishment that has contractually hired them. When funeral establishments hold out these vehicles and drivers as their own, they assume responsibility for any negligent acts or omissions. They may include limousines, hearses, and other transportation vehicles being used by – but not owned by – a funeral establishment.

2. Volunteer drivers - **Volunteer drivers** are not under the control of the funeral director and have no formal relationship with the funeral establishment. They do not act as an agent of the funeral director or the funeral establishment and would not, in most cases, expose the establishment to liability exposure for any civil **tort** claim based on the acts or omissions of the driver or the operation of their vehicles. These vehicles may include family and friends that follow the procession in their own personal vehicles.

3. Agent drivers - **Agent drivers** are under the direction and control of the funeral establishment, which is then liable for the driver's negligent actions. Agent drivers are most often employees of the funeral establishment and may drive the lead car, flower vehicles, pallbearer cars, and the hearse. They may also be called upon to park vehicles owned by visitors when they arrive for funeral service events, or be required to move vehicles into position in preparation for a funeral procession.

Funeral Establishments

The are many responsibilities that come with owning and operating a business, none the least of which is the duty of the owner to maintain the physical premises in a condition conducive to its intended use. This includes:

➤ providing for the safety and security of families and visitors, as well as the employees working in the facilities;

➤ providing for the safeguarding, care, and custody of human remains when being held or stored in a funeral establishment;

➤ compliance with laws, rules, and regulations in the construction and maintenance of funeral establishments, such as handicap access and maximum seating capacity; and

➤ compliance with all regulatory requirements associated with the transport, care, and preparation of human remains.

Premises - The level of care given to those who enter premises (land and structures thereon) depends on the status of the visitor. A **trespasser**, defined as one who intentionally and without consent or privilege enters another's property, is owed very little care. An **invitee**, defined as one who has been invited on the property by the landowner – such as visitors to a funeral establishment for the purposes of attending a funeral or **visitation** – are owed a much higher degree of care. These invitees would also include such individuals as employees, salespersons, vendors, and deliverymen.

Funeral event locations and venues - The level of care expected – and therefore the potential for any liability exposure – may also depend on the particular premises where a funeral director is engaged in providing funeral services. These locations may include:

➢ Funeral establishments. The highest degree of care is owed to funeral establishment invitees and visitors. This is especially true when funeral service events are taking place in the facility, and the funeral director is assisting others in performing related tasks. As an example, liability may attach if pallbearers are injured, even though they volunteer for the job. Liability would also exist if any person were asked by a funeral director to move a car, carry flowers, hand out programs, or provide any other assistance and was injured or harmed while under the direction and supervision of funeral establishment staff.

➢ Religious facilities, cemeteries, and crematories. Funeral directors have been found to be jointly liable for an injury or harm suffered in these locations because they are – by contract with the family – obligated to 'supervise' the funeral events taking place. The courts have held it is a reasonable expectation for a funeral director – giving direction to others and controlling various aspects of the events – to identify potentially injurious conditions and take steps to lessen any exposure to those in attendance.

➢ Other venues. Current trends in the funeral industry call for greater customization and personalization of funeral service events. As such, it is not unusual for an event to be held in a non-traditional location or setting, such as a school auditorium, outdoor theater, or private residence. All of these different venues would expose the funeral establishment to some degree of exposure because of the funeral director's direct involvement in supervising the activities taking place.

Regardless of where it takes place, any injury or loss that occurs at an event where a funeral director is performing duties, it can be assumed the funeral director and the funeral establishment may be held liable. The funeral director is the professional with the knowledge, understanding, and expertise to handle the affairs and aspects of a funeral service and, when things go wrong, they are often the target of civil litigation.

Prudent and liability conscious funeral directors should give instructions to all participants in a funeral on how to reasonably and safely carry out the tasks assigned to them. They should also be aware and alert to any potentially hazardous situation that others – with little or no experience in the funeral industry – may not notice, such as the inherent hazards of being around an open grave.

Restrictions on Funeral Establishment Sites
Municipal restrictions - Regulations enacted by local municipalities, as opposed to those enacted by federal and state authorities, are called local laws or local **ordinances**. These are often the

source of restrictions imposed on the location, construction, and operation of a funeral establishment.

Regulations may include **zoning ordinances**, defined as laws passed by a local unit of government which regulates and prescribes land use planning. These geographical zones may restrict residential, commercial, and industrial construction, as well as define acceptable uses once construction has been completed. The local governing municipality takes into consideration the character of the land, adjacent landowners, existing structures, and expected uses to minimize any negative impact on residents, visitors, businesses, schools, and other unique aspects of the community as a whole.

Building zone regulations are developed in accordance with a well-considered and written comprehensive plan intended to avoid arbitrary exercise of government power, protect the rights of landowners, and provide for the overall safety, security, health, and well-being of the public. Many plans include specific requirements or restrictions within a geographic zone that may relate to the operation of a funeral establishment, including such items as:

> ➤ larger capacity wastewater management systems;

> ➤ minimum number of required parking spaces, including handicapped spaces;

> ➤ an approved landscaping plan;

> ➤ required outdoor lighting; and

> ➤ minimum building setbacks from property lines.

If a developer wants to build a funeral establishment in a zone where it would not otherwise be permitted – such as in a residential zone instead of a business zone – a local zoning ordinance will usually require them to seek a 'special use permit' from the zoning board. The board schedules a hearing for the applicant to present their case and express their intentions for the operation of a non-permitted use in a residential zone. The board then makes a decision based on the merits of the case; potential hardship to others (including the applicant); previous board rulings and decisions; the impact on surrounding properties; and any other mitigating or amplifying information the developer wants to submit or the public wishes to have heard.

Building codes - **Building codes** are laws, ordinances, and government regulations setting forth requirements for construction, maintenance, operation, occupancy, use, or appearance of buildings. These regulations encompass a wide range of construction and site improvement needs, and anyone erecting a new building or renovating an existing structure must comply with the codes applicable to their community.

As an example, parking lot building codes may contain specifics concerning the design, layout, required green space, buffers, screening, fences, surface materials, striping, snow removal, and storm water runoff (just to name a few!).

Other regulations may specify detailed requirements for plumbing installation, general construction, wiring and electrical needs, roof structures, business signs, heating systems, and wastewater treatment plans. Contractors will also need to meet minimum standards of construction, such as using materials that will withstand established wind and snow loads for the geographical area where the structures are to be located.

Restrictive covenants in land deeds - Whenever purchasing or planning construction on real property, it is important to research the deed to determine if there are any **restrictive covenants**. These covenants (agreements) in a deed may limit or prohibit certain activities or uses. They 'run with the land,' meaning they remain with the land deed regardless of who the owner may be now or in the future. Restrictive deed covenants are often found in controlled access communities, townhouse developments, and condominiums, where the collective property owners/users wish to maintain a certain style and appearance to the buildings and grounds.

Examples might include covenants that:

➢ prohibit vehicles from being parked outside overnight;

➢ stipulate the property may never be used for any commercial or business purpose (such as a funeral establishment); or

➢ limit the display of extraordinary holiday decorations (think 12' inflatable snowman).

Nuisances - Broadly defined, a landowner's use of property which interferes with the public or another landowner's use of their property is a **nuisance**.

More specifically, an act, occupation or structure which is a nuisance at all times and under all circumstances is a **nuisance per se**, as it may be prejudicial to public morals, dangerous to life, or injurious to public rights. A funeral establishment is not usually considered a nuisance per se.

Examples of a nuisance per se might include a junkyard, landfill, sewage treatment plant, or an X-rated adult entertainment center. Municipalities often designate those occupations or enterprises to be a nuisance per se and then undertake to regulate them by imposing strict requirements, frequent inspections, and close oversight of the operations and activities taking place.

An act, occupation or structure that is not a nuisance per se but may become a nuisance by circumstances of the location or manner in which it is operated is a **nuisance in fact**. A funeral establishment is usually not a nuisance in fact but could become one if they fail to operate properly, such as exposing human remains to public view or improperly disposing of contaminated waste.

Allied Professions and Affiliations
Many states regulate potential business relationships between funeral establishments and the allied professions that work with them on a routine basis in the funeral service industry.

Crematory - States may prohibit a funeral establishment from directly operating a **crematory** or having any investment or financial interest in their operation by others. They may also restrict a funeral establishment from entering into any agreements or business relationships that provide a commission, rebate, or discount for the exclusive use of a particular crematory.

Cemetery - States may prohibit funeral establishments from leasing or using real property owned or operated by a **cemetery** or cemetery corporation. Regulations may also prohibit funeral directors from sitting on the ruling bodies (councils, boards, committees, etc.) that govern a cemetery; entering into cross-marketing agreements for goods and services with a cemetery; or the exercise, control, or management of a cemetery by a funeral entity under any circumstance.

Retail/commercial businesses - States may prohibit a funeral establishment from sharing their facility, building, or space with other specified types of businesses. For example, a state may prohibit a funeral establishment from leasing or providing space to a floral shop or monument company. Similarly, laws may prohibit profit-sharing or exclusivity agreements that provide a commission or similar incentive to purchase goods and services from one particular supplier.

Facility uses - States may prohibit a funeral establishment from leasing their facilities for purposes other than those necessary to conduct funeral events. Such prohibitions may include the use of a funeral establishment for a wedding reception, dance club, training room, or other public or private gatherings or purposes.

The regulation of relationships between funeral establishments and allied professionals described here are dependent on individual state and local laws, rules, and regulations. Funeral establishment owners must therefore be diligent in researching these matters in the geographical locations from which they operate.

Bailor and Bailee Relationships

A **bailment** is the delivery of personal property by one person to another, who then holds the property for a certain purpose under an express or implied-in-fact contract. The person who delivers the personal property is the **bailor**; the person who receives the personal property is the **bailee**.

West's Encyclopedia of American Law provides the following description of a bailment:

> *The term bailment is derived from the French bailor, 'to deliver.' It is generally considered to be a contractual relationship since the bailor and bailee, either expressly or impliedly, bind themselves to act according to particular terms. The bailee receives only control or possession of the property while the bailor retains the ownership interests in it. During the specific period a bailment exists, the bailee's interest in the property is superior to that of all others, including the bailor, unless the bailee violates some term of the agreement. Once the purpose for which the property has been delivered has been accomplished, the property will be returned to the bailor or otherwise disposed of pursuant to the bailor's directions.*

As an example, if a family member delivers a diamond necklace to a funeral director with the expectation that it will be displayed and worn by the decedent during calling hours and then returned before the burial, a bailment has been created between the parties. The family member is the bailor (delivered the necklace) and the funeral director is the bailee (received the necklace).

By virtue of the bailment agreement, the funeral director having possession of the necklace may be held responsible for exercising reasonable care in safeguarding it until returned to the family. If for any reason the necklace is lost before it can be returned, the family member (bailor) could bring a civil action against the funeral director (bailee) based on the bailment having created a duty of care the funeral director failed to meet.

Covenants Not to Compete
A covenant not to compete, also called a non-compete agreement or non-competitive clause, restricts one party from competing directly with another party. Restrictions are applicable for a specified period of time and/or a defined geographical location. These agreements are often found in contracts, although they may not violate public policy, defined by West's Encyclopedia of American Law as a principle that no person or government official can legally perform an act that tends to injure the public.

Purchase contracts - A purchase contract for a funeral establishment business may have a non-compete clause to protect the interests of the buyer. The clause may restrict the former owner from owning or operating another funeral establishment for a set period of time and/or within a specified geographic location. It may also restrict the scope of activity of the former owner, such as prohibiting them from seeking future employment as a funeral director; appearing in advertisements for competitor funeral establishments; or recommending preneed customers transfer accounts to a different funeral establishment.

Employment contracts - Employment contracts are designed to protect the interests of a funeral establishment owner from the activities of their employees, both while employed and thereafter should they be terminated or choose to resign or retire.

Employment contracts may include any of the following:

➢ covenants not to compete for a specified period of time and/or within a defined geographical location upon separation from the workplace;

➢ non-disclosure agreements to protect the confidentiality of customer lists, preneed accounts, and internal workplace operations;

➢ non-disclosure agreements to prevent the release of any valuable information (trade secrets) that provide the funeral establishment with an advantage over competitors; and

➢ restrictions on employment outside the workplace, such as working part-time for another funeral establishment; limiting the number of additional outside work hours; or restrictions on the locations or scope of any outside work.

Chapter 6: Funeral Establishment Laws

Overview
This chapter reviews federal and state laws and regulations related to the operation of funeral establishments, including the Copyright Act of 1976; Health Insurance Portability and Accountability Act; Occupational Safety and Health Administration safety standards; and the Americans with Disabilities Act.

Chapter Definitions
Americans with Disabilities Act (ADA) - a federal statute prohibiting discrimination against the disabled in employment, public transportation, telecommunication services, and public accommodations and services.

Environmental Protection Agency (EPA) - a governmental agency with environmental protection regulatory and enforcement authority.

Morgue - a place where dead human bodies are kept until identified and/or released for final disposition.

Occupational Safety and Health Administration (OSHA) - a governmental agency with the responsibility for regulation and enforcement of safety and health matters for most employees.

Preparation room - that portion or location in a funeral establishment specifically designed and equipped for embalming and otherwise preparing dead human bodies.

Music Copyrights
Music is often played in a funeral establishment as a means to augment a welcoming, reverent, and respectful atmosphere for family members and guests visiting the facility. In almost all cases, music will have copyright protections under the federal Copyright Act of 1976, and any use without prior permission would be a copyright infringement.

Songs usually have two copyrights. One copyright is for the artist that wrote the lyrics and composed the music, and the second is for the artist using the music and lyrics to record a rendition of the song. If a funeral establishment owner wishes to play copyrighted music, they must first pay a fee to the copyright holders and be given a copyright license to use the material. There are several performance rights organizations in the United States authorized to sell licenses to use copyrighted music.

The National Funeral Directors Association (NFDA) has been very proactive in this area of law on behalf of the funeral service industry. They offer a 'music license only' that:

> *... covers the performance of music (live or recorded) that is played at any funeral service, whether at the funeral establishment or at another facility as long as it is performed in connection with some type of funeral or memorial service or ceremony.*

In addition, the NFDA has a 'music webcasting license' that provides for funeral establishments to, "*broadcast musical performances over the internet*." Additional information, associated fees, and applications are available on the NFDA website.

Health Insurance Portability and Accountability Act

The Health Insurance Portability and Accountability Act (HIPPA), known informally as the Privacy Rule, establishes national standards to protect an individual's medical records and other personal health information. The Act requires appropriate safeguards to protect the privacy of this data and sets forth limits and conditions on the acceptable uses and disclosures that may be made without patient authorization.

Funeral establishment owners, directors, and employees with access to the medical records of a decedent are required to maintain the privacy of those records and employ adequate safeguards to ensure any health information they possess is not accessible to unauthorized persons or organizations. The rule applies to all forms of an individual's protected health information, whether electronic, written, or oral.

Occupational Safety and Health Administration

Under the standards of the **Occupational Safety and Health Administration** (OSHA), employers are responsible for providing a safe and healthy workplace for employees. OSHA's role is to promote the safety and health of America's working men and women by setting and enforcing standards; providing training, outreach, and education; establishing partnerships; and encouraging continual improvement in workplace safety and health.

OSHA and its state partners have dramatically improved workplace safety, reducing work-related deaths and injuries by more than 65 percent. In 1970, an estimated 14,000 workers were killed on the job – about 38 every day. In 2019, the Bureau of Labor Statistics reported this number had fallen to 5,333 – about 15 workers per day.

Mandatory reporting - Within eight hours after the death of any employee as a result of a work-related incident, the employer must report the fatality to OSHA. Within 24 hours after the in-patient hospitalization of one or more employees, or an employee's amputation, or any employee's loss of an eye as a result of a work-related incident, the employer must report the incident to OSHA.

Formaldehyde exposure standard - The OSHA Formaldehyde Standard was designed to protect workers from occupational exposures to any form of formaldehyde, including solutions, gas, or any materials that release it into the workplace. Among other things, the standard:

➢ sets workplace exposure limits;

➢ specifies personal protection equipment;

➢ sets employee training requirements;

➢ mandates periodic monitoring of workspaces; and

➢ requires emergency plans to deal with any formaldehyde exposure incident.

Note: See Guide 1 for detailed information on the OSHA Formaldehyde Standard.

Hazard communication standard - Under the provisions of the OSHA Hazard Communication Standard, employers are responsible for informing employees of the hazards and identities of workplace chemicals to which they are exposed. The standard establishes uniform requirements to make sure the hazards of all chemicals imported into, produced, or used in U.S. workplaces are evaluated and the hazard information transmitted to affected employers and exposed employees.

Note: See Guide 2 for detailed information on the OSHA Hazard Communication Standard.

Bloodborne pathogens standard - The regulations in the OSHA Bloodborne Pathogens Standard protect workers whose jobs put them at a reasonable risk of coming into contact with blood and other potentially infectious materials. Bloodborne pathogens are infectious materials in blood that can cause disease in humans, including hepatitis B and C and human immunodeficiency virus (HIV). Workers exposed to these pathogens risk serious illness or death.

Note: See Guide 3 for detailed information on the OSHA Bloodborne Pathogens Standard.

Environmental Protection Agency
The Environmental Protection Agency (EPA) sets the standards and enforces the regulations pertaining to the burial at sea of human remains and cremated remains.

Note: For information on burial at sea legal requirements, see the chapter titled, *Interment (Burial), Entombment, Natural (Green) Burial and Burial at Sea*.

Americans with Disabilities Act
The **Americans with Disabilities Act of 1990 (ADA)** is a federal statute prohibiting discrimination against the disabled in employment, public transportation, telecommunication services, and public accommodations and services. The review here focuses on the ADA as it relates to those who visit a funeral establishment as a *public accommodation*, while a future chapter reviews the ADA as it relates to *employment*.

Public accommodations - Public accommodations are private entities who own, lease, lease to, or operate facilities and are open to the public. In defining the term, the ADA lists 'funeral parlor' as an example of a public accommodation. Funeral establishments must comply with specific requirements related to architectural standards for new and altered buildings; reasonable modifications to policies, practices, and procedures; effective communication with people with hearing, vision, or speech disabilities; and other access requirements.

Additionally, public accommodations that existed prior to the Act must remove barriers where it is easy to do so without much difficulty or expense, given the available resources of the public accommodation.

Disability - To be protected by the ADA, one must have a disability or have a relationship or association with an individual with a disability. An individual with a disability is defined by the ADA as a person who has a physical or mental impairment that substantially limits one or more of the major life activities of such individual; a record of such an impairment; or being regarded as having such an impairment.

The term disability does not include:

➤ transvestitism, transsexualism, pedophilia, exhibitionism, voyeurism, gender identity disorders not resulting from physical impairments, or other sexual behavior disorders;

➤ compulsive gambling, kleptomania, or pyromania; or

➤ psychoactive substance use disorders resulting from current illegal use of drugs.

Standards - The ADA sets forth standards for compliance, and there are *two sets of standards*. For buildings and structures not occupied until *after January 1993*, the standards are not as strict because the building plans would have been architecturally designed to incorporate all of the requirements in the ADA to provide accommodations for the disabled. For buildings and structures occupied *before January 1993*, the standards are stricter, often requiring renovations and redesigns to bring them into compliance with ADA requirements that did not exist when they were initially designed and built.

For prior existing buildings, the ADA requires the removal of barriers to disabled persons whenever possible. The ADA provides over 20 examples of steps that may be taken to remove barriers, including these that may in some cases apply to a funeral establishment:

Installing ramps	Widening doors	Installing a raised toilet seat
Making curb cuts in sidewalks and entrances	Repositioning the paper towel dispenser in a bathroom	Removing high pile, low density carpeting
Creating designated accessible parking spaces	Adding raised markings on elevator control buttons	Installing offset hinges to widen doorways
Installing grab bars in toilet stalls	Rearranging tables, chairs, vending machines, display racks, and other furniture	Rearranging toilet partitions to increase maneuvering space

Removing barriers - For the purposes of removing barriers, the ADA urges public accommodations to comply with the barrier removal requirements in a priority order and lists the four priorities as being:

First, a public accommodation should take measures to provide access to a place of public accommodation from public sidewalks, parking, or public transportation. For example, measures may include installing an entrance ramp, widening entrances, and providing accessible parking spaces.

Second, a public accommodation should take measures to provide access to those areas of a place of public accommodation where goods and services are made available to the public. For example, these measures may include adjusting the layout of display racks, rearranging tables, providing

Braille and raised character signage, widening doors, providing visual alarms, and installing ramps.

Third, a public accommodation should take measures to provide access to restroom facilities. For example, these measures may include removal of obstructing furniture or vending machines, widening of doors, installation of ramps, providing accessible signage, widening of toilet stalls, and installation of grab bars.

Fourth, a public accommodation should take any other measures necessary to provide access to the goods, services, facilities, privileges, advantages, or accommodations of a place of public accommodation.

Readily achievable - When making a determination on the feasibility to provide for the removal of barriers, the ADA only requires those removals that are determined to be 'readily achievable.' The ADA defines readily achievable as meaning, "… *easily accomplishable and able to be carried out without much difficulty or expense.*"

In determining whether an action is readily achievable, the factors to be considered include:

> ➤ the nature and cost of the action needed to provide for the barrier removal;

> ➤ the overall financial resources of the site or sites involved in the action; the number of persons employed at the site; the effect on expenses and resources; legitimate safety requirements that are necessary for safe operation, including crime prevention measures; or the impact otherwise of the action upon the operation of the site;

> ➤ the geographic separateness, and the administrative or fiscal relationship of the site or sites in question to any parent corporation or entity;

> ➤ if applicable, the overall financial resources of any parent corporation or entity; the overall size of the parent corporation or entity with respect to the number of its employees; the number, type, and location of its facilities; and

> ➤ if applicable, the type of operation or operations of any parent corporation or entity, including the composition, structure, and functions of the workforce of the parent corporation or entity.

The ADA provides for the owner of the public accommodation to make the initial determination on whether or not the barrier removal being considered may be readily achievable based on the above criteria. However, if the decision is challenged for any reason, the owner has the burden of proof to demonstrate the barrier removal was not feasible or readily achievable.

For this reason, it is very important funeral establishment owners exercise due diligence and good faith in exploring the potential for the removal of a barrier. This would mean carefully taking into consideration the ADA criteria and documenting the efforts taken when considering options. For example, when cost has been a factor in making the decision to not remove a barrier, obtaining written quotes for the work that would be required to bring the barrier into compliance with ADA standards would demonstrate due diligence and a good faith effort to comply.

In addition, funeral establishment owners should explore alternative means to negate the need to remove the existing barrier, such as constructing a new ADA compliant entrance and discontinuing public use of a non-compliant entrance.

Protections - ADA protections not only apply to the individual with a disability but also those that, "... *have a relationship or association with an individual with a disability.*" This means family members or others with a priority right to control a final disposition of human remains may also be afforded ADA protections. For example, if a funeral establishment were to decline to provide funeral services for a deceased disabled person for any reason related to the disability, the family might then be in a position to file a civil claim and seek damages based on ADA protections.

Goods and services available for the funeral of a person with a disability must also be the same as for a person with no disability. This would include offering the same goods and services at the same prices as they appear on the General Price List, regardless of any existing disability at the time of death. Further, no additional fees or special charges may be assessed to handle the case of a decedent that was disabled.

State Regulations

It is of course impossible to list all of the state statutory and administrative laws that regulate the funeral service in this single book. Therefore, a generic listing of common state standards is provided here. State and local statutory and administrative laws may address these topics:

Business locations (fixed, no mobile facilities)	Arrangement of showrooms (by price, material, etc.)	Seating capacities and minimum square footage
Adequate facilities for conducting funerals	Adequate number and selection of caskets	Business telephone requirements
Health and sanitary codes	Business licenses and permits	Handicap parking and access
Access to rolling stock	Fire and safety standards	Adequate licensed personnel
Advertising	Food and beverages	Interior and exterior signage

With respect to a **preparation room**, defined as that portion or location in a funeral establishment specifically designed and equipped for embalming and otherwise preparing dead human bodies; or a **morgue**, defined as a place where dead human bodies are kept until identified and/or released for final disposition, state administrative laws may address these topics:

Walls, ceiling, and floor non-porous and easy to clean	Operating table w/sufficient instruments and chemicals	Meet sanitary codes of state and local municipality
Sufficient size for purpose	Secluded from public view	Proper ventilation/air-exchange
Sewer and disposal facilities	Hot and cold running water	Secure storage for chemicals
Eye wash stations and fountains	Emergency drench showers	Windows covered

Chapter 7: Preneed Funeral Contracts

Overview
There are a number of strategies for consumers to consider when planning to have funds available to pay for funeral expenses. These may include preneed accounts, trust accounts, burial insurance, funeral insurance, and bank accounts. These strategies are explored in this chapter, with an emphasis on preneed accounts – a strategy which relies heavily on the involvement of a funeral director.

Chapter Definitions
At-need cases - funeral service cases where funeral arrangements are made immediately after a death has occurred; as contrasted with preneed cases, where funeral arrangements are made prior to a death occurring, in preparation for use in the future [by Author].

Beneficiary - means the named individual for whom a preneed agreement is purchased. The beneficiary may also be the purchaser [by Author].

Escrow account - in funeral service, a vehicle used to hold monies on prefunded contracts and beyond the control of the funeral director.

Fiduciary - means an individual in whom another has placed the utmost trust and confidence to manage and protect property or money. The relationship wherein one person has an obligation to act for another's benefit. West's Encyclopedia of American Law, edition 2. ©2008 The Gale Group, Inc.

Guaranteed contract - an agreement whereby the funeral establishment promises that the services and merchandise will be provided at the time of need (in the future) for a sum not exceeding the original amount of the aforementioned contract plus any accruals, regardless of the current prices associated with providing the services and merchandise at the time of the funeral.

Irrevocable contract - an agreement for future funeral services which cannot be terminated or canceled prior to the death of the beneficiary.

Non-guaranteed contract - agreement in which the funeral establishment promises to apply the amount prepaid plus any accruals to the balance due. However, the cost of the funeral will be based upon the current price for the services and merchandise at the time services are provided.

Prefunded funeral arrangements - funeral arrangements made in advance of need that include provisions for funding or prepayment.

Preneed cases - funeral service cases where funeral arrangements are made prior to a death occurring, in preparation for use in the future; as contrasted with at-need cases, where funeral arrangements are made immediately following a death [by Author].

Pre-planned funeral arrangements - funeral arrangements made in advance of need that do not include provisions for funding or prepayment.

Purchaser - means the named individual paying for and purchasing a preneed account. The purchaser may also be the beneficiary [by Author].

Revocable contract - agreement which may be terminated by the purchaser at any time prior to the death of the beneficiary with a refund of monies paid on the contract as prescribed by state law.

Trust account - account established by one individual to be held for the benefit of another (as a method of payment of funeral expenses); creates a fiduciary responsibility. Money paid to a funeral establishment for future services is placed in an account with the funeral establishment as trustee for the benefit of another.

Trustee - one who holds title to property or another position of trust to a beneficiary.

Consumer Awareness
In 2017, the National Funeral Directors Association (NFDA) issued a press release relative to publication of the 2017 NFDA Consumer Awareness and Preferences Study.

In the study, the NFDA found:

> ... *consumers acknowledge the importance of preplanning their own funeral but fail to do so in practice. This year's findings reveal that 62.5 percent of consumers felt it was very important to communicate their funeral plans and wishes to family members prior to their own death, yet only 21.4 percent had done so.*

This is a puzzling statistic, as the benefits and advantages to having a preneed have been the source of numerous positive articles, reviews, and endorsements in national media outlets. In addition, consumers that have chosen to preplan a funeral have almost universally expressed satisfaction and gratitude for having made the decision to have preneed arrangements in place.

In addressing this anomaly, the NFDA went on to report that:

> *Even though nearly two-thirds of Americans acknowledge the importance of prearrangements, respondents cited several factors as preventing them from planning, namely that preplanning is not a priority, that they have not thought about it, or that prepaying is too costly.*

Preneeds as a Funding Strategy
Funeral arrangements made in advance of need are called preneeds or **preneed cases**. A preneed arrangement conference is one in which a consumer meets with a funeral service professional and makes funeral arrangements, including selection of the goods and services they wish to have provided at the time of their death. Preneeds should not be confused with other pre-death care options, such as funeral insurance policies, savings accounts, or burial insurance policies. These options plan for having the funds available to cover the costs of a funeral service but do not usually specify or provide details about exactly what goods and services are going to be included.

Preneed options - There are two preneed options, and both of them include meeting with a funeral director, making arrangements, planning funeral events, selecting goods and services, and gathering the necessary information and documentation. The difference between the two options is whether or not the funeral service is simply a **pre-planned funeral arrangement**, or a pre-planned *and* **prefunded funeral arrangement**.

Reasons for preneeds - Prefunded preneed funeral arrangements are made for many reasons. Financial considerations often play a significant role, as well as a strong desire by consumers to have control over their own final affairs.

By having a funeral preplan an individual has the opportunity to take responsibility for paying the associated expenses in advance of need. This affords them time to make the necessary financial arrangements, while relieving the burden on survivors to do so at the time of death. Other financial benefits may include prepaid discounts and guaranteed pricing, as well as reducing assets for any future Medicaid or Supplemental Security Income (SSI) eligibility applications or awards.

Beyond financial aspects, a prefunded preneed also allows a consumer to exercise considerable control over the funeral events they wish to have following their death, including the selection of the goods and services to be provided for the funeral. These selections may include:

➢ choosing the method of final disposition, e.g., burial, cremation, natural, etc.;

➢ selecting a final resting location, such as a specific cemetery or columbarium;

➢ choice of a burial container;

➢ whether or not to have calling hours;

➢ preference for an open or closed casket;

➢ where to hold a funeral or memorial service; and

➢ information to include in a death notice or obituary.

Family benefits - Putting end-of-life affairs in order prior to death is a thoughtful, considerate, and caring decision of great benefit to the survivors at the time of need. By documenting and memorializing death care decisions in advance, the family of a decedent is relieved of making difficult and emotional decisions at a time when grief and loss are a burden on their ability to cope and reason. These decisions may also eliminate or resolve potential conflicts within a family when attempting to reconcile service-related issues at the time of need.

Purchaser benefits - In addition to having the opportunity to secure the funds needed, making arrangements in advance also offers individuals the opportunity to take the time they require to make thoughtful and informed decisions. Further, the consumer is comforted by knowing they took the initiative to eliminate the need for their family to make difficult decisions under often trying and stressful circumstances. This is especially true for prefunded preneed arrangements in situations where financial resources may be limited. And lastly, many people lead an orderly and structured life, and making preneed arrangements is a logical and necessary means for them to conclude their end-of-life affairs knowing all preparations have been made.

Preneed trust accounts - A **trust account** is an account established by one individual to be held for the benefit of another. These accounts create a **fiduciary** responsibility where one person has an obligation to act for another's benefit. Generally speaking, funds in a trust account may only be withdrawn as a consumer refund or to pay for the pre-arranged funeral following death.

A limited number of states may use the term **escrow account** to describe the relationship that exists in a trust account. Caroline Banton describes escrow as:

> *... the use of a third party, which holds an asset or funds before they are transferred from one party to another. The third party holds the funds until both parties have fulfilled their contractual requirements.*

Funds received by the funeral director are usually deposited in a trust account with a financial institution. The institution is the **trustee** of the funds and has a fiduciary responsibility to both the purchaser of the preneed and the funeral establishment. The trustee distributes the funds to the establishment after the beneficiary of the preneed has died and the funeral goods and services have been provided. Many states require the funds be held in federally insured banking institutions and earn interest at prevailing rates while being held to pay for future goods and services.

Most states require preneed funds be deposited into a trust account specific to those funds alone and prohibit any funds from being commingled into one master trust account or other existing monies. Some states require or allow an amount less than 100% of the funds to be placed in trust, while other states require the full 100% of funds be placed in trust and, in addition, may mandate all interest earned be deposited into the account.

Types of Preneed Contracts

Prefunded funeral arrangements are documented in a contractual agreement between the parties. Fundamentally, the funeral director agrees to provide certain goods and services to the **purchaser** upon the death of the **beneficiary** and, in return, receives payment in advance from the consumer for those goods and services.

Many funeral establishments use the mandatory FTC Statement of Funeral Goods and Services Selected as the base document for a prefunded preneed contract by including specific contractual language, such as an express promise to pay and terms of payment. Regardless of the form the agreement takes, they are contracts, a term that has legal connotations and implications that bind the parties to the provisions it contains.

Note: The purchaser and beneficiary on a preneed contract may be the same person.

Revocable or irrevocable contracts - A **revocable contract** agreement may be terminated by the purchaser at any time prior to the death of the beneficiary and the monies paid on the contract refunded as prescribed by state law. The majority of states require the refund to also include the interest earned on any trust or other preneed account type.

An **irrevocable contract** is an agreement for future funeral services which cannot be terminated or canceled. When the beneficiary of a prefunded preneed is seeking government benefits, such as Medicaid or Supplemental Security Income (SSI), states usually mandate an irrevocable contract.

Guaranteed or non-guaranteed contracts - A **guaranteed contract** is an agreement where the funeral establishment promises services and merchandise will be provided at the time of need for a sum not to exceed the original amount of the contract, plus any accruals, regardless of the current prices associated with providing the services and merchandise at the time of need. These contracts may be guaranteed for a specified length of time, after which the guarantee is no longer in effect. Other contracts may have no time restrictions or, when they are time restricted, provide options to extend the time period for an additional fee.

A **non-guaranteed contract** is an agreement in which the funeral establishment promises to apply the amount prepaid, plus any accruals, to the balance due at the time of need. However, the final cost of the funeral will be based on current prices associated with providing the services and merchandise at the time of need.

Cash advance charges - Funeral service contracts include funeral establishment charges and cash advance charges. Cash advance funds are paid by a funeral establishment to purchase third-party goods or services, such as certified copies of death certificates and the services of a crematory. As the funeral establishment has no control over the amount third-parties charge for cash advance items, they can become an issue when a prefunded preneed is to be *guaranteed*.

For this reason, the common practice in the funeral service industry is to guarantee funeral establishment charges but *not* cash advance charges, in which case the purchaser must be made fully aware the cash advance items on a preneed are estimated and not guaranteed by the funeral establishment.

Other Funding Strategies
Burial insurance - The concept of burial insurance has its roots in 17th century London burial clubs. These clubs were formed to assist people of the working classes to defray the heavy expenses of a funeral and to perpetuate the memory of deceased friends. The costs were shared by others making weekly collections. These burial clubs were the forerunners to the modern insurance companies of today.

Burial insurance is still available in some areas and in exchange for a monthly premium provide insurance proceeds for a burial at the time of death. The cost of funeral goods and funeral services and the existence of a preneed funeral contract are not usually a part of a burial insurance policy. The policy holder simple knows the funds will be available when needed and decides how those funds are spent at the time of need to pay for funeral service events.

Funeral insurance - The purchase of a funeral insurance policy usually includes making preneed arrangements that include preselected goods and services. They provide a valuable service in offering consumers the opportunity to make scheduled payments over a period of time to pay for arrangements made in advance. In those states where not prohibited, funeral insurance policies may designate a funeral establishment as the beneficiary or assignee of the policy proceeds.

As might be expected, not all states regulate these insurance policies in the same manner. Some allow funeral directors to sell funeral insurance; become licensed insurance agents; receive a commission for a funeral insurance sale; and/or be named as a beneficiary on a funeral insurance policy. Other states prohibit some or all of these activities. These variations often create distinct advantages and disadvantages over other mechanisms available to fund preneeds. As an example, allowing a funeral director to serve as an insurance agent and receive an upfront commission payment is a distinct advantage over a 100% trust account, where a funeral director may not access any funds until the time of death.

Another advantage to an insurance funding strategy over other account types is in the area of taxes. Interest earned on a trust account is usually considered ordinary income, and the purchaser may be required to pay federal and/or state income tax on interest earned; while the accrual of benefits on an insurance policy, such as to compensate for inflation over time, are usually non-taxable.

Financial institutions - Individuals may open a savings or passbook account, purchase a certificate of deposit, or open other similar accounts with a financial institution for the deposit of funds to pay for funeral expenses. Depending on individual state regulations, these could be joint accounts naming the funeral establishment or funeral director as one of the account holders, thereby allowing access to the funds under 'right of survivorship' rules. Others may have a specific beneficiary listed by means of a TOD (transfer on death) or POD (payment on death) designation that names a beneficiary. Generally speaking, these accounts are for the purpose of holding funds intended to pay for a funeral in the future; however, the funeral arrangements for which the funds are intended may or may not be preplanned.

Preneed entrepreneurs - There are private businesses whose focus is on the administration of preneed funds for funeral establishments. They may be operated as a subsidiary to an existing company or operate as an independent service organization. Statewide funeral director associations are one of the groups that have begun to take advantage of this concept, offering a wealth of preneed-related support services to funeral establishments, such as online account records, electronic transfer of funds, and standardized forms.

Portability of Preneed Contracts
State laws address the portability (transferability) of prefunded preneed contracts when a funeral establishment is a party to the agreement, such as a trust account. The purchaser is usually entitled to transfer a preneed contract and the funds to a different funeral establishment or funeral director at any time, and the original establishment is required to facilitate the transfer within a specified number of days after receiving a transfer request.

Chapter 8: Preneed Regulatory Compliance

<u>Overview</u>
This chapter reviews issues associated with preneed accounts, including: preneed arrangement conferences; complying with the FTC Funeral Rule; identifying changes that may influence preneeds; and identifying other preneed legal considerations.

<u>Chapter Definitions</u>
At-need cases - funeral service cases where funeral arrangements are made immediately after a death has occurred; as contrasted with preneed cases, where funeral arrangements are made prior to a death occurring, in preparation for use in the future [by Author].

Beneficiary - means the named individual for whom a preneed agreement is purchased. The beneficiary may also be the purchaser [by Author].

Contract - a legally enforceable agreement.

Prefunded funeral arrangements - funeral arrangements made in advance of need that include provisions for funding or prepayment.

Preneed cases - funeral service cases where funeral arrangements are made prior to a death occurring, in preparation for use in the future; as contrasted with at-need cases, where funeral arrangements are made immediately following a death [by Author].

Purchaser - means the named individual paying for and purchasing a preneed account. The purchaser may also be the beneficiary [by Author].

Third party contracts - agreements which are incident to providing services and merchandise other than by the funeral establishment, e.g., caskets, vaults, urns, cremation services, etc.

<u>Regulatory Compliance</u>
Federal - The FTC Funeral Rule is the only federal statute with requirements specific to the funeral service industry, although other federal statutes or rules may apply indirectly or tangentially. The only mention in the Funeral Rule regarding preneeds is to note the requirements apply equally to both at-need and preneed cases.

State - A far greater influence on preneeds is wielded by state authorities that oversee business and banking laws specific to the regulation of prefunded preneeds. Practitioners must be diligent in researching and understanding the preneed laws and rules as they exist in the states where they practice.

<u>Preneed Arrangement Conferences</u>
The majority of consumers meeting to discuss preneeds with a funeral service professional want to both preplan and prefund funeral arrangements. In these cases, the funeral director agrees to provide certain goods and services, and the **purchaser** agrees to pay for those goods and services

in advance to provide a funeral for the named **beneficiary** in the agreement. The agreement is then documented in a contract and signed by the funeral director and the purchaser.

On occasion, there are consumers that wish to plan a funeral but not pay in advance for any of the goods or services. In these cases, the funeral director provides a written summary of the proposed goods and services to the consumer but does not prepare a contract or other binding agreement. A copy of the summary is maintained in the funeral establishment files and used as a guide during any future at-need arrangement conference.

Conference location - A conference to purchase **prefunded funeral arrangements** may be held in a funeral establishment, private residence, or any other suitable location. However, if the preneed arrangement conference is going to take place at any location other than the funeral establishment, funeral directors must ensure compliance with the federal Cooling-off Rule that regulates door-to-door and other similar sales. This rule provides a seller must give written notice to a consumer of the right to cancel a contract for goods and services. The rule may be triggered when a seller (funeral director) personally solicits and makes the sale at a place other than their place of business – such as in the purchaser's home.

There are various exceptions, waivers, and conditions that may require or, in some cases, negate the need to provide such written notice, but funeral directors should determine what action they must take to comply with the rule on a case-by-case basis. In addition, several states have enacted similar rules to protect consumers when funeral arrangements are made in a location other than the business location of the seller.

Note: See the chapter titled, *Consumer Protection Laws,* for a more expansive explanation of the Cooling-off Rule.

The FTC and Preneeds
The FTC Funeral Rule information that follows is limited to the influence it has on prefunded preneeds. There are four chapters in this book dedicated exclusively to a comprehensive review of the rule, and readers are encouraged to consult those chapters on any FTC Funeral Rule issue.

Generally - The FTC Funeral Rule requirements apply to all **preneed cases** (prepaid or not) and **at-need cases** when making funeral arrangements. The FTC Guide states:

> *In preneed situations, you must comply with all Rule requirements at the time funeral arrangements are pre-planned. You also need to comply with the Rule after the death of the individual who made preneed arrangements. If the survivors inquire about goods or services, alter the pre-planned arrangements, or are required to pay additional sums of money, you must give them all relevant disclosures and price lists.*
>
> *For example, survivors may be asked to pay additional amounts if the prepaid plan does not guarantee prices at the time of death. In other cases, survivors may change arrangements specified in the preneed plan, adding or subtracting certain goods or services. In both situations, the requirements of the Rule apply. You must*

give the survivors relevant price lists, as well as an itemized Statement of Funeral Goods and Services Selected.

The Funeral Rule does not apply to any preneed agreements or contracts executed (signed) before the rule went into effect in 1984. However, if they are amended or changed for any reason thereafter, the changes automatically trigger and require compliance with all of the rule requirements. It is not unusual for a prefunded preneed to have some minor changes at the time of need, and funeral directors must be vigilant to ensure FTC requirements are met when altering or changing a preneed contract, especially at the time of need.

General Price List - A copy of the current funeral establishment General Price List (GPL) must be given to a consumer when discussing the type of funerals or dispositions the establishment can provide; the specific goods and services they offer; or the prices of their goods and services. All three of these items will be a part of the conversation during a preneed arrangement conference, and the funeral director must ensure the consumer promptly receives a copy of the GPL.

The GPL must contain all of the FTC mandatory disclosures, as well as any state or local statements. Certain states may also require additional disclosures or statements related specifically to a contract for preneed arrangements.

The Funeral Rule allows for a funeral establishment to have a different GPL for preneed arrangements if they sell different goods and services on a preneed basis. However, a preneed GPL must include all of the same required disclosures and offer goods and services on an itemized basis. It is not permissible to offer only package funerals with no itemization to preneed customers.

Other price lists - In addition to the GPL, a funeral director should be prepared during a preneed arrangement conference to provide a Casket Price List and/or Outer Burial Container Price List for review if these items are being discussed or considered for purchase. These lists must be given to a consumer *before* they enter a selection room and see prices on individual products or are orally given any pricing information by the funeral director.

Embalming - Consumers must be given written notice the law does not in most cases require embalming. This is accomplished by including the mandatory FTC embalming disclosure in immediate conjunction with the price for embalming on a General Price List. The FTC requirement to have prior permission for embalming applies equally to preneed cases.

Required statement - The requirement to give a consumer a Statement of Funeral Goods and Services Selected (Statement) at the close of the arrangement conference applies equally to both at-need and preneed cases. The Statement must contain the three Funeral Rule mandated disclosures relating to legal requirements, embalming, and cash advance items.

*Non-declinable fee*s - Consumers making preneed arrangements must be made aware of the one non-declinable fee on a GPL when the funeral arrangements being chosen will include this fee. This charge is to pay for basic services and overhead and added to the total cost of the funeral arrangements the family selects, excluding arrangements for direct cremation, immediate burial, and the forwarding or receiving of human remains to or from another funeral establishment. The Basic Services section on a GPL also has an FTC mandatory disclosure.

Cash advances - The FTC Funeral Rule does not require any specific prefunded goods or services be listed as a cash advance, nor does it prohibit a funeral establishment from making a profit on a cash advance purchase. However, individual states have passed a number of legislative initiatives to regulate how cash advances are handled. Some have requirements mandating certain named items be offered *only* as cash advances, such as road tolls and certified copies of death certificates. Other states totally prohibit funeral establishments from making any profit whatsoever on cash advances. Practitioners must research all state and local laws with respect to cash advance funeral charges before developing and distributing a GPL or offering guaranteed prefunded preneeds.

Changes to Prefunded Preneeds
A prefunded preneed is a legally enforceable **contract**. As such, it must adhere to contemporary standards and practices in business law and may be subject to judicial review if any component of the contract calls into question its validity. This also applies to any changes or alterations made to a preneed contract after its execution by the parties involved.

Non-guaranteed - In the case of non-guaranteed preneeds, changes in the goods and services selected may result in a change to the total price. Both the purchaser and the funeral director would need to agree to and formalize the changes, but the contract would not necessarily be invalid or void simply because of the alterations.

Guaranteed - In the case of a guaranteed preneed, changes in the goods and services the purchaser wishes to have for a funeral will not affect the contract if the parties are in agreement. A funeral director must however be diligent in minimizing any additional financial risk as a result of the change. For example, if a purchaser wants to change from a basic wooden casket to a more expensive bronze casket, the funeral director could accept the change but refuse to guarantee the price if they thought the risk of a substantial change in future metal prices was unacceptable. The contract would then have to be re-negotiated, including whether or not it is will be guaranteed.

The duration of any guaranteed pricing may or may not be limited. If limited, extensions may be available for an additional fee. Any changes to the terms of the guarantee would again require the mutual agreement of the parties involved.

Availability - Changes that could affect a preneed contract include the unavailability of certain goods or services at the time of need. As an example, goods previously selected at the time of the preneed arrangements may no longer be available from the manufacturer, or the supplier may have gone out of business. To address the potential need to make changes, most states require language in the contract that require a funeral establishment to substitute goods or services of 'equal or greater value' for those originally selected and no longer available, at no additional cost to the consumer.

Reconciliation - Funds in a preneed contract must be reconciled at the time of need. In anticipation of this, states require preneed contracts include language on how to reconcile the account when the cost of the goods and services exceeds the amount of the monies paid or, conversely, when the amount of monies paid exceeds the cost of the goods and services. As these requirements to reconcile the account are a part of the contract, changes do not necessarily render a contract invalid.

Void or voidable - All contracts, including those for a prefunded preneed, may be void or voidable. A void contract is an agreement which has no legal effect or validity and cannot be enforced by either party; and a voidable contract is a contract which would be an enforceable agreement, but due to circumstances may be set aside by one of the parties

Kristy DeSmith explains these two contract terms – void and voidable – as follows.

> *When a contract is void, it is not valid. It can never be enforced under state or federal laws. A void contract is null from the moment it was created and neither party is bound by the terms. Think of it as one that a court would never recognize or enforce because there are missing elements.*
>
> *A contract can be **void** for the following reasons:*
>
> ➤ *The terms of the agreement are illegal or against public policy (unlawful consideration or object).*
>
> ➤ *A party was not of sound mind while signing the agreement.*
>
> ➤ *A party was under the age of consent.*
>
> ➤ *The terms are impossible.*
>
> ➤ *The contract restricts the rights of a party.*
>
> *Alternatively, a voidable contract is valid and may be enforceable in certain situations if both parties agree to move forward. One party is bound to the terms of the contract, whereas the other party can oppose the contract for legal reasons if they so choose. Therefore, if the unbound party rejects the contract, it becomes voidable.*
>
> *A contract can become **voidable** under the following circumstances:*
>
> ➤ *A party was coerced or threatened into signing the agreement.*
>
> ➤ *A party was under undue influence (one party is able to dominate the will of another).*
>
> ➤ *A party is not of sound mind or mentally competent (minor or mentally ill).*
>
> ➤ *The terms of the contract were breached.*
>
> ➤ *Mutual mistakes on behalf of both parties.*

> *The contract is fraudulent (omitting or falsifying facts or information, or the intention to not carry out the promise in the contract).*

> *Misrepresentation occurs (a false statement of fact).* [**Bold** emphasis added]

Other Legal Considerations

In addition to the preneed contract itself, there may be other laws or documentation that could impose legal obligations on the parties at the time of death.

Last will and testament - A last will and testament may contain specific instructions from the decedent on what they want for funeral goods and services following their death. In some states, these instructions may be deemed reflective of the decedent's intent and deserve consideration, while in other states they are considered absolute. When they are in conflict with instructions on a preneed account, changes may be required.

Priority right to control - State laws usually recognize the rights of the person in control of a final disposition supersede funeral arrangements in prefunded preneeds. For example, if the person in control were to find components of the preneed arrangements were not consistent with the known moral or religious beliefs of the deceased, they would be obligated to change the arrangements.

In those states that allow an individual to designate an agent to control the disposition of their remains, the document may also include specific instructions to be carried out by the agent. When those instructions are contrary to the directions or funeral arrangements contained in a prefunded preneed, most state laws provide the instructions to the agent found in the designation document will take precedence, although other states defer to the most recent set of instructions.

Court decisions - Judicial rulings, decisions, or orders may impose legal obligations on those persons with the right to control a final disposition. As an example, a court may prohibit a person from exercising their priority right when that person has been implicated in causing the death of the person for whom they would control the disposition. These situations are often referred to as 'ultimate estrangement.' Some states have statutorily restricted individuals from controlling the final disposition of human remains when charged or convicted with a crime related to the death of the decedent, such as vehicular manslaughter or murder.

Third-party contracts - These agreements are incident to providing services and merchandise other than by the funeral establishment, e.g., caskets, vaults, urns, cremation services, etc. Third-parties are not a party to the funeral service contract with the funeral establishment but have a duty and responsibility to provide certain goods and services pursuant to the funeral service contract. When they cease to exist or no longer offer the goods and services specified in a preneed contract, state laws proscribe appropriate remedies. These may include such resolutions as refunds, credits, or the substitution of like items of equal or greater value than the original item.

Supplemental Security Income (SSI) and Medicaid Programs

Certain restrictions may apply to the goods and services a prefunded preneed is paying for if the beneficiary is receiving SSI or Medicaid assistance.

SSI is a federal program that pays benefits to disabled adults and children who have limited income and resources and were either unable to work or earn enough work credit due to a disability to be eligible for similar benefits through Social Security. SSI is a means to help with medical and cost of living expenses, and the program is funded by the federal government.

Medicaid is a federal program that provides health coverage to eligible low-income adults, children, pregnant women, elderly adults, and people with disabilities. The Medicaid program is funded jointly by the states and the federal government but administered by the states, often through the counties or parishes located within the state.

Note: Medicaid should not be confused with Medicare, the national health care insurance program for Americans ages 65 and older. Medicare has no influence related to preneed contracts.

Following death - When a person receiving Medicaid benefits dies, the states, with some allowable exceptions, are required to seek reimbursement of the government funds spent on their care. Medicaid provides the following information about estate recovery and liens following death.

> *Estate Recovery and Liens*
>
> *State Medicaid programs must recover certain Medicaid benefits paid on behalf of a Medicaid enrollee. For individuals age 55 or older, states are required to seek recovery of payments from the individual's estate for nursing facility services, home and community-based services, and related hospital and prescription drug services. States have the option to recover payments for all other Medicaid services provided to these individuals, except Medicare cost-sharing paid on behalf of Medicare Savings Program beneficiaries.*
>
> *Under certain conditions, money remaining in a trust after a Medicaid enrollee has passed away may be used to reimburse Medicaid. States may not recover from the estate of a deceased Medicaid enrollee who is survived by a spouse, child under age 21, or blind or disabled child of any age. States are also required to establish procedures for waiving estate recovery when recovery would cause an undue hardship.*
>
> *States may impose liens for Medicaid benefits incorrectly paid pursuant to a court judgment. States may also impose liens on real property during the lifetime of a Medicaid enrollee who is permanently institutionalized, except when one of the following individuals resides in the home: the spouse, child under age 21, blind or disabled child of any age, or sibling who has an equity interest in the home. The states must remove the lien when the Medicaid enrollee is discharged from the facility and returns home.*

Preneeds protected - Under a variety of state laws, the beneficiary of a prefunded preneed receiving SSI or Medicaid benefits is protected from having the funds in the account seized by the government to recover benefit payments. This same protection may be afforded to certain family members as well, such as a prefunded preneed for the child of a beneficiary receiving Medicaid benefits.

As a result of these protections, states and counties have placed conditions on these special preneeds to minimize abuse and exploitation by others. There are generally three types of restrictions.

1. Identifying the customary and acceptable goods and services eligible for inclusion in a preneed, such as the initial transfer of remains; custodial care; dressing and casketing; cosmetology; supervision for visitation; supervision for a funeral service; hearse; casket; and out-of-town shipping. These 'acceptable' items may be further described by individual counties or municipalities to limit the expense, such as setting maximum allowable expenses for the burial space or casket, or limiting the number of visitation days or hours.

2. Identifying goods and services that would not be acceptable expenses, such as: food, lodging or transportation expenses for family, friends, or guests, newspaper obituaries, flowers, burial plots, and urns. These items may also be further described to more accurately reflect customary charges in specified geographical areas or regions.

3. Mandating these preneeds be irrevocable. An irrevocable account may not be closed or refunded, and the funds may not be used for any other purposes. In addition, the arrangements may not be altered or changed to facilitate a refund to any survivors.

Unfortunately, there are many instances where survivors make every conceivable attempt to take possession of preneed funds for purposes other than for which they were intended.

As an example, assume an *irrevocable* preneed account has $12,000 in funds to pay for a pre-planned funeral. At the time of death, the surviving family wants to change the services to an $1800 direct cremation and get a cash refund from the preneed account for the remaining $10,200.

In this case, the family may have the right in some states to change the arrangements to a direct cremation; however, if they do, state and federal law will require the $10,200 refund be remitted as a reimbursement to the agency that paid SSI or Medicaid benefits to provide care for the deceased prior to death. The survivors would have no legal right to any refunds.

Chapter 9: Methods of Final Disposition
Interment (Burial), Entombment, Natural (Green) Burial, and Burial at Sea

Overview
The legal and acceptable methods for the final disposition of human remains in the United States are the topics of this and the next chapter. This chapter reviews interment (burial), entombment, natural (green) burial, and burial at sea. The next chapter reviews cremation, donation, alkaline hydrolysis, and natural organic reduction.

Chapter Definitions
Cemetery - an area of ground set aside and dedicated for the final disposition of human remains.

Crypt - a chamber in a mausoleum, of sufficient size, generally used to contain the casketed remains of a deceased person.

Disinterment (exhumation) - the removal of human remains from a previous location of final disposition.

Eminent domain - the inherent power of a government to take private property for public use. In the U.S. just compensation to the property owner(s) is required.

Entombment - the placing of a human remains in a crypt in a mausoleum.

Environmental Protection Agency (EPA) - a governmental agency with environmental protection regulatory and enforcement authority.

Final disposition - the conclusive performance of services with respect to the dead human body by one of the legally recognized methods.

Inter - to bury in the ground.

Interment (burial/inhumement) - the act of placing the dead human body in the ground.

Intestate succession - the method used to distribute property owned by a person who dies without a valid will.

Mausoleum - a building containing crypts or vaults for entombment.

Natural (green) burial - an eco-friendly method of final disposition that utilizes products, services, and merchandise free of toxic/hazardous materials, are biodegradable or that minimize use of energy.

Natural (green) cemetery - a place of interment that bans the use of metal caskets, toxic embalming, and concrete vaults and may also require the use of aesthetically natural monuments.

Nuisance per se - acts, occupations or structures which are nuisances at all times under all circumstances; may be prejudicial to public morals, dangerous to life, or injurious to public rights.

Outer burial container - any container which is designed for placement in the grave around the casket including, but not limited to, containers commonly known as burial vaults, grave boxes, and grave liners.

Private cemetery - a cemetery owned by a private enterprise such as a corporation for profit, a non-profit corporation, partnership, sole owners, religious orders, etc.

Public cemetery - a cemetery owned by a governmental unit (federal, state, or municipal).

Receiving vault - a structure designed for the temporary storage of bodies not to be immediately interred.

Zoning ordinance - a law passed by a local unit of government which regulates and prescribes land use planning.

Final Disposition by Interment (Burial)
A burial is defined as the act of placing a dead human body in the ground. In the funeral service industry, a burial is formally called an **interment**, derived from the word **inter**, meaning to bury in the ground. Other disposition methods may also use the word burial in their description, but a traditional burial takes place in a 'traditional' cemetery, as compared to a burial at sea in the ocean or a green burial in a green cemetery.

An interment in some rare circumstances may be referred to as inhumation or an inhumement.

For decades, interment was the predominant choice for the disposition of human remains in North America. Today, as a whole, there are more final dispositions by cremation than there are for interment in both the United States and Canada. For a burial disposition, funeral directors may be required to file certificates of death; obtain burial permits; and, in some states, be physically present to personally supervise the interment.

Note: These two words – interment and internment – are on occasion confused with each other. An inter**n**ment is a state of confinement, such as a prisoner of war being inter**n**ed in an inter**n**ment camp. The professional practitioner will therefore be careful to use the proper pronunciation of the word **inter**ment when speaking about the burial disposition of human remains.

Traditional cemetery - There are several classifications for a traditional **cemetery**, defined as an area of ground set aside and dedicated for the final disposition of human remains. They may be a **public cemetery**, defined as a cemetery owned by a governmental unit (federal, state, or municipal), or a **private cemetery**, defined as a cemetery owned by a private enterprise, such as corporations, non-profits, partnerships, sole owners, and religious orders.

The sale of cemetery graves in a *public* cemetery are generally subject to anti-discrimination laws found in both federal and state statutes; however, *private* cemeteries are often given significantly greater latitude to identify those to whom graves may be sold and used.

As an example, a cemetery owned and operated by a Catholic Church may have rules, bylaws, or regulations that restrict interments to only those of the Catholic faith and their families.

Public cemeteries are commonly regulated by state agencies and subject to rules and regulations exercising control over such matters as:

➢ specifications for **outer burial containers** and **receiving vaults**;

➢ availability of interments on a six-day basis;

➢ maintenance of maps and the provision of directional signs;

➢ specifications and placement of markers, monuments, and other cemetery merchandise;

➢ removal or repair of damaged monuments and markers; and

➢ rights of landowner access.

Private cemeteries may adopt similar rules and regulations.

National cemetery - National cemeteries are restricted to eligible veterans and active-duty members of the United States Armed Forces, as well as certain other specified public officials and employees. Members who died while on active duty or former members who served on active duty and were *discharged under other than dishonorable conditions* are usually eligible for burial in a national cemetery. In addition, the spouse and any dependent family members of a veteran may also be eligible for burial in the same cemetery.

A military discharge is commonly referred to in the funeral service industry by the current form number, DD-214, and the document will clearly state the discharge classification in a section called *Character of Service*. The form is formally titled a Certificate of Release or Discharge from Active Duty, and the DD-214 form number has been used by all of the military branches since January 1, 1950. Prior to that date, other forms with different form numbers, in addition to the DD-214, were used by the various armed service branches.

Funeral directors should be aware there are currently eight military discharge classifications, of which the five most common are:

1. Honorable discharge.

2. General discharge under honorable conditions.

3. Other than honorable discharge.

4. Bad conduct discharge.

5. Dishonorable discharge.

The first two classifications grant veteran benefits upon separation from service, including the provision of a Military Honor Guard for a burial. The remaining three classifications generally do not grant veteran benefits. However, in unique circumstances, a family may request officials with the Department of Veterans Affairs (VA) review a discharge classification and therefore eligibility for burial in a national cemetery. With limited exceptions, VA officials are responsible for making determinations on requests for burial in a national cemetery.

If any of the three less-common discharges were to be encountered by a funeral director, the VA would need to determine if the veteran is eligible for burial in a national cemetery. The three additional discharges are:

1. Entry-level separation.

2. Medical separation.

3. Separation for the convenience of the government.

For the funeral director, the best practice is to advise the family of the need to confirm the eligibility of the decedent with the VA *before* making or announcing any plans to have a funeral ceremony with military funeral honors. There are any number of reasons why a person may not be eligible for which others may not be aware, such as certain criminal convictions and minimum required periods of service. Once approved, the role of the funeral director is to serve as a liaison between military officials and the surviving family.

Veteran cemetery (state) - Many states operate and maintain cemeteries for veterans. These are often established and improved using federal funds and have eligibility requirements similar to VA national cemeteries, but they are maintained and operated solely by the states with no VA oversight.

Funeral directors seeking to use a state cemetery for a veteran burial must contact the individual cemetery superintendent to determine the requirements, eligibility criteria, potential benefits, and any applicable cemetery rules, bylaws, or regulations. Being a legal resident of the state at the time of death is usually one notable requirement for eligibility to be buried in a state veteran cemetery.

As of this writing, there are two states with no state cemetery for veterans: Florida, and Oregon. A complete listing of all national and state cemeteries for veterans, together with addresses and contact information, may be found on the VA National Cemetery Administration website.

Pet cemetery - There are no federal laws, including the FTC Funeral Rule, that specifically regulate any aspect of death care for pets or for the burial of human remains in a pet cemetery. Legislation that does exist is coming at the state level, with most states having laws prohibiting the disposition of pet remains in a location designated for the disposition of human remains, and vice-versa. However, the rapid increase in the number of cremations being carried out in the United States has fueled a significant social movement in support of allowing human and pet remains to rest together for eternity in a common location. As such, several states have passed or are working on passing legislation to change the laws restricting such activities.

As of this writing, Pennsylvania, Virginia, New York, New Jersey, Florida, and Oregon have passed laws in varying degrees to allow for designated common burial locations for pet and human remains or cremated remains. Each of these state statutes have their own unique characteristics.

For example, Virginia provides for sections in a traditional cemetery to be designated for, "*the interment of human remains and the pets of such deceased humans, provided no pet is interred in the same grave, crypt or niche as the remains of a human,*" while New York has taken a different approach that permits, "*the disposition of human cremains in* [a] *pet cemetery.*"

It seems readily apparent the trend to loosen restrictions and thus provide greater opportunities for the remains of pets and their owners to be together in death will continue. As such, funeral service professionals should carefully research state and local laws – in addition to individual cemetery rules, bylaws, and regulations – before making any commitment to dispose of human remains in a pet cemetery, or vice-versa, as these laws and regulations are in a state of rapid transformation.

State and local laws controlling the disposition of pet and/or human remains may not include the operation of private, family, or religious cemeteries. These entities are largely regulated by their owners and operate under an adopted set of cemetery rules. Any disposition of remains (human or pet) must therefore comply with private cemetery rules, even if they are more restrictive than government rules.

Cemetery locations - Cemeteries are not a **nuisance per se** but may be regulated by local **zoning ordinances** that specify the zone or zones in which a cemetery may be built or operated. In addition to zoning, the location of a cemetery may be prohibited on any real property operated by a funeral establishment, and funeral establishments may be prohibited from engaging in any cross-marketing, shared services, or other business relationships with a cemetery corporation or similar entity. This may include the operation of a *private* crematory on cemetery property or the operation of a *public* crematory on funeral establishment property.

Eminent domain considerations - On occasion, a federal, state, or local government may want to seize private property for public use, such as the need to take real property along a designated route for the construction of a new interstate highway. The inherent power of a government to take private property for public use is most often employed by state and local municipalities through **eminent domain** proceedings.

The power of eminent domain is founded in the Fifth Amendment to the U.S. Constitution. Although more recognized for provisions related to criminal procedure, the amendment also states, "*… nor shall private property be taken for public use, without just compensation.*" This language provides the legal basis for a government to take private property for public use as long as the owner of the property is adequately compensated as required in the constitution.

Cemetery plots - Cemeteries use the terms section, block, lot, and grave, to identify where individual burial spaces are located. Each subsequent term defines a more specific cemetery location than the preceding term, making a 'section' the largest and a 'grave' the smallest. The burial grave – also known as a burial plot or funeral plot – is a piece of real estate (land) sufficient in size to hold a single casket safeguarding the human remains of one person.

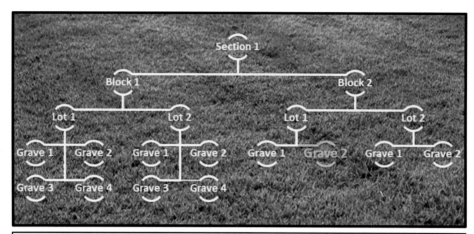

Using this schematic as an example, human remains buried in GRAVE 2 would be recorded in cemetery records as being located in Section 1, Block 2, Lot 1, Grave 2.

In most cases, a consumer will purchase a cemetery lot containing multiple burial plots. In other words, rights to a piece of land with several available graves. Cemeteries and burial plot owners are not assessed property taxes, with cemeteries often being operated as a not-for-profit entity or corporation.

When a consumer purchases one or more burial plots, they are not actually purchasing the land but rather the exclusive right to use the land for the burial of human remains. The cemetery retains ownership and grants the purchaser – or other designated persons – the right to be interred in the plot. This grant or right may be called 'interment rights' or 'grant of exclusive right to burial.'

The person with the priority right to control the final disposition of human remains has the responsibility to determine the rightful use of a cemetery space. This includes the duty to obtain the proper authorization from the property owner to inter human remains where the burial plot is located. Funeral directors are not generally responsible for ascertaining rightful ownership of a burial plot before supervising a burial but are of course expected to comply with all state laws and cemetery rules.

The purchase, sale, and use of burial plots is regulated by the states. Requirements vary but often address such matters as the ownership of burial plots, transfer of ownership, and rights of use.

State laws may include provisions that influence:

> ➤ the sale or transfer of burial plots and rights to a third-party, such as members of the next succeeding generation;

➤ the priority right of a cemetery to buy back burial plots and rights from an existing owner before the owner may offer them as a private sale to others;

➤ the transfer of burial plots and rights to others by means of a last will and testament or, where no will exists, by state **intestate succession** laws that provide for the distribution of the assets of a decedent;

➤ the right of the government or cemetery owners and operators to reclaim grave spaces that have not been used for a specified number of years; and

➤ the right of joint ownership with a right of survivorship, i.e., when one owner dies, the surviving owner(s) are automatically granted the deceased owner's share of the property.

Cemetery desecration - Cemetery desecration is the treatment of burial plots with disrespect and contempt, often associated with acts of vandalism and the destruction of cemetery monuments, markers, and other memorial paraphernalia. Various state laws address these offensive acts and often categorize them as criminal activities subject to fines and/or periods of incarceration in a local jail or lockup. A higher dollar estimate of the damages or previous convictions for the same offense are aggravating factors that in many states raise the classification of these criminal acts to felonies, which carry higher fines and incarceration in a state prison for longer periods of time.

Desecration laws usually address two types of illegal conduct.

1. Damaging real or personal property maintained as a cemetery plot, grave, burial place, or other place of interment of human remains.

2. Stealing personal property located at a cemetery plot, grave, burial place, of other place of interment of human remains.

Cemetery disinterment - **Disinterment**, also known as exhumation, is the removal of human remains from a previous location of final disposition. There are several different reasons for seeking to disinter human remains, and they may be categorized as being either private or public.

Private reasons for a disinterment may include:

➤ a desire to move human remains to a different section in a cemetery or to a different cemetery entirely;

➤ a desire to consolidate several burial plots located in different locations or cemeteries into one large family lot in one specified cemetery; or

➤ to recover improperly buried valuables or items of personal significance.

Public reasons for a disinterment may include those in which there is a substantiated public interest, such as a criminal prosecution. Other potential public interests might include eminent domain proceedings to seize real estate on which a cemetery is located, or when the government determines a disinterment is needed to ensure public health and safety.

Disinterment is regulated under state laws and – in almost all circumstances – requires a government permit authorizing the disinterment and subsequent reinterment of the human remains. However, there are states where a disinterment permit is not required when the human remains are only being moved from one burial plot location to another in the *same* cemetery. When human remains are being moved to a different location for final disposition, state vital records officials usually require a correction or annotation be made on the original certificate of death to reflect the proper location of the new final disposition.

When a disinterment is being sought for a *public* reason, the authorization to carry out the process may come in the form of a court order; however, a permit will still usually be required for the purposes of tracking the final disposition location and then using the information to correct the original certificate of death to reflect the new disposition location, as well as the date and method.

For a disinterment, a funeral director may be required to:

> ➤ coordinate with the family and public officials;
>
> ➤ file the permit application;
>
> ➤ supervise the disinterment;
>
> ➤ transport the human remains; and
>
> ➤ supervise any subsequent reinterment.

In addition, many state laws require a funeral director to examine the burial container at the time of disinterment to ensure it has retained its integrity and, in those cases where it has not, transfer the remains to another suitable container for transportation and reinterment.

When determining who has the right to request disinterment for a *private* reason, the individual with the priority right to control the disposition of human remains at the time of death may not always be the same person authorized by law to request a disinterment. State laws vary considerably on this issue and should be consulted prior to acceding to any request for a disinterment from a private person or organization.

As in all cases in the funeral service industry, if there is any conflict or dispute between the parties, it must be resolved by the parties themselves or a court of law.

Final Disposition by Entombment
Entombment is defined as the placing of human remains in a **crypt** in a **mausoleum** and provides for the safeguarding of human remains above ground in a building or structure designed specifically for this purpose. When considering this option, funeral directors should inquire about

mausoleum rules associated with entombment, such as mandatory embalming or specific requirements on the shell material or other characteristics of the casket container.

In almost all cases, mausoleums require human remains to be embalmed and may prohibit wooden caskets that could rot and deteriorate over time, thereby creating health issues and concerns. In most states, the transfer of human remains from a mausoleum for disposition in a different manner or location is handled in the same fashion as a disinterment.

Final Disposition by Natural (Green) Burial

A **green burial** is the disposition of human remains without the use of toxic chemicals or materials that are not readily biodegradable. Also known as a natural burial, this eco-friendly approach to a final disposition utilizes products, services, and merchandise that are: free of toxic/hazardous materials; biodegradable; and minimize the use of energy. The concept of a natural burial has been around for centuries. Habenstein notes the Greeks as far distant as 1600 BC prepared the deceased by anointing the body with, "*... oils, perfumes and spice, but made no serious attempt at embalming.*"

Green burial is a relative newcomer in the United States in its present form but has seen a steady growth in recent years. A funeral director planning to offer a green burial option must first acquaint themselves with the tenets and beliefs behind the movement and educate themselves to the unique goods and services this option demands. These include the rapid development of special containers and designated cemeteries. For example, a **green cemetery** is a place of interment that bans the use of metal caskets, toxic embalming, and concrete vaults. They may also require the use of aesthetically pleasing natural monuments.

The federal government has no regulations specific to natural burials; however, there are several states that have adopted legislation to ensure protection of both the environment and the public health. Many of the laws focus on the physical location where natural burials will occur, taking into consideration any evidence of underground water supplies and the potential for any ground contamination. A funeral establishment intent on offering and conducting natural burials should consult with state and local officials to determine what requirements or restrictions, if any, apply in the communities they serve.

The transportation of a deceased person for a natural burial is another area of regulatory concern. Crossing state and municipal boundaries, as well as national borders, must be taken into consideration when transporting human remains that have not been embalmed. Unfortunately, the many differences from one state or one country to the next makes it all but impossible to compile all the information needed to make an informed decision about the transportation of human remains that have not been embalmed. It is the responsibility of the funeral director to consult with international and state authorities to ensure compliance on a case-by-case basis.

Final Disposition by Burial at Sea

Dispositions at sea are regulated by the **U.S. Environmental Protection Agency** (EPA). The EPA requires the burial at sea of human remains take place at least three nautical miles from land and in water at least 600 feet deep, and funeral directors must comply with all EPA rules and regulations with respect to preparing the human remains and container for the burial at sea. As this is a unique method of disposition requiring a suitable vessel for transportation, there are private companies that offer burial at sea services to funeral establishments, similar to companies that offer burial vaults and interment service equipment at the time of a traditional burial.

Note: See Guide 4 for EPA Burial at Sea Instructions and legal requirements.

Veterans - Burial at sea for eligible veterans are handled by the United States Navy. Individuals eligible for this program include:

➤ active-duty members of the uniformed services;

➤ retirees and veterans who were honorably discharged;

➤ U.S. civilian marine personnel of the Military Sealift Command; and

➤ dependent family members of active-duty personnel, retirees, and veterans of the uniformed services.

Note: See Guide 5 for the U.S. Navy Burial at Sea Program.

Sailors aboard USS Saipan (LHA-2) conduct a burial at sea off the coast of Virginia for a former U.S. Sailor.

U.S. Navy photo by Photographer's Mate 2nd Class Robert M Schalk, January 15, 2004.

Chapter 10: Methods of Final Disposition
Cremation, Donation, Alkaline Hydrolysis, and Natural Organic Reduction

Overview
The is the second of the two chapters reviewing legal and acceptable methods for the final disposition of human remains in the United States. This chapter examines cremation, donation, alkaline hydrolysis, and natural organic reduction disposition methods.

Chapter Definitions
Alkaline hydrolysis - a process that uses water, alkaline chemicals, heat and sometimes pressure and agitation to accelerate natural decomposition, leaving bone fragments.

Alternative container - unfinished wood box or other non-metal receptacle or enclosure, without ornamentation or a fixed interior lining, which is designed for the encasement of human remains and which is made of fiberboard, pressed-wood, composition materials (with or without an outside covering) or like materials.

Body parts - organs, tissues, eyes, bones, arteries, blood, other fluids, and other portions of a human body.

Cadaver - a dead human body intended solely for scientific study and dissection.

Columbarium - a structure, room or space in a mausoleum or other building containing niches or recesses used to hold cremated remains.

Cremated remains - the final product remaining after completion of the entire cremation and pulverization process.

Cremation - the reduction of a dead human body to inorganic bone fragments by intense heat in a specifically designed retort or chamber.

Crematory - the location of the retort/cremation chamber which will perform a cremation process.

Due diligence - the attention reasonably expected from, and ordinarily exercised by, a person who seeks to satisfy a legal requirement or to discharge an obligation.

Final disposition - the conclusive performance of services with respect to the dead human body by one of the legally recognized methods.

Funeral pyre - an outdoor wooden structure upon which human remains rest and are cremated when the pyre is set on fire [by Author].

Inurnment - placing cremated remains in an urn or placing cremated remains in a niche or grave.

Niche - a recess or space in a columbarium used for the permanent placing of cremated remains.

Temporary container - a receptacle for cremated remains, usually made of cardboard, plastic, or similar materials designed to hold cremated remains until an urn, other permanent container is acquired, or other disposition is made.

Tort - a private or civil wrong against a person or his or her property, other than by breach of contract, for which there may be action for damages.

Uniform Anatomical Gift Act (UAGA) - a law permitting competent persons or others to give gifts of all or any part of the body, to take effect upon death.

Urn - permanent container for cremated remains meant for decorative or inurnment purposes.

Final Disposition by Cremation

In 2016, the average **cremation** rate for the United States reached a major milestone when it exceeded 50% and, as many in the funeral industry are aware, cremation dispositions are continuing to experience unprecedented growth. The Cremation Association of North America now projects the average rate for cremations by 2023 will be 59.4%.

When discussing cremation, some may argue it is not an actual ***final* disposition**, as further steps must be undertaken to dispose of **cremated remains**. The same argument could be made to exclude alkaline hydrolysis; however, state laws do not recognize the disposition of *cremated* remains as the final disposition of *human* remains. It is the cremation process taking place in a **crematory** that states recognize as the final disposition.

Legally - Cremation is a legal method for final disposition in all 50 states. Asian customs and practices call for cremation in an outdoor **funeral pyre**; however, with two exceptions, open-air funeral pyres are not legal in the United States. *The Crestone End of Life Project,* in Crestone, Colorado, is an open-air funeral pyre available to residents of Saguache County; and the *Shambhala Mountain Retreat Center*, also in Colorado, has a private outdoor funeral pyre. Both have Colorado Department of Public Health and Environment approvals.

Authorization - A cremation, like other disposition methods, must be authorized by the person with the priority right to control the final disposition. The form and information required for an authorization to cremate is usually regulated by the states, and the document may contain any or all of the following sections or parts.

➢ Notice to the consumer the cremation process is an irreversible and final process that will consume everything except bone and metal which are all that will be left after cremation.

➢ Acknowledgement there has been a positive identification of the human remains as required by an applicable state or local law.

➢ Affirmation of the person holding the priority right to control the final disposition they have such right and – when required or applicable – are acting to carry out the wishes of the decedent.

➤ Affirmation the human remains do not contain any hazardous items or materials, such as a pacemaker, battery pack, power cell, or radioactive implant.

➤ Confirmation personal property or things of value have been removed from the container. This is usually followed by some form of warning statement that any personal items left in the container will be destroyed by the process and cannot be retrieved after the process has finished.

➤ The name of the person authorized to receive the cremated remains from the crematory. This is usually followed by some form of warning that if the cremated remains go unclaimed after a specified period of time, the crematory has the right to dispose of them in any legal manner, such as a cemetery burial or placement in a **columbarium** wall.

➤ A description of any **urn** or other container for safeguarding the cremated remains being provided by the person authorizing the cremation or, if no container is provided, an acknowledgement the crematory will place the cremated remains in a **temporary container**. Temporary containers are usually made of cardboard, plastic, or similar materials designed to hold the cremated remains until an urn or other permanent container is provided, or some other disposition takes place.

➤ A signatory section for the person(s) authorizing the cremation to attest to the accuracy of the information provided by them to the crematory. Signatures will usually need to be witnessed, and some states require the funeral director serve as a witness.

Note: Some states allow only one person from a priority right class to sign a cremation authorization (such as one child), while others require all persons within a priority right class sign the authorization (such as all children).

Filings and permits - Before a cremation may take place, a certificate of death and request for a cremation permit must be filed with the appropriate government office. When approved, the permit authorizes the disposition method, date, and location. Some states have a universal permit with options to select the chosen method of final disposition; while others, such as Tennessee, have a special permit for cremation cases only. In addition, there are certain states, such as California, that require a permit when the disposition of the *cremated* remains is going to take place in a location other than a cemetery.

Some states, counties, or local governments may also require a medical examiner or county coroner issue a clearance (approval) for a cremation disposition before a permit may be issued by a local registrar or recorder of vital statistics.

Preparation of remains - Funeral directors are responsible for preparing and thereafter transporting human remains for cremation. The process follows a logical order and sequence that will include most, if not all of the actions listed here.

➤ Verify the name and identity of the decedent and ensure the human remains have been properly tagged for identification.

> Remove any medical devices or equipment – such as a pacemaker or other battery-operated implants – and dispose of them following hazardous material handling protocols.

> Remove any personal property or effects that may be on or with the body, such as a wallet, watch, ring, or necklace. A list of these items should be recorded, along with later notations as to their subsequent disposition as directed by the family.

> If the family has provided clothing or cosmetics, the body should be dressed and cosmetics applied according to the instructions of the person with the right to control the disposition.

> The remains should be enclosed in a leak-proof pouch or similar leak proof container to contain any bodily fluids. The pouch should also be properly tagged for identification.

> Place the pouched human remains inside a cremation casket or a suitable **alternative container**. The container may be supplied by the family, the funeral establishment, or the crematory but must always be in regulatory compliance with state or local laws, rules, and regulations related to the durability of the container and the materials from which it is constructed, so as to not impede the cremation process or endanger crematory staff.

> If the family has any personal property items – such as photographs, a stuffed animal, or blanket to be cremated with the remains – these items should be placed inside the casket or alternative container. Materials that could be hazardous to crematory staff, such as glass bottles, metal cans, batteries, and lighters should be rejected and returned to the family. Place the cover on the container and write the name of the decedent and the name of the funeral establishment on the outside of the container.

> Transport the packaged human remains in a dignified and respectful manner to the crematory, together with a government-issued cremation permit and an authorization to cremate signed by the family. In some regions, cremations must be pre-scheduled and the remains not delivered until instructed by crematory staff. In addition, many states require a licensed professional, such as a funeral director, deliver the human remains and sign a log or other document to record the transfer of custody from the funeral establishment to the crematory.

> Provide for the retrieval of the cremated remains from the crematory at a later date.

Disposition of cremated remains - The funeral director is usually responsible for assisting the family in selecting a suitable urn or similar container and transferring the cremated remains to it from the temporary container supplied by the crematory. One or more containers may be needed, as some families may wish to have the cremated remains split into smaller portion urns to provide for burials in different locations or keepsakes in a home. Typically, a funeral director will also provide for the transportation of the urn to any memorial or burial services.

An urn may be buried in the ground in a process called **inurnment**. They may also be placed in a columbarium, defined as a structure, room or space in a mausoleum or other building containing

niches (rhymes with witches) to hold cremated remains. A columbarium may also be a separate structure set apart from a mausoleum. Many of these are located outdoors and incorporate multiple niches in a cascading series of columbarium walls. Niches may be designed to hold more than one urn or container, similar to a family burial lot having more than one burial plot or grave. When located inside a mausoleum, they may have a glass face so the urn is visible from the exterior of the niche.

Cremated remains may also be separated to provide for keepsake urns, jewelry, or other mementos that remain with a family in their home or other location rather than being buried; however, funeral directors must remain vigilant to religious laws, customs, rights, or teachings that may restrict such activities. For example, in the appendix to the Roman Catholic Order of Christian Funerals, there are instructions on the proper handling of cremated remains that include prohibitions on scattering or keeping cremated remains in a home. The relevant paragraph from the appendix is provided in the textbox shown here.

> Cremated remains of a body should be treated with the same respect given to the human body from which they come. This includes the use of a worthy vessel to contain the ashes, the manner in which they are carried, the care and attention to appropriate placement and transport, and the final disposition. The cremated remains should be buried in a grave or entombed in a mausoleum or columbarium. The practice of scattering cremated remains on the sea, from the air, or on the ground, or keeping cremated remains in the home of a relative or friend of the deceased are not the reverent disposition that the Church requires. Whenever possible, appropriate means for recording with dignity the memory of the deceased should be adopted, such as a plaque or stone which records the name of the deceased (pg. 6).
>
> Source: Cremation Appendix to Roman Catholic Order of Christian Funerals ©1998

Some families may wish to use a scattering method for the disposition of cremated remains. These scatterings may take place on the land or in the water, and there are a number of devices available to provide a dignified and reverent service, such as the use of a scattering wand or tube. Some cemeteries provide designated locations for the communal scattering of cremated remains, while others may offer private lots for scattering the cremated remains of several family members.

Funeral directors must be vigilant to any laws or requirements that regulate the scattering of cremated remains, especially on or in the water. At a minimum, the scattering of cremated remains in inland waterways is often not a socially acceptable or well received practice by adjacent landowners or the community in which it takes place. To the extreme, scattering may be an illegal act subject to prosecution and penalties when a body of water is the source of drinking water. The federal Clean Water Act regulates the scattering of cremated remains in certain inland waters such as rivers or lakes, and individual states that own and maintain these waterways may have additional legal requirements – such as requiring funeral directors obtain a permit before scattering cremated remains on any public lands or waters.

Unclaimed cremated remains - State laws also set the parameters and conditions upon which unclaimed cremated remains may be disposed of by crematory operators, funeral directors, and other death care providers. Regulations may include such provisions as a prohibition on the use of scattering as a means of disposition.

Statutes dealing with unclaimed cremated remains include many of these elements:

- the identification of the person or official with the authority to dispose of unclaimed cremated remains;

- a set period of time that must pass before cremated remains are considered unclaimed and subject to disposal;

- the acceptable methods for the disposition;

- maintenance of records to support **due diligence** efforts taken by the funeral establishment, crematory, or other entity to contact the person with the right to control the disposition and request they take possession of the unclaimed cremated remains; and

- a permanent record of the date and location for the disposal.

For the unclaimed cremated remains of a veteran, there are often state regulations that allow for the transfer of cremated remains to an authorized veteran organization for disposition. These regulations frequently prohibit scattering as the disposition method and require the organizations to maintain permanent records of the date, method, and location of all such dispositions.

Torts - Cremation as a final disposition method of human remains exposes a funeral director and the funeral establishment they work for to many of the same **tort** actions or omissions described in the chapter titled, *Funeral Practitioners and Staff*. Cremation errors due to misidentifications and mistakes that result in a wrong body being cremated are often cited as the underlying actions or omissions resulting in claims against funeral service professionals.

Ways to minimize liability exposures associated with cremation cases include:

1. Having comprehensive operational manuals that detail the proper procedures and measures to be taken by staff to reduce exposures when handling cremation cases.

2. Implementing a tracking program requiring human remains in the care of the funeral establishment be immediately tagged with a wrist or ankle bracelet bearing a unique ID barcode or the decedent's name. Every movement thereafter should then be tracked from location to location and recorded by either scanning the barcode or making manual entries in a log.

3. Documenting the activities and actions taken with respect to safeguarding human remains and thereafter cremated remains. This brings a level of accountability to the staff and provides a means for the funeral establishment owner to actively monitor compliance. More importantly, it establishes a written track record that demonstrates the consistent intent and practice of the establishment to exercise due diligence in carrying out their duties and responsibilities. If a civil claim is made, these records may serve to diminish the level of liability exposure and any potential penalties or settlements.

4. Periodically meet with crematory operators to discuss how they track and document individual cases, and review the procedures used by the funeral establishment to ensure they are consistent and compatible with those of the crematory. Adjustments to the funeral establishment policy should be made when any inconsistencies are found that might hinder proper identification procedures for either organization.

5. Periodically conduct on-site inspections of crematory facilities to verify and observe the steps being taken to ensure no identification errors occur. If later confronted with a liability claim, these proactive actions also demonstrate to the court the due diligence undertaken by the funeral establishment to minimize any chance for a mistake.

Final Disposition by Body Donation

Medical colleges and universities, as well as scientific research and testing facilities, regularly need sources to supply **cadavers** for use in their respective studies and programs. One such source are those individuals that make preneed arrangements and therein provide for their body to be donated upon the occasion of their death. Family members are another source, as those holding the right to control a final disposition may elect to choose body donation at the time of an at-need arrangement conference.

Body and **body part** donations are regulated by individual states using the **Uniform Anatomical Gift Act (UAGA)** as a guide. According to West's Encyclopedia of American Law, "*Uniform Acts are laws designed to be adopted by all of the states so that the law in one jurisdiction is the same as in another jurisdiction.*"

These uniform acts are prepared and sponsored by the National Conference of Commissioners on Uniform State Laws (Conference), whose members are experienced lawyers, judges, and professors of law generally appointed to the commission by state governors. States are free to adopt the act as written by the Conference or modify it through the state legislative process to make it compatible and consistent with other existing state laws.

Body donation – as a final disposition method for human remains – is not the same as the donation of body parts for transplantation or other medical purposes. In the UAGA, 'body part' is defined as organs, tissues, eyes, bones, arteries, blood, other fluids, and other portions of a human body.

The Conference describes the UAGA as follows:

> *UAGA governs organ donations for the purpose of transplantation, and it also governs the making of anatomical gifts of one's cadaver to be dissected in the study of medicine. The law prescribes the forms by which such gifts can be made. It also provides that in the absence of such a document, a surviving spouse, or if there is no spouse, a list of specific relatives in order of preference, can make the gift. It also seeks to limit the liability of health care providers who act on good faith representations that a deceased patient meant to make an anatomical gift. The act also prohibits trafficking and trafficking in human organs for profit from donations for transplant or therapy.*

The UAGA was passed in 1968, and most recently revised in 2006. Amendments have included such revisions as eliminating the need to have a witness to the signature of the person making a donation; mandating uniform donor cards be recognized as legally binding in all 50 states; and allowing individuals to express their desire to donate their remains on a driver's license, through verbal expression, or in writing by a will or other advance directive. Properly completed body donation authorizations include liability protections for the funeral director and funeral establishment dealing with this method of final disposition.

By 2017, all states had adopted the core components of the UAGA; however, there may be subtle differences from one state to the next. Funeral directors must therefore be familiar with body donation requirements as they exist in the state or states where they offer funeral services.

When discussing body donation with a family, *anatomical gift* is the preferred terminology.

Final Disposition by Alkaline Hydrolysis
Alkaline hydrolysis, also known alternatively as resomation, is one of the newest entries in the field of final disposition methods.

New York Times reporter Jonah Engel Bromwich describes the alkaline hydrolysis process as:

> *... a chemical bath to dissolve protein, blood and fat, leaving only a coffee-colored liquid, powdery bone and any metal implants, like dental fillings.*

The liquid and metal implant waste products Bromwich identifies are properly discarded, while the bone fragments are ground into a powdery ash and returned to the family, similar to the return of cremated remains. In fact, the hydrolysis process may alternatively be known as water cremation, bio-cremation, or flameless cremation. As of January 2022, about 20 states have approved the process, while others are considering legislation to include it as a legal means for the final disposition of human remains.

Alkaline hydrolysis has been used to dispose of animal waste and carcasses for many years and is considered to be eco-friendly, safe, and cost-effective.

Bones and bone fragments after alkaline hydrolysis process completion.

Final Disposition by Natural Organic Reduction (NOR)

Natural organic reduction – also known informally as human composting – is another emerging method for the final disposition of human remains that has only recently shown progress in being adopted by the states. NOR is powered by beneficial microbes that occur naturally on human remains and in the environment.

There are several steps to the NOR process:

1. The human remains are placed in a special cradle for preparation, which includes surrounding them with wood chips, alfalfa, and straw. They are then moved into a processing vessel, where the cradle and any material that will not break down in the organic process are removed.

2. Additional plant material is added and the complete package remains in the vessel for 30 days. During this time, the microbes break down everything on the molecular level and form a nutrient-dense soil.

3. Each decedent creates roughly one cubic yard of soil amendment, and this is removed from the vessel for further processing. Any non-organics, such as false teeth or dental metal, is sorted out, removed, and recycled in the same manner as in a cremation.

4. Any bones or fragments that remain are processed mechanically and reintroduced into the soil so that a curing period can begin. During the curing process, they break down further and absorb into the soil.

5. The soil itself is processed so that it has a fairly even texture size, which in turn makes a healthier soil more capable of retaining moisture. The curing process takes between two and three weeks, during which time the soil is cooling off and the reduction process is continuing.

6. After passing all regulatory testing requirements – such as those for harmful microbes, pH levels, and heavy metal content – the process is finished.

The soil created returns the nutrients from the human remains back to the natural world. It restores forests, sequesters carbon, and nourishes new life.

Environmental impact - The minimal impact on the environment when using the NOR method for a final disposition – compared to burial or cremation – is one of the major positive influences of this method.

Recompose, one of only a handful of companies offering NOR, has stated:

> *For every person who chooses Recompose over conventional burial or cremation, one metric ton of carbon dioxide is prevented from entering the atmosphere. In addition, our approach to human composting requires ⅛ the energy of conventional*

burial or cremation. Recompose allows you to choose an end-of-life option that strengthens the environment rather than depleting it.

Legal status - As of late 2021, only the state of Washington (in 2019), and the states of Oregon and Colorado (in 2021) have legalized this method for the final disposition of human remains. The states of California, New York, Delaware, and Massachusetts are considering authorizing this method and other states will undoubtedly be looking to explore this alternative.

Colorado has banned selling NOR soil for commercial use but the public is allowed to use the soil for any purpose, such as in their own garden or on private property.

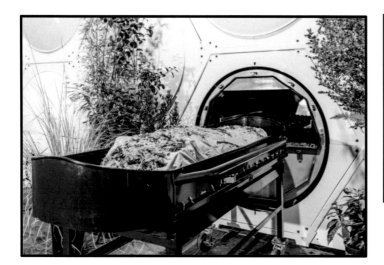

This image simulates human remains (surrounded by wood chips, alfalfa, and straw) after being prepared for the NOR process. The remains will be moved into the processing vessel, at which time the cradle and any material that will not break down in the organic process is removed.

This vessel has the capacity to handle ten NOR cases. The human remains and plant material remain in the vessel for 30 days. Microbes break everything down on the molecular level, resulting in a nutrient-dense soil.

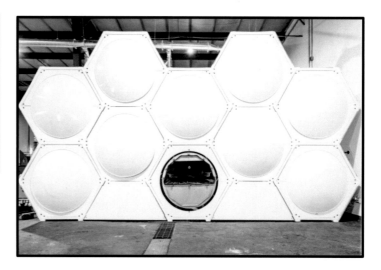

Images on this page are courtesy of Recompose
Kent, Washington, July 2021
URL: https://recompose.life/

Chapter 11: Last Will and Testament

Overview
A last will and testament is a legal document that allows a person to choose who they want to control and settle their end-of-life affairs after they have died. A last will may include such things as directions for the distribution of assets to beneficiaries and instructions for the final disposition of their remains. Recognizing state regulations vary, this chapter reviews the common elements found in estate laws as they relate to a last will and testament.

Chapter Definitions
Abatement - a proportional reduction of a devise when estate assets are not sufficient to pay it in full.

Ademption - the extinction or withdrawal of an inheritance because decedent did not own the named property at the time of death.

Codicil - an addition or amendment of a last will and testament executed with the same formality of the will.

Devise - a gift of real or personal property by will.

Devisee - the person who receives a devise.

Escheat - forfeiture of a decedent's property to the state in the absence of heirs.

Heir - one who inherits, or is entitled to receive property by laws of intestacy.

Holographic will - a will written entirely by the hand of the testator.

Intestate - the state or condition of dying without having made a will; intestacy.

Intestate succession - the method used to distribute property owned by a person who dies without a valid will.

Nuncupative will - oral will declared or dictated by testator during last illness before appropriate witnesses to dispose of personal property and afterwards reduced to writing (not valid in all states).

Per capita - the method of dividing an estate by which an equal share is given to each of a number of persons, all of whom stand in equal degree of kindred to the decedent.

Per stirpes - the method of proportionately dividing an estate between beneficiaries according to their deceased ancestor's share.

Revocation - the omission or cancellation of an instrument, act, license, or promise.

Testate - the condition of leaving a will at death.

Testator - a person who makes a valid will.

Will - an instrument executed with required formality, by persons making disposition of their property to take effect upon their death.

Last Will and Testament

Legal age - Forty-eight states require a person to be at least 18 years of age before they can legally execute a last will and testament. In Georgia, the minimum age is 14, and Louisiana has no minimum age. There is an exception for members of the Armed Forces of the United States, who may execute a will at the age of 17.

Testamentary capacity - 'Testamentary' refers to the activities described in a will, such as making appointments, distributing assets to beneficiaries, and leaving instructions for the final disposition of human remains. 'Capacity' refers to the mental state and ability of a person. Testamentary capacity therefore refers to the mental capacity a person must possess to be capable of making a will. It may be referred to as being 'of sound mind and memory.' A person making a will is called the **testator**, and the estate of a decedent who had a will is called a **testate** estate.

Adults are presumed to have the necessary testamentary capacity to make a will; however, this presumption may be challenged in a court of law if it can be shown the individual – at the time the will was executed – suffered from a mental handicap, diminished capacity, senility, dementia, or other condition that would impair mental health. In addition, a person making a will must do so with intent, a mental state of being. If they were coerced or forced into signing a will, they would not have had the required mental state at the time, thus making the will invalid. With very limited exceptions, wills must be in writing and signed in the presence of one or more witnesses.

To have the mental capacity to execute a will, a person must:

> ➢ know the nature and extent of the real property and personal property that will make up the assets of the estate;

> ➢ know the 'natural objects of bounty,' meaning the closest surviving blood-relatives in the family;

> ➢ know the intended disposition of the property; and

> ➢ have the ability to connect all of these elements together to form a coherent plan.

Special Wills

Nuncupative will - This is an oral will dictated by a person during a final illness before appropriate witnesses to dispose of personal property. Thereafter, the witnesses reduce the information to writing. West's Encyclopedia of American Law defines a **nuncupative will** as:

> *The oral expression of a person's wishes as to the disposition of his or her property*
> *to be performed or to take effect after the person's death, dictated by the person in*

his or her final illness before a sufficient number of witnesses and afterward reduced to writing.

Nuncupative wills are valid for the disposition of *personal* property but not *real* property. As of this writing, there are roughly 20 states that recognize a nuncupative will, and these states have specific requirements that must be met before one may be deemed valid. Requirements may include:

- ➢ a minimum number of witnesses to the oral declaration;

- ➢ limitations on the type or value of personal property subject to disposition by the terms of a nuncupative will;

- ➢ a written memorialization by the witnesses to the terms of a nuncupative will;

- ➢ requirements for the written memorialization to be submitted to proper authorities within a certain time frame;

- ➢ limiting them to a 'final illness' or period of sickness when the person making a nuncupative will is unable to make a written will; and

- ➢ prohibitions on a nuncupative will superseding a written will.

Holographic will - This is a will written entirely by the hand of the testator. West's Encyclopedia of American Law defines a **holographic will** as:

> *… a will entirely handwritten, dated and signed by the testator (the person making the will), but not signed by required witnesses.*

Similar to a nuncupative will, holographic wills are only valid for the distribution of personal property. They are not recognized in all 50 states and, for those states that do accept them, there are usually specific requirements that must be met for the will to be valid.

The requirements for a holographic will may include:

- ➢ proof it was the intent of the person to write a holographic will;

- ➢ evidence to establish the person was of sound mind and memory and had the testamentary mental capacity to write a will at the time it was actually written and signed;

- ➢ the identification of the personal property to be distributed;

- ➢ the names of the intended beneficiaries to receive the property; and

- ➢ proof the person signed the holographic will.

Holographic wills often open up issues of validity based on one or more of the requirements bulleted previously. When questions are raised, the will may be contested by those who believe they have a rightful or superior claim to the personal property being distributed. Validity may be challenged on such issues as illegible or scrawled handwriting, especially as it applies to the signature; the mental capacity of the person at the time the will was written; a failure to fully or completely identify beneficiaries; or descriptions of personal property are either too broad in scope or lack any specificity to be clearly identified.

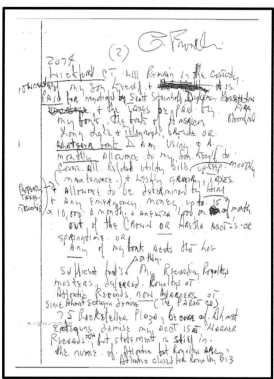

Page from holographic will allegedly written by Aretha Franklin.

In August of 2018, legendary soul singer Aretha Franklin died in Detroit, Michigan. At the time it was believed the assets of her estate would be distributed evenly among her four sons. This all changed in May of 2019 when more than one holographic will was discovered, all allegedly written by Ms. Franklin.

Ben Sisario and Steve Friess described the wills as, "*… scrawled documents - found in a locked cabinet and under the sofa cushions of Franklin's home in suburban Detroit.*" The validity of the most recent holographic will, dated 2014, is currently being questioned by at least two of her sons. If it is found to be valid, it will significantly change the dynamics of estate distribution had there been no will.

Revocation and Amendments
Revocation is the omission or cancellation of an *instrument*, act, license, or promise. A last will and testament is a *written instrument* and may be legally cancelled by revocation.

There are three methods to revoke a will:

1. *As an act by the testator* - This method to completely revoke a will requires the owner of the will (testator) to either destroy the written instrument (the will) or write a new will that includes a provision to revoke any previous wills.

2. *As an operation of law* - This method to partially revoke or amend a will takes place automatically following some other significant act, such as a divorce (with respect to the former spouse), marriage or remarriage (to allow a new spouse to inherit a share), or the birth or adoption of a child (to allow for them to inherit a share). As an example, if a person were to marry *after* executing a will and then die *before* having had an opportunity to amend the will to include the spouse, the law would recognize the likely right of the spouse to inherit under the will and – as an operation of law – write the spouse into the will.

West's Encyclopedia of American Law describes the 'operation of law' concept as follows:

Operation of Law

The manner in which an individual acquires certain rights or liabilities through no act or cooperation of his or her own, but merely by the application of the established legal rules to the particular transaction.

For example, when an individual dies intestate [without a will], *the laws of descent and distribution provide for the inheritance of the estate by the heir. The property of the deceased is said to be transferred by operation of law.* [Bracketed material by author.]

3. *As an amendment or addition to a will* - The legal term to describe an amendment or addition to a will is **codicil**. Depending on the terms of a codicil, it may partially or completely revoke the terms of the original will, and it must be executed with the same legal formality as the original last will and testament. Wills do not expire or have expiration dates but may be revoked or amended.

Distribution Issues

A gift of real or personal property by means of a last will and testament is the definition of **devise**, and the person who receives a devise (gift) is called the **devisee**.

On occasion, problems may occur that impact the distribution of devises from an estate to the designated devisees. In anticipation of these potential issues, states have established the legal means to resolve the most common of them.

Insufficient funds - When making a will, the testator describes the estate property and identifies to whom this property will be distributed following their death. As an example, in a will, Mr. Smith has identified his bank savings account as an asset and named his three children as beneficiaries to receive $30,000 each from the account. However, following his death, it is determined there is only $12,000 in the account. In these situations, the law requires an **abatement** of the devise (gift), defined as a proportional reduction of a devise when estate assets are not sufficient to pay it in full. Therefore, in our example, each child would receive a reduced proportionally equal amount from the savings account, i.e., $12,000 divided equally between three children equals $4,000 each.

Ownership of property - To describe this second potential distribution problem, assume Mr. Smith also stipulated in his will that his 2022 Chevy Corvette was to be given to his neighbor. Following his death, it is discovered the Corvette was actually stolen by Mr. Smith from a little old lady in Pasadena, California, while she was out shopping for new hearing aids. In this case, the law will require an **ademption** of the devise, defined as the extinction or withdrawal of a devise because the decedent did not own the named property at the time of death. I.e., no fancy new car for the neighbor.

Spousal election - This concept provides legal remedies for a person whose spouse has attempted to disinherit them from the spousal assets in an estate distribution. While the number of married people that want to disinherit their spouse is relatively low, there are times when long-standing differences and grievances, a failure to follow through on a divorce, or other contentious issues inspire a person to try and block a spouse from receiving any estate assets when they die.

These spousal 'right of election' statutes generally provide for a spouse to receive assets even when they have been specifically disinherited in a will or were left minimal assets. These rights vary significantly from state-to-state. For examples, a snapshot of spousal election rights in Ohio, New York, and Hawaii are provided here.

State of Ohio - A spouse electing against a will may take up to one-half of the net estate, unless there are more than two surviving children, in which case they can take up to one-third of the net estate. Source: Ohio Revised Code Section 2106.

State of New York - A surviving spouse exercising a right of election is entitled to the greater of $50,000 or, if the estate value is less than $50,000, one-third of the net estate of the deceased spouse. Source: Estates, Powers, and Trusts Law Section 5-1.1-A.

State of Hawaii - The surviving spouse of a decedent has a right to take an elective-share amount equal to the value of the estate, determined by the length of time the spouse and the decedent were married to each other. For example, the share for 2 years of marriage is 6%; 12 years, 38%; and 15+ years, 50%. Source: Hawaii Revised Statutes Section 560:2-202.

Note: The election rights provided here are significantly abbreviated and do not include factors that may influence application in real-life situations. Individuals seeking information about spousal elections should always consult with legal counsel.

Disinheritance - An owner of a will can deliberately disinherit someone who may have a natural right to assets of an estate, such as an immediate blood relative. To do so, a disinheritance clause is usually included in the will to clearly identify the individual to whom it applies and, in some instances, the reason. When someone is simply left out of a will with no explanation, a court may take the position it was a simple error or omission and restore rights to the party excluded. Whether in the will or not, disinheriting someone may result in the settlement of the estate being contested by the aggrieved party and ultimately put the administration of the estate into the hands of the court, rather than the person who wrote the will. For anyone contemplating a disinheritance, the best practice is to seek legal counsel for advice.

Intestacy

Intestate (or intestacy) is the state or condition of dying *without* having made a will, and the estate of a decedent who did not have a will is called an intestate estate. **Intestate succession** is the method used to distribute property owned by a person who dies intestate (without a valid will). Exactly who is entitled to receive assets from an estate is dependent on the intestacy laws of the individual states, and where the decedent lived or where the assets were located at the time of death may determine which state has jurisdiction.

Intestate succession laws list the hierarchy order in which the spouse and next-of-kin receive the distribution of assets from an estate. Typically, when there is a surviving spouse and surviving children, the entire estate will be split among them, meaning there would be no need to go farther down the hierarchy list to identify additional heirs. In these situations, the surviving spouse will often receive half of a decedent's estate, while the children will split the remaining half. When there are no surviving children, the surviving spouse will typically inherit the entire estate, once again meaning there would be no need to go farther down the list.

Intestate succession laws provide a comprehensive listing of blood relatives that may inherit from the estate of a person that dies with no will. These may include such kin relationships as children, siblings, parents, grand-children, grand-parents, nieces, nephews, and cousins. In addition, states generally recognize legally adopted children have the same standing as a biological child when it comes to intestate succession. Potential heirs do not include friends, neighbors, unmarried couples, or institutions – such as charities; however, state intestate laws may accommodate certain domestic or common law partnerships.

Methods of distribution - There are two methods to distribute assets from an estate: '**per capita**" and '**per stirpes**' (pronounced *per stir peas*).

The 'per capita' (by head) method divides the estate by giving an equal share to each **heir** holding an equal degree of kindred. For example, assume a man has been predeceased by his wife and has three surviving sons. When the father dies, each of his three sons would receive an equal share of the estate. If one or more of the sons were to die before the parent, their shares would be divided equally among the surviving sons.

The 'per stirpes' (by branch) method divides an estate by giving proportional shares according to a deceased ancestor's share. Using the same example, the per stirpes method would take the share of a son that dies before the father and pass it down to the deceased son's children (the father's grandsons), as opposed to dividing the shares per capita among the remaining sons.

This is a base illustration of the example showing the hierarchy of the father, his three sons and his two grandsons. ➲

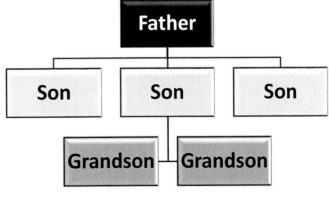

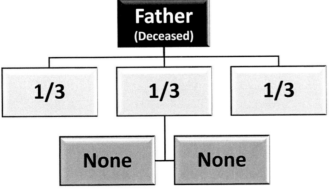

➲ This illustrates how assets would be distributed when the father dies and is survived *by all of his sons*. Both *per capita* and *per stirpes* distribution methods would have the same result. Only when an heir predeceases the person for whom the estate is being settled will the results differ. Notice all three sons get an equal one-third share of the estate.

This illustrates how assets would be distributed by the *per capita* method when the father dies and is predeceased *by one of his sons*. The share of the deceased son is divided among the two surviving sons, now giving them each one-half of the estate. ➲

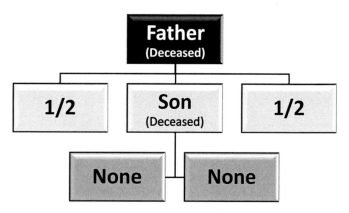

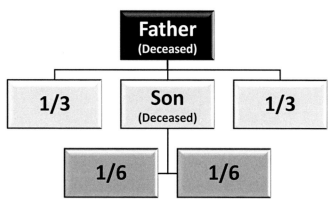

➲ And finally, this illustrates how assets would be distributed using the *per stirpes* method when the father dies and is predeceased *by one of his sons*. Note the share of the deceased son does not get divided between the two surviving sons but is instead divided among the deceased son's two children, giving them each one-sixth of the estate.

Escheat - **Escheat** laws grant a legal right to transfer estate assets and property to a state government if a person has died and there are no known legal heirs.

West's Encyclopedia of American Law describes 'escheat' as follows:

> *Escheat*
>
> *The power of a state to acquire title to property for which there is no owner. The most common reason that an escheat takes place is that an individual dies intestate, meaning without a valid will indicating who is to inherit his or her property, and without relatives who are legally entitled to inherit in the absence of a will. A state legislature has the authority to enact an escheat statute.*

Escheat usually takes place on a revocable basis, meaning if a rightful heir is found, the property would be returned. There are other conditions that might trigger an escheat law, such as a determination the rightful heir is incompetent to manage the inheritance. Escheat laws vary among the 50 states.

Chapter 12: Estate Administration

Overview

The administration of an estate follows a number of progressive steps that must be undertaken by the personal representative, including an inventory of estate assets, payment of taxes and claims, and the distribution of the assets to the proper heirs or devisees. This chapter provides a general overview of these steps and concludes with an examination of additional estate and health care documents a funeral director may need to deal with in funeral service matters.

Chapter Definitions

Devise - a gift of real or personal property by will.

Devisee - the person who receives a devise.

Durable power of attorney - a power of attorney that remains in effect after the disability or incapacity of the principal (see also power of attorney).

General power of attorney - a written instrument granting the agent broad powers to act for the principal.

Heir - one who inherits, or is entitled to receive property by laws of intestacy.

Inheritance - the estate assets which pass from the decedent to his/her heirs.

Insolvent estate - the condition of the estate of a deceased person which is unable to pay the debts of the decedent and/or the estate.

Inventory - listing and valuation of a decedent's assets by personal representative of the estate.

Living will - a document which governs the withholding or withdrawal of life-sustaining treatment from an individual in the event of an incurable or irreversible condition that will cause death within a relatively short time, and which becomes effective when such person is no longer able to make decisions regarding his/her medical treatment.

Mortgage - a secured loan on a parcel of real property.

Personal representative - person who is appointed by the court to represent and administer the estate of a deceased person.

Power of attorney - an instrument granting someone authority to act as agent or attorney-in-fact for the principal; an ordinary power of attorney is revocable and automatically terminates upon the death or incapacity of the principal.

Preferred claim - a claim which is accorded a priority, advantage, or privilege.

Probate - the process of administering the estate and determining the validity of a will.

Probate court - a court having jurisdiction over estates.

Probate estate - the property and debts of a decedent that is subject to administration by the personal representative of an estate.

Secured claim - a debt which is supported by a pledge, mortgage, or lien on assets belonging to the debtor.

Solvent estate - an estate in which the assets exceed the liabilities.

Springing power of attorney - a written instrument authorizing one person to act as an agent for another effective only upon a certain event occurring.

Uniform Probate Code - a model law intended to achieve uniformity in probate proceedings throughout the U.S.

Unsecured claim - a claim which is not supported by a pledge, mortgage, or lien on other assets.

Probate Court

Probate is the process of administering an estate and determining the validity of a will. The probate process is supervised by a **probate court,** the name of the court most often associated with having jurisdiction over estates in the United States. However, there are states that assign probate duties to a court of a different name, such as the Superior Court in California; Court of Chancery in Delaware; and Surrogate Court in New Jersey. Probate courts also supervise the administration of estates for cases where the decedent did not have a will at the time of death.

Sixteen states adopted the **Uniform Probate Code** for the administration of estates when it was first released in 1969. The code is a model law written by the National Conference of Commissioners on Uniform State Laws and intended to achieve uniformity in probate proceedings throughout the United States. Since then, several other states have adopted selected portions of the code and written other portions themselves to develop probate laws unique to the needs of a particular state. Suffice it to say, funeral directors must be knowledgeable with the probate process in the state or states where they practice.

Appointment of Personal Representative

One of the first steps to administering an estate is for the probate court to appoint a **personal representative** (executor) who is going to represent and settle the estate of the deceased.

Testate estates - A testate estate exists when the decedent *had a will* at the time of death. For these estates, the court will appoint the person named in a will to carry out the administration of the estate assets. However, the court may appoint a different representative if there is any question of the competency or fitness of the person named in the will to serve, or if any potential conflict of interest or dispute exists, or develops, while the estate is being settled.

Intestate estates - An intestate estate exists when the decedent *did not have a will* at the time of death. For these estates, the court will appoint a personal representative. The most common practice is for the court to appoint an immediate family member, such as a spouse or adult child.

However, the court may elect to appoint a different representative if it is believed to be in the best interest of the parties involved, especially when family members cannot agree on who in the family should get the appointment or there is any readily evident family dispute.

Before the administration of an estate may begin, a probate court must approve of the appointment of the personal representative. Once approved, the court issues a 'letter of testamentary' to identify the personal representative and grant them the authority to act on behalf of the estate. Funeral directors should be aware the person named as an executor in a will may not always be the same person with the priority right to control the final disposition of the human remains. In addition, many states provide liability protections for funeral directors who take actions reasonably and in good faith based on authorizations and directions regarding the disposition of human remains found in a will, regardless of whether the will is later probated or subsequently declared invalid.

Duties of Personal Representative

Probate estate is defined as the property and debts of a decedent subject to administration by the personal representative of an estate. It is the duty and responsibility of the representative to identify the property (assets) and debts (liabilities); provide for the payment of the debts against the estate; and thereafter distribute any remaining estate assets, known as the **inheritance**, to the **devisees** pursuant to the terms of a will (when there is one) <u>or</u> to the **heirs** pursuant to intestate succession laws when there is no will. In the majority of cases, a representative will seek legal counsel to assist them in complying with state probate statutes and requirements.

Calculation date - The initial step in determining the value of a probate estate is to identify a calculation date from which all assets and liabilities will be based. The calculation date is often the date of death but may, in certain states, be a later date, such as six months after death.

Duty to inventory assets - An **inventory** of the estate assets will determine the value of the probate estate, and each item on the estate inventory must be valued. Value may be determined using any number of methods, such as fair market value, comparison value, book value, or professional appraisal.

Accounting - When determining the value of marketable securities for an estate inventory – such as stocks and bonds – the common accounting formula is 'value plus income less expenses.' This takes into consideration income generated from stock ownership, such as dividends; as well as any expenses associated with their ownership or management, such as broker fees.

Duty to inventory debts - Any outstanding debts or claims against the estate must be identified. These may include outstanding amounts owed for utilities, credit cards, loans, mortgages, medical bills, and other accounts due or incurred before the date of death or date of calculation.

Duty to file and pay taxes - The estate representative is also responsible for paying any taxes owed by the decedent or the estate. These may include such taxes as property, school, income, and estate taxes. All outstanding federal, state, and local taxes must be accounted for and paid before the remaining estate assets may be distributed to heirs or devisees.

Duty to pay claims - Claims against the estate must be paid according to probate law requirements that list the order of priority for payment.

Solvent or insolvent estate - Once an inventory has been taken to determine the value of the estate assets and the process of identifying all the claims (liabilities) against the estate has been accomplished, it is possible to determine if an estate is solvent. A **solvent estate** is one in which the assets exceed the liabilities. An **insolvent estate** in one in which the estate does not have sufficient assets to pay the debts (liabilities) of the decedent and/or the estate.

Probate laws address the issue of an insolvent estate and the distribution of whatever assets are available to be used toward the claims. These laws may specify rates and formulas to provide proportional payments to claimants based on the priority of the claims.

Payment of Claims
Payment of claims follows a specified order by priority. There are three major priority levels in the order of distribution:

1. **Preferred claims**. These are a debt which is accorded a priority, advantage, or privilege. The expenses for administering the estate and expenses for funeral services are two preferred claims found in virtually all probate laws. The administration expenses would include payment to the personal representative for their services and may also include such other expenses as an estate attorney or professional appraiser.

   The payment of funeral expenses is often listed as being second only to the estate administration expenses. It is therefore very important funeral directors are cognizant of the need to file a claim with the probate court against an estate if the funeral bill is not paid under the terms of the funeral arrangement contract. Claimants have a limited time frame within which they must file claims against an estate, and any failure to meet those deadlines may legally preclude them from being included in the payment of claims from the assets of the estate.

2. **Secured claims**. These claims are a debt which is supported by a pledge, mortgage, or lien on assets belonging to the debtor (person owed money). One of the most common types of a secured claim is a car loan, but claims could include lesser items, such as furniture or a desktop computer purchased from a retail outlet using a credit agreement.

   A similar situation to a secure claim or lien on personal property is a secure **mortgage** on *real* property, such as a residential home purchased with a loan (mortgage) from a bank. The mortgage is 'secured' because the bank that loaned the funds to the mortgagee to purchase the real property has a legal right to take possession of the mortgaged property in a foreclosure proceeding if the mortgagor fails to keep up the mortgage payments.

3. **Unsecured claims**. These claims are not supported by a pledge, mortgage, or lien on other assets. They represent the lowest priority when it comes to the payment of claims against an estate.

After all claims against the estate have been paid, the distribution of the remaining assets takes place. In the case of an intestate estate, the assets will be distributed to *heirs* according to state intestate succession laws. In the case of a testate estate, the assets will be distributed to the *devisees* pursuant to the terms of the will.

Estate Asset Distribution

After taxes and claims against an estate are paid, the personal representative will be in a position to distribute the remaining assets to the heirs or devisees. This may be accomplished by formal distribution through a probate court or an informal distribution by agreement. An informal distribution is usually authorized for estates when the value does not reach a specified amount that would require formal probate of the estate. For example, a state may not require the formal distribution of assets for an estate valued at $30,000 or less. In these cases, the personal representative could file information with the court seeking approval for the informal distribution of the assets for a small estate.

Another informal option used in some states is to present the probate court with a family settlement agreement, the term used for an agreement reached by all of the heirs as to how an estate should be distributed. A family settlement agreement does not usually need the consent of the court but must be signed by all of the heirs and persons receiving real estate or personal property from the estate, and the agreement must be filed with the probate court.

Other Estate and Health Care Documents

Power of attorney (POA) - A **power of attorney** document is a legal instrument used by one person (called the Principal) to delegate legal authority to another person (called an Agent or Attorney-in-Fact), to make property, financial and other legal decisions on their behalf. A POA is frequently used in the event of illness or disability of the Principal, or in legal transactions where the Principal cannot be physically present to sign necessary legal documents.

A person with authority over the affairs of another by means of a Power of Attorney ceases to have such authority once the person they represented has died.

There are three common power of attorney types funeral directors should be familiar with.

1. A **general power of attorney** is a written instrument granting an Agent broad powers to act for the Principal. They may be called an *ordinary* power of attorney. This type of POA ceases to exist upon the disability or incapacity of the Principal.

2. A **springing power of attorney** is a written instrument authorizing one person to act as an Agent for another, effective only upon a certain event occurring (springing). They are commonly employed by individuals that wish to delegate an Agent to manage their affairs in the event they become disabled or mentally incompetent. They typically will require a medical doctor or mental health professional to attest to any disability or mental condition when the delegated Agent believes they should start making decisions for the Principal. They may also be called a *conditional* power of attorney.

3. A **durable power of attorney** provides the authority granted under a power of attorney will remain in effect even *after* the disability or incapacity of the Principal.

The three most common power of attorney types described here are found in the majority of states, but some may use a slightly different name based on the authority granted to the Agent. For example, some states recognize a medical power of attorney to grant authority to act in matters of health and well-being; a limited power of attorney for a very specific purpose, such as signing a legal document when the Principal is not available to do so for themselves; or a financial power of attorney with respect to fiscal and monetary matters. In virtually all cases, the addition of the word 'durable' to the name of a power of attorney type extends the power being granted to remain in effect even after the disability or incapacity of the Principal.

The statutes on the use of a power of attorney to delegate authority to an Agent are not consistent across the 50 states, although the differences are usually not significant. Regardless, funeral directors must be familiar with the laws pertaining to these very powerful documents in the states where they practice.

Living will - A living will – known in some states as a health care directive or advance directive – governs the withholding or withdrawal of life-sustaining treatment from an individual in the event of an incurable or irreversible condition that will cause death within a relatively short time.

A living will may have language similar to this:

> *I direct my attending physician to withhold or withdraw treatment that merely prolongs my dying, if I should be in an incurable or irreversible mental or physical condition with no reasonable expectation of recovery.*

> *These instructions apply if I am in a terminal condition; permanently unconscious; or minimally conscious but have irreversible brain damage and will never regain the ability to make decisions and express my wishes.*

> *I direct that treatment be limited to measures to keep me comfortable and to relieve pain, including any pain that might occur by withholding or withdrawing treatment. While I understand that I am not legally required to be specific about future treatments, if I am in the condition(s) described above I feel especially strongly about the following forms of treatment:*
> - *I do not want cardiac resuscitation.*
> - *I do not want mechanical respiration.*
> - *I do not want tube feeding.*
> - *I do not want antibiotics.*
> - *I do want maximum pain relief.*

Health care proxy - A health care proxy is similar to a power of attorney in that the Principal is naming someone they trust to serve as their proxy (agent) to make health care decisions if they are unable to do so themselves. A health care proxy may be called a durable medical power of attorney or an appointment of a health care agent or surrogate. Naming a proxy can help ensure the Principal gets the health care they prefer in the event they cannot communicate those preferences for themselves. A proxy will typically make health care treatment decisions when the Principal is incapacitated and unable to communicate due to a temporary or permanent illness or injury.

A Principal does not have to be terminally ill to designate a health care proxy or for the proxy to make decisions on their behalf.

Chapter 13: Funeral Director
Qualifications, Duties, and Responsibilities

Overview
In addition to federal codes and acts that influence and regulate the funeral service industry, states have numerous laws and countless administrative rules and regulations to control and manage the operation of funeral establishments and the conduct of funeral directors. These regulations are of course state specific with no two states having identical requirements. This chapter therefore provides a review of the most common elements found in state laws, with a focus on the qualifications, duties, and responsibilities of funeral directors. The following chapter continues exploring common requirements with a focus on state oversight and enforcement activities.

Chapter Definitions
Apprenticeship (internship/resident training) - the process a person engages in to learn the practice of funeral directing and/or embalming under the instruction, direction, or personal supervision of a duly licensed funeral director and/or embalmer.

Common carrier - any carrier required by law to convey passengers or freight, without refusal, if the approved fare or charge is paid (e.g., airline, train, etc.).

Contract carrier - provides transportation for compensation only to those with whom it desires to do business (e.g., livery service).

Due diligence - the attention reasonably expected from, and ordinarily exercised by, a person who seeks to satisfy a legal requirement or to discharge an obligation.

Embalmer - a person, properly licensed, who disinfects, preserves, and/or restores a dead human body.

Funeral director (funeral service practitioner) - a person properly licensed, engaged in, or conducting, or holding himself/herself out as being engaged in preparing, other than by embalming, for the burial or disposition of dead human bodies.

Interstate - between two or more states.

Intrastate - within a state.

Private carrier - those who transport only in particular instances and only for those they choose to contract with (e.g., funeral establishment vehicles and livery).

Reciprocity - the relationship existing between two states whereby each extends some privileges of licensure to licensees of the other state.

Vital statistics - the registration, preparation, transcription, collection, compilation, and preservation of data pertaining to births, adoptions, deaths, stillbirths, marital status, etc.

Use of Titles: Funeral Director, Undertaker, and Mortician

A cursory review of funeral service titles used in the 50 states reveals the vast majority have adopted the term **funeral director** to identify funeral service professionals. Mortician is still seen sporadically but now viewed by many within the service as sounding too morbid and gloomy. The term undertaker is virtually non-existent, as state legislators have gradually phased them out of the modern lexicon. For the purposes of this chapter, the term Funeral Director is used to represent all three titles equally, unless otherwise noted. However, it must be recognized some states offer both a funeral director and an **embalmer** license and allow professionals to hold one or both at their choosing.

Funeral Director Qualifications

Age and citizenship - Most states have a minimum age to be a funeral director, with some requiring a minimum age of 18 years and others an age of 21 years. Funeral directors must also be a natural citizen or permanent legal resident of the United States.

Domicile - States may have a requirement for funeral directors to be a resident of the state in which they practice; however, the trend today is for states to allow dual-licensure in two or more states with no residency requirements.

Moral and legal character - Funeral directors must be of good moral and legal character. By definition, moral character is the existence or lack of virtues such as integrity, courage, fortitude, honesty, and loyalty. Legal character – also known as legal personality – is possessing the quality or state of being a person who respects the norms and acceptable standards of society and the rule of law. Taken together, they define a good person that contributes a positive and beneficial influence on their community.

Formal education - Funeral directors must possess a high school diploma and complete an accredited funeral service program in a higher education academic institution. The requirements for these college-level programs are set by the American Board of Funeral Service Education, the only organization recognized by both the U.S. Department of Education and the Council on Higher Education Accreditation for this purpose. As of May 2019, there were 57 accredited funeral service academic institutions in the United States authorized to offer funeral service programs of study.

Field training - Practical (on-the-job) training in the field may be for periods of one to three years and are supervised by the state agency that enforces funeral service laws, rules, and regulations. The training may run concurrent with formal education requirements or take place after the completion of those requirements. These periods of practical training may be called an **apprenticeship, internship, resident training**, or other similar title.

Programs afford prospective funeral directors the opportunity to engage and learn the practice of funeral directing and/or embalming under the instruction, direction, and personal supervision of a duly licensed funeral director and/or embalmer.

Examinations - Upon completing the requirements for a college level academic program, students are required to take and pass the two-part national board examination. Upon successful completion of this examination, the results are recognized nationwide.

Some states may also require the successful completion of written and/or oral exams that test an applicant's knowledge on state requirements to practice in the fields of funeral directing and/or embalming. In addition, practical examinations for embalmer licenses exist in some states.

Continuing education - Annual or biannual continuing education is a state requirement that mandates funeral directors attend a minimum number of hours of in-service training specific to funeral service issues. These regulations often include a breakdown of the training categories that must be included, such as one hour of OSHA training or two hours of funeral service law; while other requirements may specify how much of the training must be offered in a classroom setting with an instructor versus webinars and other online mediums. To ensure compliance, proof of continuing education attendance is required when funeral directors apply for state registration and/or license renewals.

Fees - There are state fees associated with virtually all phases of obtaining a funeral director license and thereafter renewing it on a routine basis. These may include fees for such activities as:

> ➤ registration as a funeral service student;

> ➤ registration as a funeral service apprentice, intern, or resident;

> ➤ filing an application to take a state funeral service examination;

> ➤ receipt of an initial funeral director license; and

> ➤ routine periodic renewals of a funeral director license.

Reciprocity and Dual Licensure

Reciprocity - **Reciprocity** is the relationship existing between two states whereby each extends specific privileges of licensure to licensees of the other state. These agreements permit funeral directors to enter the reciprocal state and be treated the same as if they were licensed in that state. Some states issue courtesy cards to funeral directors for this purpose, while others issue temporary permits on a case-by-case basis to perform a specified funeral service activity.

Reciprocity agreements may provide for a visiting funeral director to perform such services as:

> ➤ removing human remains;

> ➤ supervising delivery or removal from a common carrier of human remains; and

> ➤ supervising funeral service events for human remains.

Dual licensure - Dual licensure exists when one funeral director maintains licenses in more than one state or jurisdiction. The requirements to obtain dual licensure are similar but not universal all across the nation, with applicants required to submit any or all of these items:

- a letter of introduction to briefly outline current and past experience in the funeral service community;

- records attesting to the successful completion of an accredited funeral service education program and certified copies of student transcripts;

- copies of national board examination scores from the International Conference of Funeral Service Examining Board;

- records to document the successful completion of an apprenticeship or other similar field training experience;

- records of all current or previous funeral director, embalmer, or undertaker licenses held in other states, including the disclosure of any disciplinary actions or proceedings initiated against the applicant;

- proof of United States citizenship or permanent residency status; and

- applicant fees, if any.

Note: Some states waive the requirement to provide apprenticeship records if the applicant can authenticate a minimum number of years full-time experience as a funeral service practitioner.

Duties and Responsibilities

Individual states regulate which funeral service tasks must be undertaken or supervised by licensed funeral practitioners. These activities may include:

- the removal or transfer of human remains from the place of death or where released by legal authority;

- the supervision of calling hours and/or a funeral service where human remains are present;

- the supervision of the interment of human remains in the ground, entombment of human remains in a mausoleum, or other final disposition method with human remains present;

- delivery of human remains to a crematory;

- delivery of human remains to a common carrier;

- pickup of human remains from a common carrier;

- embalming and restoration of human remains for viewing;

- sale of funeral service goods and services to a consumer;

- care, preparation, shipment, and transportation of human remains; and

➢ the disinterment of human remains.

In addition to these duties, states may have laws, rules, or regulations that require funeral service professionals to:

➢ adhere to reasonable standards of care and exercise **due diligence** when performing duties;

➢ comply with all legal and reasonable requests of the person having a priority right to control the final disposition of human remains;

➢ obey all applicable government laws, rules, and regulations, as well as rules and regulations of private allied services and professionals, such as cemeteries and crematories; and

➢ comply with all health and safety regulations related to the safeguarding, handling, and final disposition of human remains.

Regulatory Compliance Related to Vital Statistics

Funeral directors also have legal duties and responsibilities when it comes to reporting deaths and filing certificates of death. The information these records contain are used to compile **vital statistics**, defined as the registration, preparation, transcription, collection, compilation, and preservation of data pertaining to births, adoptions, deaths, stillbirths, and marital status.

Certificates of death - Funeral directors have an obligation to obtain personal and biographical data and other information for inclusion on a certificate of death, as well as recording the disposition method, date, and location. Many states also require a funeral director's signature on a certificate of death before submitting it to a local registrar, recorder, or clerk for filing.

Fetal certificates of death - Fetal death certificates are usually handled differently than standard certificates in order to maintain the strictest privacy and confidentiality, especially as it relates to the identity of the mother of the fetus. Any breach of confidentiality related to these certificates may subject an offender to fines and penalties in a criminal court and/or a tort claim for damages in a civil court.

Burial, transit, cremation, and disinterment permits - Human remains may not be disposed of until a certificate of death has been filed and recorded with a local registrar, and the registrar has in turn issued a permit authorizing the disposition. Most states have permits that cover all methods of disposition, while others may have a special permit for cremation or transit cases. A permit is also required, in most cases, to authorize the disinterment of human remains.

Regulatory Compliance for Transportation of Human Remains

Purposes - Human remains present health and safety concerns for not only those required to handle and transport the remains but also for the general public when transports take place. For these reasons, states often have rigorous regulatory compliance requirements for the handling, packaging, and transporting of human remains to mitigate any potential health or safety concerns for all applicable parties.

Transports may be needed for such purposes as the transfer of human remains to or from:

- a preparation room or morgue for embalming;

- the location where the final disposition is to take place, such as a mausoleum, cemetery, or crematory;

- a funeral establishment in a different state;

- the place of death;

- an authorized institution for anatomical donation purposes;

- a medical facility for a post-mortem examination (autopsy); and

- the arrival/departure location for a common carrier.

Permits - Transportation permits are required for many but not all of the activities where human remains are being transferred from one location to another. For example, states usually require a permit to ship human remains by common carrier; while no permit is usually required to transport remains to another funeral establishment or place of final disposition when in the same state.

Methods - There are three methods for the transportation of human remains: **common carrier**, **contract carrier**, and **private carrier**.

1. Common carriers are those required to convey passengers or cargo, without refusal, if the fare or charge is paid. Airline and rail services, bus lines, and shipping companies are typical common carriers, with airline and rail services the two most prominent in the funeral service industry. Common carriers post rates for the services they offer and must offer these services to the general public. For example, American Airlines is a well-known common carrier. Anyone can schedule a flight or ship cargo on their aircraft by simply paying the applicable charges and fees.

2. Contract carriers provide transportation for compensation only to those with whom it desires to do business. In other words, a contract carrier only serves specific customers with whom they have a contract. They are not open to the general public and not required to publish rates. For example, ABC Transportation Company may have a contract with the U.S. Postal Service to transfer mail to and from Postal Service distribution centers. The services they offer are not available to the general public and they are not required to publish rates for service. These carriers can be as small as one man and a large van and up to hundreds of employees and vehicles in multiple locations nationwide.

3. Private carriers transport only in particular circumstances and only for those they choose to contract with. They include funeral establishment vehicles, such as a removal vehicle; and livery services offered to families, such as a funeral coach (hearse) or a limousine.

Preparation (common carrier) - States often have rules and regulations specific to transportation of human remains by common carrier. These are in addition to any requirements the carriers themselves may impose. State rules and regulations may include such items as:

> - the body must be encased in a rigid container constructed to withstand hazards associated with the method of transportation used;

> - to prevent the leakage of body fluids, the body must be placed in a leak-proof pouch in the container, or the container itself must be leak-proof;

> - bodies must be clothed or covered by a shroud or other suitable covering;

> - external body orifices must be closed with absorbent cotton to contain body fluids;

> - a name tag must be affixed to the body with the name of the deceased as it appears on the certificate of death; and

> - a state issued transit permit (or copy) must be attached to the exterior of the transportation container.

Preparation (private carrier) - For the transportation of human remains by private carrier, state rules and regulations may include such items as:

> - the body must be encased in a casket or container, or enclosed in a waterproof pouch and secured on a rigid litter or stretcher;

> - the body must be obscured from public view;

> - a funeral director must take steps necessary to prevent leakage of body fluids from the container in which the remains are encased; and

> - the interior of the vehicle and equipment used for transportation must be maintained in a clean and sanitary manner.

Preparation (cremated remains) - The United States Postal Service offers the only available method for shipping cremated remains domestically or internationally, and they must be shipped using Priority Mail Express Service. United Parcel Service (UPS), Federal Express (FedEx), and DHL do not accept *human remains* or *cremated remains* for shipment. Each company specifically lists them as prohibited items on their respective websites. USPS shipping includes standard tracking. If requested at the time of purchase, a proof of delivery signature record is also available. It is recommended this proof of delivery option always be chosen to provide a signed, written record of the cremated remains being received.

The USPS has issued Publication No. 139 containing very detailed and explicit instructions for the selection and preparation of containers, packing materials, and labels; as well as information on special requirements, such as the need for two containers per shipment – one interior and one exterior. There are also special requirements related to international shipments. USPS Priority Mail Express *International* Services may not always be available and, in rare cases, the destination country may prohibit mailing cremated remains to their homeland.

Note: See Guide 6 for the full text of USPS Publication 139.

Restrictions - Additional requirements and restrictions may be imposed for the transportation of human remains in unique cases, such as when the cause of death is a contagious disease or the remains being shipped have not been embalmed. Each state handles these cases differently, but requirements may include using sealed containers for contagious cases, or using dry ice to slow decomposition for human remains that are not embalmed.

Transportation - The transportation of human remains will be required when forwarding or receiving remains from one funeral establishment to another. Local and **intrastate** (within a state) transportation will usually be handled by private carrier and subject to the preparations and conditions listed above. **Interstate** (between two or more states) transportation will usually be handled by common carrier and subject to carrier rules. If interstate transportation is by roadway, funeral directors may need to comply with the rules and regulations in force in each state where the remains will be in transit; however, the majority of states have reciprocity agreements that recognize a government issued transit permit from another state fully meets the requirements to transit across their state.

The international transfer of human remains is far more complicated and requires compliance with legal requirements for *both* the shipping country and receiving country.

Note: See Guide 7 for detailed information on International Shipping of Human Remains.

Enforcement of state and local laws, rules, and regulations - The general enforcement of laws, rules and regulations is a function of the offices, divisions, boards, and departments in state and local governments. They may be specific to the funeral service industry, such as a state department of public health that has a division of cemeteries and a division of funeral directing.

Federal transportation requirements are regulated by the Transportation Security Administration, United States Coast Guard, Federal Aviation Administration, and Surface Transportation Board.

Chapter 14: Oversight and Enforcement Actions

Overview

A state agency charged with oversight responsibilities related to funeral service activities will have the authority and responsibility to enforce laws applicable to the operation of funeral establishments and the conduct of funeral directors. This responsibility includes the implementation of enforcement practices and discipline. This chapter reviews the regulatory procedures associated with enforcement efforts; prohibited conduct in funeral service activities; grounds for revocation or suspension of operators and licensees; and disciplinary procedures.

Chapter Definitions

Administrative agency - a governmental body created by legislation empowered to make and enforce rules and regulations.

Administrative law - the rules and regulations created by Federal and State administrative agencies (e.g., OSHA, FTC, state board rules and regulations).

Crime - an action against society as a whole in violation of constitution, statues, or ordinances, e.g., treason, felony, misdemeanor.

Embalmer - a person, properly licensed, who disinfects, preserves, and/or restores a dead human body.

Funeral director (funeral service practitioner) - a person properly licensed, engaged in, or conducting, or holding himself/herself out as being engaged in preparing, other than by embalming, for the burial or disposition of dead human bodies.

Funeral establishment - a facility used in the care and preparation for the funeral and/or final disposition of dead human bodies.

Moral turpitude - an act showing inherent baseness or vileness of principle or action; shameful wickedness; depravity.

Tort - a private or civil wrong against a person or his or her property, other than by breach of contract, for which there may be action for damages.

State Oversight

Administrative agencies are government bodies created by legislation and empowered to make and enforce rules and regulations. They are the agencies that oversee and supervise **funeral directors**, **embalmers**, and **funeral establishments**. The rules and regulations the agencies create and enforce are known as **administrative law**.

Rules and regulations in the funeral service industry characteristically detail the expected or prohibited conduct of a funeral director, in addition to setting out the requirements for the operation of funeral establishments. When a violation occurs, the regulatory agency may take action and impose sanctions on the funeral director and/or funeral establishment owner. Typically, penalties include warnings, suspensions, revocations, monetary fines, and/or the forfeiture or loss of licensing credentials. These actions are independent of any civil actions for **tort** offenses that may be related to the same incident or case.

The potential grounds for a state agency to initiate enforcement action has been broken into two categories and presented below in two tables. One table lists grounds for enforcement action that may be taken against funeral directors; and the second table lists grounds for enforcement action that may be taken against a funeral establishment. The entries in these tables are reflective of the most common state administrative rules and regulations as they relate to funeral service activities. The entries are not exhaustive and not always found in all state administrative laws. They are provided as a guide. Each funeral director must familiarize themselves with rules and regulations as they exist in the states where they practice.

Potential Grounds for Enforcement Action Against Funeral Directors	
Removal of human remains without proper authority	Failure to surrender or dispose of human remains upon request
Embalming without authority	Committing acts which are illegal
Conducting a funeral without proper authority	Unfit by reason of substance abuse
Disposition of human remains without authority	Unfit by reason of alcohol abuse
Performing duties outside scope of licensure	Misleading advertisements
Possession of an altered certificate, license, registration, or diploma	Soliciting or employing solicitors for human remains
False statements to obtain a license	Unfit due to a state of insanity
Removal or embalming human remains without approval	Conviction of a criminal act involving a felony or **moral turpitude**
Use of indecent or obscene language in the immediate vicinity of the family	Mutilation in preparation or restoration of human remains
Performing service outside authorized geographical limits	Refusing to surrender a body when properly ordered to do so
Willful false statement on a death certificate	Untrustworthiness in financial dealings
Failure to fulfill continuing education requirements	Possession of a fraudulent certificate, license, registration, or diploma

Potential Grounds for Enforcement Action Against Funeral Establishments	
All of the grounds for action as listed previously for funeral directors	Engaging in prohibited cross-marketing activities with allied professionals
Failure to comply with OSHA standards in a preparation room	Failure to meet minimum requirements for an arrangement room, chapel, or prep room
Failure to have a general price list	Failure to comply with ADA standards
Failure to properly display an establishment registration or license	Failure to provide casket and outer burial container price lists to consumers
Failure to publicly display a general price list	Operating from a mobile location

Regulatory Agency Procedures

Regulatory agencies must follow established procedures for receiving and then investigating potential violations of the rules and regulations over which they have jurisdiction. Procedures commonly follow a sequence of connected events similar to the one provided here as an example.

Complaint - Complaints may come from any source but, when filed by a consumer, most states require they be in writing and either verified under oath or by the witness of others. The majority of formal complaints are initiated by enforcement agency investigators as the result of their daily work in routinely conducting facility inspections.

Investigation - The regulatory agency conducts an investigation and makes a determination on how the matter should be handled. This may include:

> dismissal of the complaint;

> informal resolution by the parties involved; or

> the filing of formal administrative charges against the offender.

Formal charges - When formal charges are filed, the funeral director and/or funeral establishment is the respondent (person or entity being charged). Respondents must be given a written copy of the charges and provided with a date and time to appear for a hearing before the regulatory agency. The regulatory agency is the plaintiff (charging party).

Hearing - A hearing – sometimes referred to as a disciplinary action hearing – may take place before an administrative judge, state commissioner, or other government official authorized to hear administrative law matters. In some states, the hearing may be held before a panel of several officials, in which case one is the designated lead, presiding, or chief official.

Plaintiff - The plaintiff is the enforcement agency, represented by an agency official that presents the case against the respondent in front of the hearing officer. They may call witnesses and submit evidence to prove the case. Strict rules of evidence are not usually followed in administrative proceedings, although evidence must be relevant and credible.

Respondent - The respondent has a right to address (respond to) the charges presented by the plaintiff. They may be represented by legal counsel and are allowed to call witnesses and submit evidence to counter the charges.

Ruling - After due consideration, the hearing officer pronounces judgment on the case. Each separate charge is judged to be either founded or unfounded. If a charge is judged to be unfounded, the charge is dismissed. If a charge is judged to be founded, the hearing officer may then impose sanctions and/or penalties.

Appeal - If any of the charges against the respondent are judged to be founded by the hearing office, the respondent has the right to dispute the ruling. They may file an appeal before a judicial court of competent jurisdiction, such as a state district court or an appeals court. Both the plaintiff and the respondent would then be required to go before the applicable judicial forum to defend their respective positions on the case.

Criminal and Civil Actions
In addition to sanctions that may be imposed on a funeral director or the owner of a funeral establishment for violating administrative rules and regulations, the activities underlying the violation could result in a case being filed in a civil or criminal court.

Civil courts - If a **tort** – a private or civil wrong against a person or his or her property – occurred as a consequence of violating administrative rules, a consumer could file a civil tort claim. With this claim they could pursue compensation for any injury or loss they believe was the result of an act or omission by the funeral director, the funeral establishment, and/or the funeral establishment owner.

Criminal courts - If a **crime** – an action against society as a whole in violation of a constitution, statute, or ordinance – occurred as a consequence of violating administrative rules, the funeral director or funeral establishment owner could face criminal charges in a criminal court. States generally classify a crime as a misdemeanor for a minor offense or a felony for a major offense. Penalties for a criminal conviction may include fines and/or incarceration in a local jail or lockup for minor offenses, or a fine and incarceration in a state prison or penitentiary for major offenses.

Chapter 15: FTC Funeral Rule - Introduction

Overview
The Federal Trade Commission, Federal Regulation Rule for Funeral Industry Practices, is the one federal regulation that specifically addresses funeral services. Known simply as the Funeral Rule, it has significant regulatory compliance requirements for funeral service owners, operators, and practitioners. This chapter is an introduction to the rule, while the three succeeding chapters go into greater depth and detail on the requirements for compliance.

Chapter Definitions
At-need cases - funeral service cases where funeral arrangements are made immediately after a death has occurred; as contrasted with preneed cases, where funeral arrangements are made prior to a death occurring, in preparation for use in the future [by Author].

Commission - refers to the Federal Trade Commission.

Federal Trade Commission (FTC) - an agency of federal government created in 1914 to promote free and fair competition by prevention of trade restraints, price fixing, false advertising, and other unfair methods of competition.

Funeral director (funeral service practitioner) - a person properly licensed, engaged in, or conducting, or holding himself/herself out as being engaged in preparing, other than by embalming, for the burial or disposition of dead human bodies.

Funeral goods - the goods which are sold or offered for sale directly to the public for use in connection with funeral services.

Funeral provider - any person, partnership or corporation that sells or offers to sell funeral goods and funeral services to the public.

Funeral services - any services which may be used to: (1) care for and prepare deceased human bodies for burial, cremation, or other final disposition; and (2) arrange, supervise, or conduct the funeral ceremony or the final disposition of deceased human bodies.

Prefunded funeral arrangements - funeral arrangements made in advance of need that include provisions for funding or prepayment.

Preneed cases - funeral service cases where funeral arrangements are made prior to a death occurring, in preparation for use in the future; as contrasted with at-need cases, where funeral arrangements are made immediately following a death [by Author].

Mission and Goals of the FTC
The mission of the **Federal Trade Commission** is to protect consumers and competition by preventing anticompetitive, deceptive, and unfair business practices through law enforcement, advocacy, and education, without unduly burdening legitimate business activity.

The goals of the Federal Trade Commission are to:

➢ protect consumers from unfair and deceptive practices in the marketplace;

➢ maintain competition to promote a marketplace free from anticompetitive mergers, business practices, or public policy outcomes; and

➢ advance the FTC's performance through excellence in managing resources, human capital, and information technology.

History of the FTC and the Funeral Rule
When the FTC was created in 1914, its purpose was to prevent unfair methods of competition in commerce as part of an on-going battle at the time to break up monopolies and trusts. In subsequent years, Congress passed legislation giving the agency greater authority to police anticompetitive practices and administer other consumer protections. As a result, the FTC is responsible for such initiatives as the Telemarketing Sales Rule; Pay-Per-Call Rule; and Equal Credit Opportunity Act. In 1975, Congress gave the FTC the responsibility of adopting industry-wide trade regulation rules, and the Funeral Rule is a direct result of this far-reaching authority.

The Funeral Rule was adopted in 1984 and revised in 1994, and it was not until 26 years later, in early 2020, that the FTC announced it was considering a review of the rule with the intent of revising and updating the various provisions to more accurately reflect contemporary practices in the industry. However, with the onset of the Covid pandemic in February of 2020, the initial timeline for making a decision on whether or not revisions are needed has been pushed back several times. If the decision is made to move forward with a full review, it will take a year or more to conduct a thorough review process, submit proposed changes to the public for comment, and submit a final plan to the Commission for approval.

Consumer Rights
The purpose of the Funeral Rule is to provide certain rights to consumers when making funeral arrangements, either at the time when death occurs or when making arrangements in advance of need. The Funeral Rule specifically prohibits funeral directors from:

➢ misrepresenting legal, crematory, and cemetery requirements;

➢ embalming for a fee without permission;

➢ requiring the purchase of a casket for a direct cremation;

➢ requiring consumers to buy certain funeral goods or services as a condition for furnishing other funeral goods or services; and

➢ engaging in other deceptive or unfair practices.

In practice, the Funeral Rule allows consumers to comparison shop for prices from any number of different funeral establishments. With this pricing information in hand, consumers can make an informed decision on which establishment they want to provide them with funeral goods and services. The Funeral Rule is centered around provisions that require **funeral directors** to provide consumers with accurate, up-to-date, itemized price lists and information. These price lists and other mandates are reviewed in-depth in the next three chapters that follow, including:

> Chapter 16 - Reviews general price lists, including the required items and disclosures, distribution requirements, and use for preneed funeral arrangements.

> Chapter 17 - Reviews casket price lists and outer burial container price lists, as well as the mandatory Statement of Funeral Goods and Services Selected that must be given to a consumer at the conclusion of an arrangement conference.

> Chapter 18 - Reviews miscellaneous provisions found in the Funeral Rule, such as embalming approvals, record retention schedules, direct cremation mandates, and telephone price disclosures.

<u>Who Must Comply?</u>
All **funeral providers** must comply with the Funeral Rule. The FTC defines a funeral provider as any person, partnership or corporation that sells or offers to sell funeral goods and funeral services to the public.

Funeral goods are goods sold or offered for sale directly to the public for use in connection with funeral service events, while **funeral services** are any services which may be used to:

> care for and prepare human remains for burial, cremation, or other final disposition; and

> arrange, supervise, or conduct the funeral ceremony or the final disposition of human remains.

A more concise means to describe the difference between goods and services in the industry is to define <u>goods</u> as *tangible* merchandise items *purchased* by the consumer, such as a register book, flag case, or crucifix; and <u>services</u> as *non-tangible* items *provided* to a consumer for a fee, such as the use of the funeral establishment for calling hours or the personal supervision of a graveside service by a funeral director.

The definition of a funeral provider states the provider, "… *sells or offers to sell funeral goods <u>and</u> funeral services to the public.*" A provider may not always be a funeral director or a funeral establishment, as other individuals, businesses, and organizations may be defined as a provider simply because they offer to sell both funeral goods and funeral services. Sellers that offer only funeral goods or only funeral services (not both) do not meet the definition.

For example, the Costco Wholesale Company sells caskets online and from wholesale outlets, but they do not offer or sell any type of funeral services, such as the preparation of human remains. They therefore do not meet the definition of a funeral provider and are not subject to the Funeral Rule. In recent years, several state and local funeral director associations have sought to have the rule revised to require all those who sell funeral goods <u>or</u> funeral services comply with the rule provisions, assuming this change would deter third-party vendors from selling funeral goods or, at the very least, level the playing field for competition between third-party vendors and funeral establishments. This issue may be addressed if the FTC proposes changes to the Funeral Rule.

Preneeds and the Funeral Rule

The requirements of the Funeral Rule apply to all **at-need cases** and **preneed cases** when making funeral arrangements. In addition, when a preneed case becomes an at-need case following the death of the person for whom the preneed was arranged, the rule must be complied with again when making at-need funeral arrangements. If a family asks about additional goods or services, alters or changes pre-planned arrangements, or is required to pay additional sums of money, they must be given all relevant disclosures and price lists as required in the rule.

As an example, if the prices listed on a **prefunded funeral arrangement** were not guaranteed by the funeral establishment, the family may need to pay the difference between the preneed pricing and the current pricing at the time of death. This would trigger the requirement for the funeral director to provide all applicable price lists and disclosures under the Funeral Rule. Similarly, any addition or change to the goods or items in the preneed would require compliance with the rule.

Preneed contracts completed before the rule went into effect in 1984 do not have to be retro-actively brought into compliance; however, if they are going to be amended or modified for any reason thereafter, the changes automatically trigger all of the rule requirements and mandatory disclosures.

Note: See the chapter titled, *Preneed Regulatory Compliance,* for additional information on prefunded preneed requirements.

Enforcement

The Federal Trade Commission enforces federal consumer protection laws that prevent fraud, deception, and unfair business practices. It also enforces federal antitrust laws that prohibit anticompetitive mergers and other business practices that could lead to higher prices, fewer choices, or less innovation. As such, the FTC is the agency charged with the responsibility to enforce compliance with the Funeral Rule.

Consumer education - The FTC promotes consumer education as one means to ensure compliance. Toward that end, the FTC publishes several articles in a series titled, *Shopping for Funeral Services.* The series includes information on topics of interest to a consumer, including these titles.

The Funeral Rule

Funeral Costs and Pricing Checklist

Types of Funerals

Choosing a Funeral Provider

Buying a Cemetery Site

Planning Your Own Funeral

Funeral Terms

Consumers may view these publications online or request they be sent to them by mail. In addition to these articles, the FTC also provides consumers with information on how to file a consumer complaint.

Funeral providers - The FTC uses self-enforcement and direct enforcement actions to facilitate funeral providers in complying with the rule.

For *self-enforcement* actions, the FTC has published a set of guidelines titled, *Complying with the Funeral Rule*, to assist funeral directors in understanding and applying the provisions of the rule in the workplace. These guidelines include detailed information on the three required price lists, as well as the mandatory itemized statement that must be given to consumers. These guidelines are available online and in print.

For *direct enforcement* actions, the FTC conducts annual undercover inspections to observe whether or not funeral establishments are complying with the Funeral Rule. Undercover enforcement officers randomly go into funeral establishments in a targeted area and inquire about funeral goods and services. These 'shoppers' observe actions taken by the establishment staff to verify they are complying with the rule in such areas as timely providing a consumer with a General Price List when discussing goods and services, the prices for funeral goods and services, or the types of dispositions or funerals offered. Typically, when undercover officers have observed non-compliance issues on at least two separate occasions, enforcement action will be taken.

In addition to undercover shoppers, FTC staff may also respond to a specific consumer complaint by conducting a compliance review or investigation of a particular funeral establishment.

Offender program - A funeral establishment found to be in violation of the rule may be offered an opportunity to enter the Funeral Rule Offender Program (FROP), a multi-year training program designed to increase compliance. The one-time FROP training opportunity is an alternative to an enforcement action, court order, and civil penalties up to $40,654 per violation (as of 2018).

FROP is a joint project of the FTC and the National Funeral Directors Association (NFDA). The NFDA administers the program and provides participants with a legal review of the price disclosures required by the rule, along with ongoing training, testing, and monitoring of compliance. Participants must make a voluntary payment to the U.S. Treasury in lieu of a civil penalty and pay annual administrative fees to the National Association.

In an April 2018 press release, the FTC reported investigators – working undercover in 11 states – found failures to disclose pricing information required by the Funeral Rule in 29 of the 134 funeral establishments they visited in 2017. This same press release provided insight into what the investigators were looking for by including this paragraph:

> *The FTC conducts undercover inspections to monitor funeral establishment's compliance with the Funeral Rule. The Rule gives consumers important rights when making funeral arrangements. For example, **funeral establishments must provide consumers with an itemized general price list at the start of an in-person***

discussion of funeral arrangements, a casket price list before consumers view any caskets, and an outer burial container price list before they view grave liners or vaults. The Rule also prohibits funeral establishments from requiring consumers to buy any item, such as a casket, as a condition of obtaining any other funeral good or service. By requiring the provision of itemized prices, the Funeral Rule enables consumers to compare prices and buy only the goods and services they want. [**Bold** *emphasis added.*]

Note: In addition to federal compliance efforts, many states have similar programs to ensure compliance with state requirements as they relate to the conduct of funeral directors and the operation of funeral establishments.

Chapter 16: FTC Funeral Rule - General Price Lists

Overview
The Funeral Rule requires up to three different price lists to inform consumers of the goods and services a funeral establishment offers, and the prices they charge for those goods and services. The most significant of these lists is the General Price List, described by the FTC as 'the keystone of the Funeral Rule.' This chapter is dedicated to a review of this important price list.

Chapter Definitions
Alternative container - an unfinished wood box or other non-metal receptacle or enclosure, without ornamentation or a fixed interior lining, which is designed for the encasement of human remains and which is made of fiberboard, pressed-wood, composition materials (with or without an outside covering) or like materials.

Direct cremation - disposition of human remains by cremation without formal viewing, visitation, or ceremony with the body present.

Forwarding of remains - one of the 16 items required on a GPL (if the funeral provider offers this service). This involves services of the funeral provider in the locale where death occurs and preparation for transfer to another funeral provider as selected by the family (consumer). The Funeral Rule requires package pricing of this service with a description of the components included.

Funeral ceremony - service commemorating the deceased with the body present.

General price list (GPL) - a printed or typewritten list that must be given for retention to all persons who inquire in person about the funeral goods, funeral services, or prices of funeral goods or services offered by a funeral establishment.

Graveside service - for the purposes of Funeral Rule pricing, a service intended for those situations where there is no funeral ceremony at the funeral establishment or elsewhere.

Immediate burial - a disposition of human remains by burial, without formal viewing, visitation, or ceremony with the body present, except for a graveside service.

Itemization - a method of listing goods and services on a General Price List that treats each individual good or service being offered as a separate line item that includes the price for the item [by Author].

Memorial service - a ceremony commemorating the deceased without the body present.

Non-declinable service fee - with respect to a GPL basic services fee, the only fee for services, facilities or unallocated overhead permitted in the Funeral Rule that may be non-declinable, unless otherwise required by law.

Package pricing - a pricing method whereby several items of goods and/or services are bundled together and offered for one price for all the included items [by Author].

Receiving remains - one of the categories required to be itemized on the GPL (if the funeral provider offers the service). This involves services of the funeral provider after initial services have been provided by another firm at the locale of death. Funeral Rule requires package pricing of this service with a description of the components included.

Services of funeral director and staff - basic services, not to be included in prices of other categories on a General Price List, that are furnished by a funeral provider in arranging any funeral, such as conducting the arrangements conference, planning the funeral, obtaining necessary permits, and placing obituary notices.

Transfer (removal) of remains - The transportation of human remains from a place of death or other location from where the remains are released by legal authority [by Author].

Triggering event - the event (discussion) that occurs requiring a GPL be given to a consumer for retention; the triggering event for giving out the GPL is a face-to-face meeting to discuss funeral goods, services, and prices.

Requirement for a General Price List

A printed or typewritten **General Price List** (GPL) must be given to all individuals who inquire in person about the funeral goods, funeral services, or prices of funeral goods or services offered by a funeral establishment. A funeral director must provide the list to a consumer upon beginning discussion of any of the following:

1. The prices of funeral goods or funeral services.

2. The overall type of funeral service or disposition.

3. Specific funeral goods or funeral services offered by the funeral provider.

These three activities are referred to as **triggering events,** or the face-to-face meetings that then require a funeral director to give the consumer a GPL for review and retention (to keep).

The requirement for a consumer to be given a GPL applies regardless of the location where the discussion takes place. There is however one exception to this requirement at the time when a decedent is being transferred from the place of death and a funeral director is requesting authorization to embalm.

For this purpose and time only, a GPL does not need to be given to a consumer; however, the funeral director must disclose embalming is not required by law (except in certain cases) and refrain from any further discussion that would trigger the requirement to provide a GPL. If any other triggering event discussions take place, a GPL must be given to the consumer for their retention.

Providing a General Price List

In-person - A GPL must be given to anyone who asks – in person – about funeral goods, funeral services, or the prices of such goods and services. Funeral establishment competitors, news media representatives, clergy members, government officials, and consumer advocacy groups are just a few of the possible individuals or groups that may request a GPL. There are no exceptions.

By phone - Certain information must be provided to those who telephone a funeral establishment and inquire about the price of funeral goods and funeral services, but the rule does not require funeral establishments to mail or otherwise provide callers with a GPL based on a telephone call. However, there is also nothing in the rule to prohibit a funeral establishment from mailing a GPL to someone if they choose to do so.

Note: Additional information on telephone price disclosures is provided in the chapter titled, *FTC Funeral Rule - Miscellaneous Provisions*.

By mail - Funeral establishments do not have to mail a GPL upon request but, once again, there is nothing to prohibit them doing so, and some states may have rules and regulations that do require a GPL be mailed upon request.

For retention - A GPL cannot be shown in a booklet or binder where it appears there is only one copy available, as an individual hard copy must be physically offered to consumers so they can take it home with them when they leave. A consumer does not have to accept or review a GPL, and a funeral director is not required to do anything beyond offering and making one available to them. However, a funeral director also may not do or say anything to discourage a consumer from accepting, reviewing, or keeping a GPL. Additionally, no fees or conditions may be set for a consumer to receive a GPL, as they must be provided free of charge.

Information Required on a General Price List

Heading - A GPL must contain at least the following information in the heading:

1. The name, address, and telephone number of the funeral provider's place of business.

2. A caption describing the list as a 'General Price List'.

3. The effective date of the list.

The effective date is the date on which the GPL is first made available to be given or offered to persons requesting funeral service information.

Itemized prices - Following the heading, a GPL must itemize *16 specific items of goods and services*, together with the price for each item. **Itemization** – the pricing method used on a GPL – is a method of listing goods and services that treats each individual good or service being offered as a separate line item that includes the price for the item.

A funeral establishment must list each of the 16 FTC specified items on their general price list; however, they do not need to list any of the 16 items they do not offer to consumers. They may also list items they offer that are not included in the 16 FTC items, such as prayer cards or a flag case.

Note: Many states require all items offered by a funeral establishment must be listed on the general price list, regardless of whether or not they are included in the 16 specified by the FTC. The best practice in the industry is to include all goods and services regularly offered by a funeral establishment on the GPL.

Disclosures - In addition to the 16 specific items, there are *six disclosures* required in the rule that must be included within the itemized listings. These disclosures must use the identical wording provided in the rule and be located in specific locations on the GPL. Additional information, such as state laws or regulations relevant to an item, may be added, but a funeral establishment may not change the FTC language or add anything that would modify the FTC language.

Packages - A funeral establishment may offer **package pricing** on a GPL, but these packages must be in addition to – not in place of – the required itemized prices. For example, an establishment could offer a memorial package that includes prayer cards, acknowledgement cards, and a register book; but they must then also list and offer each of these three same items individually. There is nothing in the rule to prohibit the package price for the items being lower than the cost of the three items if purchased individually. Some states prohibit package pricing.

Discounts - The rule allows a discount in pricing for special circumstances, such as arrangements for a friend or relative, or a family that otherwise could not afford the services; however, funeral establishments may not inflate the prices in order to offer all or most of their customers a discount. If that were the case, the discounted prices would be the accurate prices and should be reflected on the price list.

Order of the items list - The rule does not require the 16 items be listed in any particular order, although some states have regulations that mandate a specific order to make it easier for consumers to comparison shop for the items they want for a funeral. In those states, prices may be quickly compared item-by-item by reviewing them in the same order on two or more GPLs from the same state.

The 16 Items and Six Disclosures
For the review that follows, the 16 FTC items and six disclosures have been listed in an order designed to facilitate the learning process. Regardless of the items or their order, the first thing seen on a GPL following the heading is the first of the six required disclosures: 'right of selection.'

This "right of selection' disclosure informs consumers they have a right to select only the goods and services they wish to purchase. It must be placed right *after* the heading and right *before* the listing of goods and services being offered.

> **DISCLOSURE 1 of 6 - Right of Selection**
> *The goods and services shown below are those we can provide to our customers. You may choose only the items you desire.* ***However, any funeral arrangements you select will include a charge for our basic services and overhead.*** *If legal or*

other requirements mean you must buy any items you did not specifically ask for, we will explain the reason in writing on the statement we provide describing the funeral goods and services you selected. [**Bold** emphasis added.]

Funeral establishments must include the third sentence of the disclosure – highlighted in bold – if consumers cannot decline the basic services fee. The phrase 'and overhead' may be placed after the word 'services' as shown, if the fee also includes the recovery of overhead costs.

ITEM 1 of 16 - Basic Services of Funeral Director and Staff, and Overhead

The charge for **services of funeral director and staff** is a fee for the basic services a funeral establishment provides that are not otherwise itemized. It includes services common to virtually all forms and types of funeral arrangements for the disposition of human remains, such as conducting the arrangement conference, securing necessary permits, preparing notices, sheltering of remains, and coordinating arrangements with a cemetery, crematory, or other third party. The fee should not include charges related to other items that must be separately listed on the GPL that the consumer may decline to purchase.

There are two options to how the Basic Services Fee may be listed on a GPL:

Option 1 - If a funeral establishment lists a separate Basic Services Fee and the charge is non-declinable – the consumer does not have the option of declining the charge – the GPL must include a disclosure that reads as follows:

DISCLOSURE 2 of 6 - Basic Services Fee (For option 1 - Fee is on GPL)
This fee for our basic services and overhead will be added to the total cost of the funeral arrangements you select. (This fee is already included in our charges for direct cremations, immediate burials, and forwarding or receiving remains.)

If a funeral establishment chooses Option 1, this disclosure must appear together with the price for the basic services and with a description of the services included for that price. It may not be placed on a separate page or anywhere else on the GPL apart from the basic services price. If this fee is non-declinable, the price must also include all charges for the recovery of overhead expenses not allocated elsewhere on the GPL. In this situation, the first sentence of the disclosure can include the phrase 'and overhead' after the word services as shown above.

There are four GPL items for which the Basic Services Fee must be included in the item price: direct cremations, immediate burials, forwarding of remains, and receiving remains. These are known as minimal services. If a consumer chooses one of these four items, they are not prohibited from selecting other goods and services offered. However, the Basic Services Fee may not be charged for any goods and services purchased when they are in addition to any of the four minimal services.

As an example, if a consumer chooses an immediate burial for a service but would also like to purchase a flag display case, they can be charged for the immediate burial and the flag case but not the Basic Services Fee. As required, the Basic Services Fee must already be included in the immediate burial charges because it is a minimal service.

Option 2 - Instead of charging a separate Basic Services Fee, a funeral establishment may include this fee in the casket prices, in which case the establishment must include a disclosure that reads as follows:

> **DISCLOSURE 2 of 6 - Basic Services Fee (For option 2 - Fee is in casket price)**
> *Please note that a fee of $_____ for the use of our basic services and overhead is included in the price of our caskets. This same fee shall be added to the total cost of your funeral arrangements if you provide the casket. Our services include (specify) _____.*

If a funeral establishment chooses Option 2, the fee should include all charges for the recovery of overhead costs not allocated elsewhere, and the establishment may add the phrase 'and overhead' after the word services in the first sentence. The disclosure must appear on the GPL together with the prices for the individual caskets or on the GPL together with the casket price range if the establishment has a separate Casket Price List.

The Basic Services Fee may include overhead from various aspects of a funeral establishment operation, such as the parking lot, reception and arrangements rooms, and other common areas. It may also include insurance, staff salaries, taxes, and fees that a funeral establishment must pay to operate the business. Alternatively, instead of including all overhead in the Basic Services Fee, a funeral establishment may spread overhead charges across the various individual goods and services offered.

As a third alternative, a funeral establishment may combine the first two approaches by spreading some portion of the overhead charges across the individual items, while including the remainder of the charges in a Basic Services Fee on the GPL.

Note: The Basic Services Fee is the only *non-declinable service fee* allowed for services, facilities, or unallocated overhead, unless a state or local law requires otherwise.

ITEM 2 of 16 - Forwarding of Remains to Another Funeral Home
This is the first of the four minimal services. The GPL must list one price for this item and describe all services the funeral establishment will provide for the quoted price. It must include all charges, including the Basic Services Fee and any facility or equipment fees.

ITEM 3 of 16 - Receiving Remains from Another Funeral Home
This is the second of the four minimal services and has the same requirements as Item 2.

ITEM 4 of 16 - Direct Cremation
This is the third of the four minimal services. It must state a price range, include a mandatory disclosure, and list the prices for each of two options. The required disclosure must be placed in immediate conjunction with (directly next to) the price range for the direct cremation options and read as follows:

DISCLOSURE 3 of 6 - Direct Cremation

If you want to arrange a direct cremation, you can use an alternative container. Alternative containers encase the body and can be made of materials like fiberboard or composition materials (with or without an outside covering). The containers we provide are (specify) _____

_____.

At the end of the last sentence in the disclosure, the funeral establishment must describe the specific kind of containers they offer for a direct cremation. If a funeral establishment does not offer direct cremations, they do not need to include this disclosure on the GPL.

The listing for direct cremation must include two options:

Option 1 - A price for direct cremation if the consumer provides the casket or container.

Option 2 - A price for each direct cremation selection the funeral establishment offers with an alternative container.

An **alternative container** is defined as an unfinished wood box or other non-metal receptacle or enclosure, without ornamentation or a fixed interior lining, which is designed for the encasement of human remains and which is made of fiberboard, pressed-wood, composition materials (with or without an outside covering) or like materials.

If a funeral establishment offers direct cremation, the Funeral Rule mandates they must offer at least one option that includes an alternative container. They may offer multiple options, each with a different alternative container, and every option must be separately listed with a description of the alternative container and the price.

The GPL must also describe the services a funeral establishment will provide for each type of direct cremation they offer, such as direct cremation with a memorial service or direct cremation with scattering of the cremated remains.

If the crematory fee to have human remains cremated is included in the direct cremation price, the words 'and cremation' must be included in the GPL description of what goods and services are provided. If a funeral establishment uses a third-party crematory, they may want to treat the cremation charge as a cash advance item. In these cases, the words 'and cremation' would not be included in the description, but it must be explained to the consumer the crematory charge will be estimated or itemized separately on the Statement of Funeral Goods and Services Selected.

ITEM 5 of 16 - Immediate Burial

This is the fourth of the four minimal services. The GPL must state a price range and list the prices for each of two options.

Option 1 - The price for an immediate burial where the consumer provides the casket.

Option 2 - The price for each form of immediate burial offered where the funeral establishment provides a casket or alternative container. Unlike direct cremation, a funeral establishment is not required to make an alternative container available for an immediate burial; however, they are not prohibited by the rule from offering an alternative container option to consumers.

The GPL must describe the services and container provided for each price. If the immediate burial option is available with any casket a funeral establishment is offering on the casket price list, the GPL can simply state the price of the service and refer the consumer to the casket price list for the casket prices.

ITEM 6 of 16 - Transfer of Remains to Funeral Establishment

This item is for the **transfer (removal) of human remains** to a funeral establishment. This may be from the place of death or some other location from which the remains are released by legal authority. The pricing method for this service may be a flat fee, an hourly rate, a mileage charge, or a combination of these methods. Many funeral establishments charge a flat fee for a transfer up to a specified number of miles, and use the mileage charge method for any additional miles outside the radius of the flat fee. The fee must include costs for personnel, equipment, and a vehicle. This charge is not used for the transportation of human remains beyond the initial transfer, such as transportation to an airport or crematory.

ITEM 7 of 16 - Embalming

The price for embalming must include the use of the preparation room, as well as the professional services, equipment, and materials involved in performing an embalming. It does not include other related services, such as cosmetic or restoration work, which would be listed in Item 8 - Other Preparation of the Body. The embalming disclosure must read as follows:

DISCLOSURE 4 of 6 - Embalming

[Except in certain special cases,] [E]mbalming is not required by law. Embalming may be necessary, however, if you select certain funeral arrangements, such as a funeral with viewing. If you do not want embalming, you usually have the right to choose an arrangement, such as direct cremation or immediate burial, that does not require you to pay for it.

This disclosure informs consumers the law usually does not require embalming. However, there are states that do not, *by law*, require an embalming for any reason, including for a visitation or a funeral, in which case the Funeral Rule allows a funeral establishment in those states to delete the phrase [Except in certain special cases] from the embalming disclosure. The first sentence would then read: *Embalming is not required by law.* The rule also allows states to add information about state law requirements, as long as they do so *after* the mandated FTC disclosure.

This disclosure must be placed in immediate conjunction with the price for embalming. The price cannot be on one page and the disclosure placed on another page or anywhere else on the GPL apart from the embalming price.

ITEM 8 of 16 - Other Preparation of the Body

This charge includes such services as dressing and casketing; topical disinfection (when there is no embalming); cosmetic work; and restoration work to prepare the remains for viewing.

ITEM 9 of 16 - Use of Facilities and Staff for Viewing

A funeral establishment may charge a flat fee or an hourly fee for the use of facilities for a viewing. The price must include charges for both the services of staff and the facilities used in connection with a viewing. If a funeral establishment provides staff services for a viewing held at another facility – such as a church or home – they may list a separate fee for the staff services, as a facilities charge would not be appropriate because the funeral establishment facilities are not being used.

ITEM 10 of 16 - Use of Facilities and Staff for Funeral Ceremony

The charge for a funeral ceremony at a funeral establishment must include both the use of facilities and the necessary staff services. Staff charges and facilities charges may not be listed as two separate charges; however, staff services provided at any other facility – such as a church – may be listed as a separate fee.

ITEM 11 of 16 - Use of Facilities and Staff for Memorial Service

The charge for a memorial service has the same requirements as Item 10 - Use of Facilities and Staff for Funeral Ceremony.

ITEM 12 of 16 - Use of Equipment and Staff for Graveside Service

The charge for this service should include both staff services and any equipment, such as a tent and folding chairs, needed for a **graveside service**. Equipment charges and staff charges may not be listed as two separate charges. A funeral establishment may include a committal service at the grave in their charge for a funeral ceremony or have a separate charge for a graveside service.

Note: The separate charge for a graveside service is intended for those situations where there is no funeral ceremony at the funeral establishment or elsewhere.

ITEM 13 of 16 - Hearse

The pricing method for this service may be a flat fee, an hourly rate, a mileage charge, or a combination of these methods. Similar to pricing methods for Item 6 - Transfer of Remains, a funeral establishment may charge a flat fee with or without an additional mileage charge for distances beyond a certain specified radius.

ITEM 14 of 16 - Limousine

The available pricing methods for this service are the same as Item 13 - Hearse.

ITEM 15 of 16 - Casket Prices

There are two options for listing casket prices on a GPL:

Option 1 - List a casket price range on the GPL with a disclosure about the availability of a casket price list. The disclosure when this option is chosen must read as follows:

DISCLOSURE 5 of 6 - Casket Prices
A complete price list will be provided at the funeral establishment.

Option 2 - List all the prices of individual caskets directly on the GPL and not have a separate casket price list. There is no required disclosure when this option is chosen.

ITEM 16 of 16 - Outer Burial Container Prices
There are two options for listing outer burial container prices on a GPL:

Option 1 - List an outer burial container price range on the GPL with a disclosure about the availability of an outer burial container price list. The disclosure when this option is chosen must read as follows:

DISCLOSURE 6 of 6 - Outer Burial Container Prices (For option 1)
A complete price list will be provided at the funeral establishment.

Option 2 - List all the prices of individual outer burial containers directly on the GPL and not have a separate outer burial container list. With this option, a disclosure is required on the GPL that must read as follows:

DISCLOSURE 6 of 6 - Outer Burial Container Prices (For option 2)
[In most areas of the country], [S]tate or local law does not require that you buy a container to surround the casket in the grave. However, many cemeteries require that you have such a container so that the grave will not sink in. Either a grave liner or a burial vault will satisfy these requirements.

If no state or local law requires an outer container surround a casket in the grave, such as a burial vault or grave box, the rule allows a funeral establishment to delete the phrase [In most areas of the country] from the disclosure. The first sentence would then read: *State or local law does not require that you buy a container to surround the casket in the grave.*

If a funeral establishment chooses option 1 for outer burial container prices (providing a range on the GPL), the required disclosure shown above for option 2 (listing all the prices on a GPL) must instead be placed on the separate outer burial container price list.

Note: See Form 1 to view a typical General Price List.

Chapter 17: FTC Funeral Rule
Other Price Lists and a Required Statement

Overview

The first part of this chapter examines the Funeral Rule requirements for a funeral establishment to have a Casket Price List and an Outer Burial Container Price List for consumers to review when selecting these items. The latter part of the chapter reviews the Funeral Rule Statement of Funeral Goods and Services Selected, a document which must be provided to a consumer at the conclusion of an arrangement conference.

Chapter Definitions

Alternative container - an unfinished wood box or other non-metal receptacle or enclosure, without ornamentation or a fixed interior lining, which is designed for the encasement of human remains and which is made of fiberboard, pressed-wood, composition materials (with or without an outside covering) or like materials.

Cash advance items - any item of service or merchandise described to a purchaser as a 'cash advance,' 'accommodation,' 'cash disbursement,' or similar term. A cash advance item is also any item obtained from a third party and paid for by the funeral provider on the purchaser's behalf.

Casket - a rigid container which is designed for the encasement of human remains and which is usually constructed of wood, metal, fiberglass, plastic, or like material, and ornamented and lined with fabric which is usually constructed of wood, metal, fiberglass, plastic, or like material, and ornamented and lined with fabric.

Casket price list (CPL) - a printed or typewritten list containing at least the retail prices of all caskets and alternative containers offered by a funeral establishment which do not require special ordering, enough information to identify each, and the effective date for the price list.

Itemization - a method of listing goods and services on a General Price List that treats each individual good or service being offered as a separate line item that includes the price for the item [by Author].

Outer burial container - any container which is designed for placement in the grave around the casket including, but not limited to, container commonly known as burial vaults, grave boxes, and grave liners.

Outer burial container price list - a printed or typewritten list containing at least the retail prices of all outer burial containers offered by a funeral establishment which do not require special ordering, enough information to identify each container, and the effective date for the prices listed.

Package pricing - a pricing method whereby several items of goods and/or services are bundled together and offered for one price for all the included items [by Author].

Statement of Funeral Goods and Services Selected - an itemized list of goods and services that a consumer has selected during an arrangement conference that allows them to evaluate the selections and make any desired changes.

Other Price Lists

Three price lists and the requirement to provide consumers with a written **itemization** of the goods and services they selected during the arrangement conference are the four core elements of the Funeral Rule. The price lists required by the rule include the general price list, explained in the previous chapter, and these two additional lists: casket price list and outer burial container price list.

The Casket Price List

Casket prices may be included on and made a part of the General Price List or, in the alternative, be provided on a separate **casket price list** (CPL). When using a separate casket price list, the list must provide the following basic information:

1. The name of the business (funeral establishment).

2. A caption describing the list as a Casket Price List.

3. The effective date for the price list.

4. The retail price of each **casket** and **alternative container** that does not require special ordering, along with enough information to identify them.

Alternative containers - If a funeral establishment offers direct cremation as a service option, they must also offer at least one direct cremation selection that includes an alternative container. The prices of alternative containers must be listed together with the caskets on the CPL. Caskets may not be on one list and alternative containers on a different list.

Item descriptions - Descriptions of the different caskets and alternative containers must be sufficient enough to clearly identify them. The rule does not go into any detail on what the descriptions must include, but most states require any or all of the following:

➤ the make, model, and name of the casket or alternative container;

➤ a description of the interior cloth weave and style, such as a velvet, crepe (rhymes with cape), or satin weave; and a tailored, shirred (rhymes with bird), or tufted style;

➤ the exterior finish, such as polished, brushed, painted, natural, or cloth-covered;

➤ the gauge of metal, for metal caskets; and

➤ the species of wood, for wooden caskets.

Providing a photograph or simply a manufacturer name and model are not sufficient to identify a casket or alternative container.

Caskets to be listed - The Funeral Rule requires a funeral establishment list only those caskets and alternative containers they *usually offer* for sale and that do not require special ordering. The FTC has defined special ordering to mean purchasing a casket or container that is not in stock and not a part of a funeral establishment's regular offerings to consumers. Except for the requirement that a funeral establishment have an alternative container available if they are going to offer direct cremation, the rule does not require any particular caskets or alternative containers be listed.

The CPL does not have to include customized caskets or caskets maintained in inventory to fill pre-existing preneed contracts, unless the caskets are also regularly offered for sale. It is also not necessary to prepare a new CPL if a casket or alternative container is temporarily out-of-stock.

If a particular casket or alternative container is available in a variety of interior or exterior materials, designs, colors, or other optional items that do not change the overall price, a funeral establishment can simply note the availability of those options on the CPL. There is no requirement or need to list each variation individually.

Format - The Funeral Rule does not require any particular format for the list, nor is there any requirement on the order in which caskets and alternative containers must be placed on the list. It may be in any form, including in a notebook or on a chart, as long as it contains the required information. All of the CPL information must be displayed in a clear and conspicuous manner.

Casket Price List Requirements

In-person - A funeral establishment must give a CPL for review to anyone who asks, in person, about the caskets or alternative containers they offer or the prices they charge for them. The list must also be offered to a consumer any time discussions *begin* about caskets or alternative containers. The offer must be made *prior* to showing any caskets or alternative containers to a consumer, thereby providing them the opportunity to look at the price list before discussing the options or viewing the actual products.

The FTC is very specific in stating consumers should not first learn of casket prices by entering a casket showroom or selection room and reading price cards placed on individual caskets or by having the funeral director recite price information to them orally.

Price cards - A funeral establishment may use individual price cards on caskets and containers, but this pricing method must be *in addition to* having a CPL.

For review - The casket price list must be given to a consumer for review, but it does not need to be given to them to keep, as is required for a General Price List; however, there is no prohibition on allowing a consumer to keep the CPL if the funeral establishment wants to do so.

Display - The Funeral Rule does not require caskets or containers be displayed in any specific manner or arrangement, and there are no requirements to have caskets and containers on display if a funeral establishment does not want or have the necessary space for a casket selection showroom. Some establishments present selections by using a book containing photographs of the various caskets and containers they offer. When using a book, catalog, or other media format for presentations, it must include all the information required for a CPL, including the business name, a caption describing the presentation materials as a Casket Price List, and the effective date of the list.

For funeral establishments that use a manufacturer or supplier casket showroom outside the funeral establishment facility, they must offer the CPL when and where the discussion of casket offerings and prices begins. This may occur at the funeral establishment, if this is where discussions begin; or at the manufacturer or supplier casket showroom, if this is where the discussion begins.

Note: Some states and municipalities have rules and regulations that address the issue of casket displays, such as requiring the least expensive casket offered for sale be displayed in the same manner and visual presentation as other caskets are displayed.

Preneed arrangements - The CPL requirements are the same for at-need or preneed funeral arrangements. In addition, if the purchaser of a preneed funeral arrangement later wants to change or amend a casket or container selection for any reason, the CPL must be offered to them again for review under the same conditions as provided above.

Note: See Form 2 to view a typical Casket Price List listing caskets and alternative containers.

The Outer Burial Container Price List

Outer burial container prices may be included on and made a part of the General Price List or, in the alternative, be provided on a separate **outer burial container price list** (OBC Price List). When using a separate price list, it must provide the following basic information:

1. The name of the business (funeral establishment).

2. A caption describing the list as an Outer Burial Container Price List.

3. The effective date for the price list.

4. The retail price of each **outer burial container** that does not require special ordering, and enough information to identify them.

5. The mandatory Funeral Rule disclosure for an outer burial container price list.

Item descriptions - Descriptions must be sufficient enough to clearly identify the items listed. The Funeral Rule does not go into any detail on what the descriptions must include, but most states require any or all of the following:

➢ the name of the supplier;

➢ the name of the manufacturer;

> ➤ the model name or number; and

> ➤ a description of the construction material, such as concrete, carbon steel, stainless steel, copper, aluminum, or polymer (plastic) derivatives.

Providing a photograph or simply a manufacturer name and model are not sufficient to identify an outer burial container.

Containers to be listed - The Funeral Rule requires a funeral establishment list only those outer burial containers they *usually offer* for sale and that do not require special ordering. The FTC has defined special ordering to mean purchasing an outer burial container that is not in stock and not a part of a funeral establishment's regular offerings to consumers.

The OBC Price List does not have to include containers maintained in inventory to fill pre-existing preneed contracts, unless the outer burial containers are also regularly offered for sale by the funeral establishment. It is also not necessary to prepare a new OBC Price List if an outer burial container is temporarily out-of-stock.

Format - The Funeral Rule does not require any particular format for the list, nor is there any requirement on the order in which outer burial containers must be placed on the list. It may be in any form, including in a notebook or on a chart, as long as it contains the required information. All of the OBC Price List information must be displayed in a clear and conspicuous manner.

Disclosure - The following disclosure must be included on an OBC Price List:

> *[In most areas of the country], [S]tate or local law does not require that you buy a container to surround the casket in the grave. However, many cemeteries require that you have such a container so that the grave will not sink in. Either a grave liner or a burial vault will satisfy these requirements.*

If no state or local law requires an outer burial container – such as a burial vault or grave box – surround a casket in the grave, the Funeral Rule allows a funeral establishment to delete the phrase [in most areas of the country] from the disclosure. The first sentence of the disclosure would then read: *State or local law does not require that you buy a container to surround the casket in the grave.*

Outer Burial Container Price List Requirements
In-person - A funeral establishment must give an OBC Price List for review to anyone who asks, in person, about the outer burial containers they offer or the prices they charge for them. The list must also be offered to a consumer any time discussions *begin* about outer burial containers. The offer must be made *prior* to showing any outer burial containers to a consumer, thereby providing them the opportunity to look at the price list before discussing the options or viewing the actual products.

Price cards - A funeral establishment may use individual price cards on outer burial containers or miniature models of containers, but this pricing method must be *in addition to* having the required price list.

For review - The outer burial container price list must be given to a consumer for review, but it does not need to be given to them to keep, as is required for a General Price List; however, there is no prohibition on allowing a consumer to keep an OBC Price List if the funeral establishment wants to do so.

Display - The Funeral Rule does not require outer burial containers be displayed in any specific manner or arrangement, and there are no requirements to have outer burial containers on display if a funeral establishment does not want or have the necessary space to have an outer burial selection showroom. Some establishments present selections by using a book containing photographs of the various outer burial containers they offer. When using a book, catalog, or other media format for presentations, it must include all the information required for an OBC Price List, including the business name, a caption describing the presentation materials as an Outer Burial Container Price List, the mandatory Funeral Rule disclosure, and the effective date of the list.

Preneed arrangements - The OBC Price List requirements are the same for at-need or preneed funeral arrangements. In addition, if the purchaser of a preneed funeral arrangement later wants to change or amend an outer burial container selection for any reason, the OBC Price List must be offered to them again for review under the same conditions provided above.

Note: See Form 3 to view a typical Outer Burial Container Price List.

Statement of Funeral Goods and Services Selected
Following arrangements, the Funeral Rule requires a funeral establishment provide the consumer with a **Statement of Funeral Goods and Services Selected** (Statement). The purpose of the Statement is to allow the consumer to evaluate the selections they made and make any desired changes.

When to provide - If the funeral arrangements take place in person, the Statement must be given to the consumer at the conclusion of the arrangements. It is not acceptable to mail or give the Statement to the consumer on a later date or time. In those cases where arrangements are made by telephone, the consumer must be given the Statement at the earliest possible date. If all of the arrangements are made by telephone and the consumer is not going to visit the funeral establishment before the final disposition takes place, the Statement should be given or sent to the consumer as soon as possible.

Format - The Funeral Rule does not require any specific form, heading, or caption on the Statement. The information required may be included on a contract or other similar type written document; however, it should be noted many states have laws that require a specific form and format be used to meet the Funeral Rule requirement for a Statement.

Funeral home charges - All of the goods and services selected by the consumer must be listed on the Statement, and the order of the items must correspond to the same order as the items are listed on the GPL. Each item must be listed separately with the price, along with any disclosure required by the Funeral Rule. Similar to the requirements for a GPL, **package pricing** is allowed as long as they are offered *in addition to*, not in place of, itemized prices for each of the items in the package. If the consumer selects a package, the Statement should describe the package by listing each of the individual goods and services that are included and then state the package price.

Cash advance charges - **Cash advance items** are items of goods or services that are:

➢ described to a consumer as a 'cash advance,' 'accommodation,' 'cash disbursement,' or similar term; or

➢ obtained from a third party and paid for by the funeral establishment on behalf of the consumer.

Cash advance items may include such items as cemetery or crematory services, pallbearers, public transportation, clergy honoraria, flowers, musicians or singers, obituary notices, gratuities, and death certificates. When the price for a cash advance item is not immediately known, the funeral establishment must enter a good faith estimate; however, a written statement of the actual charges with no estimates must be provided to the consumer before the final bill is paid. Each cash advance item selected must be listed on the Statement with the price.

Total funeral expenses - The Statement must include the total cost of the funeral arrangements selected by the consumer, including the cost of the goods and services (funeral home charges), plus any cash advance items (cash advance charges).

~ Funeral Home Charges + Cash Advance Charges = Total Cost of Funeral Arrangements ~

Required Disclosures on a Statement
There are three Funeral Rule disclosures required on the Statement, and they must use the identical wording provided in the rule. Additional information – such as state laws or regulations relevant to the item – may be included, but a funeral establishment may not change the FTC language or add anything that would modify the FTC language.

1: Legal Requirements Disclosure
This first disclosure informs a consumer they will only be charged for the items they selected or that were required by law, or required by a cemetery or crematory. And further, that the funeral establishment will explain those legal, cemetery, or crematory requirements in writing. The disclosure reads as follows:

> *Charges are only for those items that you selected or that are required. If we are required by law or by a cemetery or crematory to use any items, we will explain the reasons in writing below.*

> _____
> _____
> _____

The Statement form should leave enough space for the funeral establishment to identify and explain any legal, cemetery, or crematory requirements that compel a consumer to purchase a specific funeral good or service. These explanations must be entered on the Statement form *before* it is given to the consumer.

2: Embalming Disclosure
This second disclosure relates to embalming and the need to have prior approval to embalm human remains. The disclosure reads as follows:

> *If you selected a funeral that may require embalming, such as a funeral with viewing, you may have to pay for embalming. You do not have to pay for embalming you did not approve if you selected arrangements such as a direct cremation or immediate burial. If we charged for embalming, we will explain why below.*

_____
_____
_____

The Statement form should leave enough space for the funeral establishment to explain the reason for charging for embalming, and this explanation must be entered on the Statement *before* it is given to the consumer.

Note: See the next chapter titled, *FTC Funeral Rule: Miscellaneous Provisions*, for a more in-depth review of the requirement to have express permission to embalm.

3: Cash Advance Items Disclosure
The Funeral Rule does not prohibit a funeral establishment from adding a service charge (profit) to a cash advance item or require disclosure to the consumer of the amount of the service charge. However, if a service charge is to be collected, or the funeral establishment retains a rebate, commission, or trade or volume discount for a cash advance item, a disclosure is required.

Disclosures must be placed in immediate conjunction with (directly next to) the list of cash advance items on the Statement, and specify the items to which the disclosure applies. This disclosure cannot be on a separate page or elsewhere on the Statement apart from the list of itemized cash advance items, and reads as follows:

> *We charge you for our services in obtaining*: _____
_____
_____
_____

It is important to note, each of the 50 states may *expand* on the Funeral Rule requirements in their home state. As an example, some states prohibit a funeral establishment from making any profit whatsoever on a cash advance, while other states have laws that enumerate those items which *must* be cash advance items and cannot be listed as a funeral home charge.

Note: See Form 4 to view a typical Statement of Funeral Goods and Services Selected.

Chapter 18: FTC Funeral Rule - Miscellaneous Provisions

Overview

Previous chapters dealt with major provisions related to prices lists and providing consumers with an itemized statement at the conclusion of funeral arrangements. This chapter reviews the remaining provisions of the rule that address such areas as embalming approvals, record retention schedules, direct cremation mandates, and telephone price disclosures.

Chapter Definitions

Alternative container - an unfinished wood box or other non-metal receptacle or enclosure, without ornamentation or a fixed interior lining, which is designed for the encasement of human remains and which is made of fiberboard, pressed-wood, composition materials (with or without an outside covering) or like materials.

Alternative price lists - price lists which may be prepared for use in certain limited situations such as children/infants, for government agencies to provide for indigent persons, for agreements with religious groups, burial societies, or memorial societies for members of their group.

Authorizing agent - the person(s) with the paramount right to authorize cremation and disposition.

Casket handling fees - a fee charged to a consumer who exercises the right to purchase a casket from another seller; these fees are prohibited under the Funeral Rule.

Direct cremation - disposition of human remains by cremation without formal viewing, visitation, or ceremony with the body present.

Disclosures - required statements on Funeral Rule price lists that must be placed exactly as provided in the Rule; use the identical wording provided in the Rule; cannot be edited or paraphrased; and must be presented in a clear, conspicuous, and legible manner.

Due diligence - the attention reasonably expected from, and ordinarily exercised by, a person who seeks to satisfy a legal requirement or to discharge an obligation.

Free items - none of the 16 specified items required to be separately itemized on the GPL can be listed as free or no charge. Items not required by the rule can be listed as free.

Itemization - a method of listing goods and services on a General Price List that treats each individual good or service being offered as a separate line item that includes the price for the item [by Author].

Telephone price disclosures - a mandate in the FTC Funeral Rule that requires funeral establishments to provide consumers who inquire about prices or offerings any available information from required price lists.

Third party merchandise - funeral goods a consumer purchases from a source other than the funeral establishment with whom the consumer is making funeral arrangements [by Author].

Tying arrangements - a condition that exists when a consumer is required to purchase funeral goods or funeral services they do not want, to be able to acquire or receive funeral goods or funeral services they do want [by Author].

<u>Approval for Embalming</u>
The Funeral Rule stipulates there are only three circumstances under which a funeral establishment may embalm human remains.

1: Law Requires Embalming
This first circumstance applies when a state or local law requires embalming. In these cases, the legal requirement would supersede any contrary instructions or requests of the family or person with the priority right to control the final disposition. If embalming does take place because of a legal requirement, it must be explained to the consumer on the Statement of Funeral Goods and Services Selected.

2: Prior Approval Required
This second circumstance applies when a funeral director has been given the prior approval of the **authorizing agent** or a designated representative of the agent as determined by state or local law. The permission must be *express*, not implied. Express permission is consent given – either verbally or in writing – from one person to another to carry out a specific and explicit action. Implied permission is the consent one person infers or understands based on the actions of another.

For example, if a family informs a funeral director during the transfer of remains from the place of death they are considering a public viewing, the director cannot infer from this statement they are approving embalming. The director must make a specific request to embalm, and the family must give their explicit express permission and approval to embalm. The family must also be made aware embalming is usually not required by law or, in those states where it applies, never required by law.

Permission may be given at any time. For example, if express permission to embalm is given at the time preneed funeral arrangements are made, no further permission is required at time of need.

In all cases, when embalming is performed, the reason a family has been charged for embalming must be explained on the Statement of Funeral Goods and Services Selected. The reason may be as simple as the family requested embalming for a public viewing, but if the consumer has been told the embalming is *required* for a specific reason, such as a public viewing or to meet a legal requirement, this specific reason must be listed on the Statement. Writing something similar to 'family consent' or 'family request' does not provide the reason, only that the family consented.

Note: While the Funeral Rule allows for express permission to be given orally or in writing, some state laws require permission be given in writing.

3: No One Available to Give Approval
This third circumstance applies when there is no one available to give permission. To meet the threshold for using this circumstance to embalm, these three elements would need to be present:

1. The funeral establishment is unable to contact a family member or other authorized person after exercising **due diligence**. The establishment must exhaust all means known and available given the time constraints. To fully demonstrate the exercise of due diligence, an establishment that has refrigeration available may need to take more expansive and aggressive attempts to reach someone for permission to embalm.

2. The establishment has no reason to believe the family does not want embalming.

3. After embalming, the establishment obtains subsequent approval.

When requesting approval after the fact, the establishment must inform the family that if they select a funeral where embalming would be required (such as a funeral with formal viewing), the establishment will charge a fee; if the family selects a funeral where embalming would not be necessary (such as a direct cremation) there would be no fee. If the family then *expressly* approves embalming or chooses a funeral where embalming is required, the establishment may charge for the services.

The FTC mandatory disclosure in the embalming section of the Itemized Statement explains this consumer right with the inclusion of this sentence:

> *You do not have to pay for embalming you did not approve if you selected arrangements such as a direct cremation or immediate burial.*

Telephone Price Disclosures

The Funeral Rule requires funeral establishments provide consumers who inquire by telephone about goods and services with accurate information from the General Price List, Casket Price List, and Outer Burial Container Price List. In addition, the establishment must answer any other questions about offerings and prices with any *readily available* information that reasonably answers the question.

No conditions - Providing price information cannot be conditioned on the caller first identifying themselves, such as requiring a name, address, or telephone number. In addition, a funeral establishment cannot require consumers to physically come to the establishment to get the information being requested by telephone.

Answering options - If an establishment uses an answering machine to record calls, or a third-party answering service to handle incoming calls and take messages, someone from the establishment must respond to questions from callers on an individual basis by returning a call to them at the earliest convenience.

Staff - Non-licensed staff members in a funeral establishment must provide the information they have available on the required price lists. For inquiries that go beyond the price lists or other available information, they may pass the call on to a licensed funeral service practitioner. If no practitioner is immediately available, such as being in an arrangement conference or supervising a funeral, staff members must take a message and refer it to a practitioner for a call back at the earliest convenience.

Business hours - If not the normal practice, funeral establishments are not required to provide information on goods, services, or prices to a consumer after regular business hours. Consumers may be told to call back during regular business hours and the information being requested will be provided. However, there is nothing in the rule to prohibit a funeral establishment from answering questions after hours, and many funeral establishments do so on a routine basis.

Alternative Price Lists for Special Groups
In certain limited situations, a funeral establishment may use **alternative price lists**. When an alternative price list is used, it must comply with all Funeral Rule provisions, including required headings, disclosures, and the use of **itemization** to list items and prices.

Children and infants - Alternate items and prices may be offered for children and infant funeral arrangements. This information may be listed on the regular general, casket, and outer burial container price lists, or the establishment may prepare separate price lists for children and infants. If the option to provide separate price lists is chosen, a funeral establishment is not required to give those lists to anyone except individuals inquiring about a funeral for a child or infant.

Government agencies - Funeral establishments may enter into agreements with government agencies to provide funeral arrangements for a certain classification of individuals, such as indigents or other persons entitled to a government benefit or assistance. These price lists must be provided to government officials when making or discussing funeral arrangements. Items and prices may be listed on the regular price lists, or separate price lists may be prepared. If the option to provide separate price lists is chosen, there is no requirement to give those lists to anyone except government representatives or persons who qualify for the special pricing.

Government agencies often choose to contract funeral arrangements for a specified classification of individuals on a package basis. In these cases, the rule allows package pricing, as long as the packages are offered *in addition to*, not in place of itemized prices. When qualifying individuals inquire in person about funeral packages, they must be given a copy of the GPL to keep.

Religious groups and memorial societies - Funeral establishments may enter into agreements with religious groups and burial or memorial societies to arrange funerals for their members at special prices. The establishment may list these special prices on the regular price lists or separate price lists for members of these special groups only. Price lists must be provided to representatives of these groups when they inquire about funeral arrangements on behalf of their membership. If an individual member of the group inquires in person about funeral arrangements, they must be provided a copy of the GPL to keep.

Preneeds - Because a funeral establishment may sell different goods and services for preneed arrangements, the Funeral Rule allows a funeral establishment to have a preneed GPL that is not the same as an at-need GPL. A preneed GPL must include all required disclosures and offer goods and services on an itemized basis, and establishments are prohibited from offering only package funerals to preneed consumers.

<u>Misrepresentations Prohibited by the Funeral Rule</u>
The Funeral Rule prohibits six specific misrepresentations in the following areas:

1. Embalming requirements.

2. Caskets for direct cremations.

3. Legal and cemetery requirements.

4. Outer burial containers.

5. Preservative and protective claims.

6. Cash advances.

1: Embalming Requirements
Some states have laws that require embalming in specific circumstances; while other states do not require embalming by law under any circumstance. Consumers may not be told the law requires embalming if that is not accurate.

If a state or local law does require embalming, the funeral director must notify the family in writing that embalming is required by law and identify the specific circumstance (reason) in the law that triggered the requirement. If state or local law does not require embalming, the family must be notified in writing of this fact. In both scenarios, written notification is provided in the mandatory FTC embalming disclosure on the General Price List. The disclosure reads as follows:

> *[Except in certain special cases,] [E]mbalming is not required by law. Embalming may be necessary, however, if you select certain funeral arrangements, such as a funeral with viewing. If you do not want embalming, you usually have the right to choose an arrangement, such as direct cremation or immediate burial, that does not require you to pay for it.*

This disclosure informs consumers the law usually does not require embalming. However, in those states where embalming is not required by law under any circumstance, the Funeral Rule allows a funeral establishment to delete the phrase [Except in certain special cases] from the disclosure. The first sentence would then read: *Embalming is not required by law.*

When embalming is required by law, the special circumstance (reason) must be recorded on the Statement of Funeral Goods and Services Selected provided to the consumer at the conclusion of the funeral arrangements.

Note: See Form 4 to view a Statement that includes a location to record the reason for embalming.

Unless state or local law requires embalming, a funeral establishment may not tell consumers embalming is required for 'practical purposes' for a direct cremation; an immediate burial; or, when refrigeration is available, a closed-casket funeral with no formal viewing or visitation.

FTC guidelines provide these two examples:

> *Example 1: A family wants to arrange a funeral with a formal viewing. The funeral will take place three days after death has occurred on a hot summer day. Your state does not require embalming. You do not have refrigeration facilities. In this situation, you can tell the family that the funeral establishment requires embalming as a practical necessity to delay decomposition of the remains and to preserve them for viewing. You may not tell the family that the law requires embalming in this case because that is not true.*

> *Example 2: A family wants to arrange an immediate burial, but does not want to pay for embalming. Embalming is not required by your state law. Before burial takes place, one family member wants to look briefly at the deceased by lifting the lid of the casket. Here, you may not tell the family that embalming is required. The request to see the deceased does not constitute a formal viewing.*

> *In situations like Example 2, you also cannot require the family to pay for 'other preparation of the body,' if they decline embalming.*

2: Casket for Direct Cremation

Consumers cannot be told any state or local law, or any other reason, requires them to buy a casket if they are arranging a **direct cremation**. If a funeral establishment offers direct cremation, the rule requires they offer and make available an **alternative container**. This is accomplished by including the required alternative container disclosure on the General Price List and listing the containers with their prices on the Casket Price List. The disclosure reads as follows:

> *If you want to arrange a direct cremation, you can use an alternative container. Alternative containers encase the body and can be made of materials like fiberboard or composition materials (with or without an outside covering). The containers we provide are (specify) _____.*

_____
_____
_____
_____

Note: The Funeral Rule allows crematories to set standards for the type and durability of alternative containers they will accept.

3: Legal and Cemetery Requirements

Consumers cannot be told any federal, state, or local law, or any particular cemetery or crematory rule or regulation, requires them to buy a specific good or service if that is not accurate. If a consumer must buy a specific item because of any legal, cemetery, or crematory requirement, the reason must be recorded in the legal requirement disclosure on the Statement provided to the consumer at the conclusion of the funeral arrangements.

The disclosure reads as follows:

> *Charges are only for those items that you selected or that are required. If we are required by law or by a cemetery or crematory to use any items, we will explain the reasons in writing below.*

_____
_____
_____
_____

4: Outer Burial Container

Consumers cannot be told any state or local law requires them to buy an outer burial container if that is not accurate, and the funeral establishment is obligated under the Funeral Rule to notify consumers if there is no state law that requires them to purchase these containers. Notification is provided by including the mandatory FTC disclosure on the Outer Burial Container Price List.

The disclosure reads as follows:

> *[In most areas of the country], [S]tate or local law does not require that you buy a container to surround the casket in the grave. However, many cemeteries require that you have such a container so that the grave will not sink in. Either a grave liner or a burial vault will satisfy these requirements.*

If no state or local law requires a container – such as a burial vault or grave liner – surround a casket in the grave, the rule allows a funeral establishment to delete the phrase [In most areas of the country] from the disclosure. The first sentence would then read: *State or local law does not require that you buy a container to surround the casket in the grave.*

When an outer burial container is required by law, the reason must be recorded on the Statement provided to the consumer at the conclusion of the funeral arrangements.

5: Preservative and Protective Value Claims

A funeral director cannot make any representations to a consumer that funeral goods or services will delay the natural decomposition of human remains for a long term or an indefinite time. Although the rule prohibits making these representations, the FTC has recognized it is possible for some funeral goods or services to delay decomposition for a short period of time.

FTC guidelines provide this example:

> *Example: A family selects a funeral with a viewing. You may explain to the family that embalming will temporarily preserve the body to make it suitable for viewing, but you cannot tell them that the embalming will preserve the body indefinitely.*

A funeral establishment cannot tell consumers funeral goods – such as caskets, vaults, or outer burial containers – have protective features or will protect the body from gravesite substances when that is not accurate. In addition, a funeral establishment must provide consumers with all the warranty information they have on the goods they offer for sale, and consumers should be allowed to read the manufacturer warranties for themselves. The establishment should indicate any claims or warranties are made by the manufacturer and not by the funeral establishment.

FTC guidelines provide this example:

> *Example: Mr. Morton has chosen casket A. You should allow him to read the written warranty that the manufacturer offers, but you must not adopt as your own any statement about preservation or protection that you know to be in violation of the Rule. You may want to inform Mr. Morton that the manufacturer has made certain statements about the product, but that you do not have personal knowledge of the protective value of the merchandise.*

Note: See the chapter titled, *Consumer Protection Laws,* for additional information on how to handle implied warranties in compliance with the Magnuson-Moss Warranty Act.

6: Cash Advance Items. A funeral establishment may mark up the charge on cash advance items or receive a commission, discount, or rebate that is not passed on to the consumer, but they cannot state the price charged for the cash advance item is the same as the cost to the funeral establishment. If there is an added charge – or if the establishment receives and keeps a rebate, commission, or trade or volume discount – they must tell the consumer the price is not the same as the cost to the establishment. The rule does not prevent a funeral establishment from adding a service charge to a cash advance, nor does it require them to disclose the amount of that service charge.

The notice of cash advance charges is provided to a consumer by including the mandatory FTC cash advance disclosure on the Statement. The disclosure states: *"We charge you for our services in obtaining …"* This statement is followed with the cash advance items that have service charges.

Note: Some states have laws that prohibit a funeral establishment from making any profit whatsoever on cash advance items, while others may identify certain funeral goods and services that *must* be listed as a cash advance charge and not a funeral establishment charge.

What Consumers Cannot be Required to Purchase
Tying arrangements prohibited - A funeral establishment cannot employ **tying arrangements**, defined as a condition that exists when a consumer is required to purchase funeral goods or funeral services they do not want, to be able to acquire or receive funeral goods or funeral services they do want. With certain limited exceptions, consumers must be able to choose only the goods and services they wish to purchase.

A funeral establishment may not refuse to serve a family because they do not select one particular item or a certain combination of items or services from the establishment. In addition, the charge for optional service items, such as embalming, cannot be included in the non-declinable Basic Services Fee. To do this would require every consumer to pay for what is supposed to be an optional service, with no opportunity to decline the service.

The rule prohibits a funeral establishment from charging any fee as a condition of furnishing any funeral goods or services, other than the fees for:

> ➢ the basic services of funeral director and staff (the only non-declinable fee allowed);

> ➢ the funeral goods and services selected by the consumer; and

> ➢ the funeral goods and services required to be purchased by law, or by a cemetery or crematory, as identified and explained on the Statement.

Therefore, a funeral establishment may not charge an additional fee or surcharge to consumers who purchase a third-party casket, as this fee would not fall within any of the three categories of allowable charges listed above.

As a stated exception in the Funeral Rule, a funeral establishment does not have to comply with requests for funeral goods and funeral services that are impossible, impractical, illegal, or excessively burdensome, but a funeral establishment cannot refuse a request simply because they do not like or approve of it.

The FTC Guidelines provide this example:

> *Example: During July, a family requests that a funeral occur five days after death, but does not want embalming. You don't have refrigeration facilities. Your state law does not require embalming under any circumstances. However, in this situation, you can refuse to provide these arrangements, unless the family buys embalming. You can consider such a request impractical or excessively burdensome.*

Free items - A funeral establishment may not list any of the 16 required items on the GPL as 'free' or 'no charge.' Because the funeral establishment will recover the cost of the free item in the prices of other items on the GPL, the consumer would not have the choice to reject the charge if it was listed as free. Unless restricted by state law, establishments can offer other items *not on the list of 16 required items* for free or no charge, such as prayer cards or a cross.

Third-Party Merchandise

When the Funeral Rule was implemented in 1984, the issue of **third-party merchandise** was not of much interest to the funeral establishments of that era. Today, with the proliferation of third-party casket vendors and fierce competition in selling caskets to an ever more cost-conscious and skeptical consumer, the issue is one of great interest to the funeral service industry. As a result, the FTC has been compelled to issue numerous advisory opinion letters related to consumer's purchasing third-party merchandise and the responsibilities of the funeral establishment.

A significant number of FTC opinion letters concerning third-party merchandise focus on one specific section of the Funeral Rule that, in part, states:

In selling or offering to sell funeral goods or funeral services, it is an unfair or deceptive act or practice for a funeral provider to: condition the furnishing of any funeral good or funeral service to a person arranging a funeral upon the purchase of any other funeral good or funeral service ...

The collective opinions expressed in these opinion letters *prohibit* certain activities related to third-party caskets, including:

1. A funeral establishment may not refuse the delivery of a third-party casket. To do so would set a condition for the consumer whereby they would have to buy a casket from the funeral establishment if they want the funeral establishment to provide other services and merchandise.

2. A funeral establishment may not require a family's presence for the delivery of a third-party casket. This would place an unreasonable burden on a consumer's choice to purchase a casket from a third-party seller.

3. A funeral establishment may not refuse to sign for the merchandise or acknowledge delivery of a third-party casket, because it would place an unreasonable burden on a consumer's choice to purchase a casket from a third-party seller.

    Note: The FTC, in an advisory opinion dated June 22, 2004, acknowledged a Receipt of Third-Party Merchandise form developed by the National Funeral Directors Association, *"... does not constitute an unreasonable burden on the consumer,"* when used as a record of the receipt and acceptance of a third-party casket.

4. A funeral establishment may not refuse to use third party merchandise until the consumer inspects it.

5. A funeral establishment may not charge any **casket handling fees** for handling a third-party casket. Casket handling fees are defined as a fee charged to a consumer who exercises the right to purchase a casket from another seller, and these fees are prohibited under the Funeral Rule. These prohibited charges include:

    ➢ fees for receiving the casket;

    ➢ disposing of the container or packaging in which it is shipped;

    ➢ storage when delivered in advance of time needed;

    ➢ inspection; and

    ➢ preparation for use.

6. A funeral establishment may not refuse the delivery of a third-party casket under any conditions applied *exclusively* to third-party casket retailers, including a refusal to accept delivery:

   ➤ 'more than' a specified number of days in advance of its use;

   ➤ 'less than' a specified number of days in advance of its use;

   ➤ during regular business hours, except by prior appointment; and

   ➤ during regular business hours at a particular date and time, unless the funeral establishment is unable to accept caskets from *any supplier* at that date and time.

7. A funeral establishment may not withhold the use of a funeral establishment's standard equipment, such as a utility church truck to assist in bringing a casket into the funeral establishment at the time of delivery. Such equipment is part of a funeral establishment's overhead costs charged to and paid by consumers in the form of the non-declinable basic services fee. It would be an unreasonable burden to deny consumers the benefit of the equipment for which they must pay simply because they have exercised their right to purchase a casket from a third party.

Following a close examination of the FTC advisory opinion letters, it becomes abundantly clear third-party merchandise vendors must be treated *exactly* the same as a funeral establishment's regular wholesale vendors. Any special requirements or treatment in the delivery or handling of a third-party casket or other goods could subject a funeral establishment to potential enforcement action by the FTC based on the 'unreasonable burden' prohibition.

Recordkeeping
The federal required retention period for a funeral establishment to archive price lists is at least one year from the date the lists were last distributed to consumers. Similarly, they must archive a copy of each completed Statement of Funeral Goods and Services Selected for at least one year from the date of the arrangement conference. These records must be available for inspection by FTC representatives upon request.

Note: Most states have significantly longer retention periods for these same records that require they be archived for a much lengthier period of time than the federal government.

Comprehension of Disclosures
Disclosures are defined as required statements on Funeral Rule price lists that must be:

   ➤ placed exactly as provided in the rule;

   ➤ use the identical wording provided in the rule;

   ➤ cannot be edited or paraphrased; and

➤ must be presented in a clear, conspicuous, and legible manner.

The disclosure print or type face must be large and prominent enough that consumers can easily notice and read the information. Price lists cannot include any information that alters or contradicts the information the Funeral Rule requires a funeral establishment to provide, although additional state or local information may be included as long as it does not confuse or obscure the required information.

State Exemption Provisions
State agencies may apply to the Federal Trade Commission for a statewide exemption from certain provisions in the rule, and the Commission may grant an exemption if it finds:

➤ there is a state requirement in effect that applies to the same transactions that the Funeral Rule covers; and

➤ the state requirement provides an overall level of protection that is as great as, or greater than, the protection provided by the rule.

If a state is granted an exemption, funeral establishments are only required to comply with the state regulations. If a state does not seek an exemption – or is not granted an exemption – funeral establishments must comply with all state regulations, as well as the Funeral Rule.

As of this writing, the author is not aware of any state that has been granted a complete exemption from complying with the Funeral Rule, although certain provisions proposed for exemption by some states have been approved.

Chapter 19: Workplace Laws

Overview
Statutes that deal with workplace requirements provide protection for all employees, not just those in the funeral service industry. Therefore, this chapter provides a summary of the most influential of these laws and, when of importance, reflects on how a particular provision may apply to a funeral establishment workplace.

The review includes these five acts:

Fair Labor Standards Act	Civil Rights Act - Title VII	Family Medical Leave Act
Age Discrimination in Employment Act		Americans with Disabilities Act

Fair Labor Standards Act
Introduction - The Fair Labor Standards Act (FLSA) establishes minimum wage, overtime pay, recordkeeping, and child labor standards affecting full-time and part-time workers in the private sector. It is enforced by the Wage and Hour Division (WHD) of the U.S. Department of Labor.

The FLSA has jurisdiction over funeral establishments if they have gross annual sales that exceed $500,000. According to the National Funeral Directors Association, the average cost of a funeral in 2019 was $7640. A funeral establishment would therefore only need to handle approximately 65 funerals to reach the threshold and be required to comply with the provisions of the FLSA.

Adult minimum wages - As of this writing, covered workers are entitled to a minimum wage of $7.25 per hour and must be paid overtime pay at a rate of not less than one and one-half times their regular rate of pay after 40 hours of work in a workweek.

Wages required by the FLSA are due on the regular payday for the pay period covered. Deductions made from wages for such items as cash or merchandise shortages, employer-required uniforms, and tools of the trade, are not legal to the extent they reduce the wages of employees below the minimum rate required by the FLSA or reduce the amount of overtime pay due.

Youth minimum wages - A minimum wage of not less than $4.25 an hour is permitted for employees under 20 years of age during their first 90 consecutive calendar days of employment. Employers are prohibited from taking any action to displace employees in order to hire individuals at the youth minimum wage. Also prohibited are partial displacements, such as reducing employee's hours, wages, or employment benefits.

Overtime pay - Covered employees must receive overtime pay for hours worked over 40 in a workweek at a rate not less than time and one-half their regular rates of pay, and there is no limit in the FLSA on the number of hours employees aged 16 and older may work in any workweek. The FLSA also does not require overtime pay for work on Saturdays, Sundays, holidays, or regular days of rest, unless overtime is worked on such days.

An employee's workweek is a fixed and regularly recurring period of 168 hours (seven consecutive 24-hour periods). The workweek does not need to coincide with the calendar week, but may begin on any day and at any hour of the day. Different workweeks may be established for different employees or groups of employees. Averaging of hours over two or more weeks is not permitted. Normally, overtime pay earned in a particular workweek must be paid on the regular pay day for the pay period in which the wages were earned.

Exemptions - Certain employees are exempt from overtime provisions of the FLSA, including executives, administrators, and professionals.

To qualify for the *executive* exemption, all of the following tests must be met:

➤ the employee must be paid on a salary basis at a rate not less than $684 per week;

➤ the employee's primary duty must be managing the enterprise, or managing a customarily recognized department or subdivision of the enterprise;

➤ the employee must customarily and regularly direct the work of at least two or more other full-time employees or their equivalent; and

➤ the employee must have the authority to hire or fire other employees, or the employee's suggestions and recommendations as to the hiring, firing, advancement, promotion, or any other change of status of other employees must be given particular weight.

To qualify for the *administrator* exemption, all of the following tests must be met:

➤ the employee must be paid on a salary or fee basis (as defined in the regulations) at a rate not less than $684 per week;

➤ the employee's primary duty must be the performance of office or non-manual work directly related to the management or general business operations of the employer or the employer's customers; and

➤ the employee's primary duty includes the exercise of discretion and independent judgment with respect to matters of significance.

To qualify for the *learned professional* exemption, all of the following tests must be met:

➤ the employee must be paid on a salary or fee basis at a rate not less than $684 per week;

➤ the employee's primary duty must be the performance of work requiring advanced knowledge, defined as work which is predominantly intellectual in character and which includes work requiring the consistent exercise of discretion and judgment;

➤ the advanced knowledge must be in a field of science or learning; and

> ➤ the advanced knowledge must be customarily acquired by a prolonged course of specialized intellectual instruction.

With respect to the funeral service industry and the learned professional exemption, the regulation states:

> *Licensed funeral directors and embalmers who are licensed by and working in a state that requires successful completion of four academic years of pre-professional and professional study, including graduation from a college of mortuary science accredited by the American Board of Funeral Service Education, generally meet the duties requirements for the learned professional exemption.*

Recordkeeping - The FLSA requires employers to keep records on wages, hours, and other items. Most of the information is of the kind generally maintained by employers in ordinary business practice and in compliance with other laws and regulations. The records do not have to be kept in any particular form and time clocks are not required.

Equal pay - The equal pay provisions of the FLSA prohibit sex-based wage differentials between men and women employed in the same establishment who perform jobs that require equal skill, effort, and responsibility and which are performed under similar working conditions. This act also applies to all employment positions, including any members of an exempt class; however, unequal pay may be acceptable if appointments or promotions are based on a seniority or merit-based system. These provisions, as well as several other statutes prohibiting discrimination in employment, are enforced by the Equal Employment Opportunity Commission.

Enforcement activities - WHD enforcement of the FLSA is carried out by investigators stationed all across the United States. As authorized representatives, they conduct investigations and gather data on wages, hours, and other employment conditions in order to determine compliance with the law, regardless of a workers' immigration status. Where violations are found, they recommend changes in employment practices to bring an employer into compliance.

Statute of limitations - The FLSA allows the Department of Labor or an employee to recover back wages and an equal amount in liquidated damages where minimum wage and overtime violations exist. Generally, a 2-year statute of limitations applies to the recovery of back wages and liquidated damages. A 3-year statute of limitations applies in cases involving willful violations.

Civil litigation - The FLSA may file suit on behalf of employees for back wages, an equal amount in liquidated damages, and civil monetary penalties where appropriate. They may also seek a U.S. District Court injunction to restrain violations of the law, including the unlawful withholding of proper minimum wage and overtime pay, failure to keep proper records, and retaliation against employees who file complaints or cooperate with the U.S. Department of Labor.

Criminal prosecution - The FLSA has the authority to take action against non-compliant funeral establishments and, for willful violations, the proprietors of funeral establishments may be subject to criminal penalties, including fines and imprisonment. Penalties for civil cases include payment of back wages and overtime, with the potential for double awards under the liquidated damages provision in the law. All penalties, fines, and jail times increase if steps are not taken to bring a funeral establishment into compliance.

Retaliation prohibited - Employees who have filed complaints or provided information cannot be discriminated against or discharged on account of such activity. If adverse action is taken against an employee for engaging in protected activity, the affected employee or the Secretary of Labor may file suit for relief, including reinstatement to his/her job, payment of lost wages, and damages.

Civil Rights Act - Title VII
Introduction - In 1964, the United States passed the Civil Rights Act, one of the strongest civil rights laws in history. The act bans discrimination because of a person's color, race, national origin, religion, or sex. Major features of the Civil Rights Act include the freedom to vote and use hotels, restaurants, theaters, parks, and all other public places. The law also encouraged the desegregation of public schools and authorized the withdrawal of federal funds from programs practicing discrimination. Other significant features include the prohibition of job discrimination and the creation of the Equal Employment Opportunities Commission (EEOC). The Act applies to all employers having 15 or more employees.

Discrimination - Title VII forbids discrimination in any aspect of employment, including:

Hiring and firing	Job advertisements	Use of company facilities
Assignment or classification of employees	Pay, retirement plans and disability leave	Any other terms and conditions of employment
Recruitment	Testing	Fringe benefits
Transfer, promotion, layoff, or recall	Training and apprenticeship programs	Compensation of employees

Enforcement - The EEOC is the agency tasked with administering and enforcing federal workplace laws that prohibit discrimination in the workplace, including Title VII of the Civil Rights Act. For those cases that may warrant special attention due to suspicion of a systemic pattern of discrimination, a referral may be made to the U.S. Department of Justice, whose offices may file criminal or civil charges in a court of law.

Retaliation - Title VII prohibits employers from retaliating against any employee for filing a charge of discrimination or speaking out against discrimination in the workplace. It also protects employees from retaliation if they choose to participate in an investigation, proceeding, or hearing on behalf of a co-worker who they believe had their rights violated.

Pregnancy discrimination - In 1978, Title VII of the Civil Rights Act was amended to add the Pregnancy Discrimination Act. The Act makes it unlawful for an employer to discriminate against a pregnant woman in the workplace. Pregnancy discrimination occurs when expectant mothers are fired, not hired, or otherwise discriminated against due to their pregnancy or intention to become pregnant. The Act applies to all employers having 15 or more employees.

Common forms of pregnancy discrimination include:

➢ not being hired due to visible pregnancy or likelihood of becoming pregnant;

➢ being fired after informing an employer of a pregnancy;

➢ being fired after maternity leave; and

➢ receiving a pay dock due to pregnancy.

Family and Medical Leave Act

Introduction - The Family Medical Leave Act (FMLA) was passed by the federal government in 1993. It entitles eligible employees of covered employers to take unpaid, job-protected leave for specified family and medical reasons, with continuation of group health insurance coverage under the same terms and conditions as if the employee had not taken leave.

Covered employers - The FMLA applies to employers that have 50 or more employees in 20 or more workweeks in the current or preceding calendar year.

Eligible employees - Only eligible employees are entitled to take FMLA leave. An eligible employee is one who:

➢ works for a covered employer;

➢ has worked for the employer for at least 12 months;

➢ has at least 1,250 hours of service for the employer during the 12-month period immediately preceding the leave; and

➢ works at a location where the employer has at least 50 employees within 75 miles.

The 12 months of employment do not have to be consecutive. Any time previously worked for the same employer (including seasonal work) could, in most cases, be used to meet the 12-month requirement. If the employee has a break in service that lasts seven years or more, the time worked prior to the break would not count.

Benefits - Eligible employees are entitled to 12 workweeks of leave in a 12-month period for:

➢ the birth of a son or daughter, or placement of a son or daughter with the employee for adoption or foster care;

➢ to care for a spouse, son, daughter, or parent who has a serious health condition;

➢ for a serious health condition that makes the employee unable to perform the essential functions of his or her job; or

> ➤ for any qualifying exigency (urgent need) arising out of the fact that a spouse, son, daughter, or parent is a military member on covered active duty or called to covered active-duty status.

An eligible employee may also take up to 26 workweeks of leave during a single 12-month period to care for a covered military servicemember of the Armed Forces of the United States with a serious injury or illness, when the employee is the spouse, son, daughter, parent, or next of kin of the servicemember. The single 12-month period for military caregiver leave is different from the 12-month period used for other FMLA leave reasons.

Note: Many states have passed legislation similar to the FMLA that significantly expand on the benefits available, including longer periods of leave and, in some states, *paid* leave.

Age Discrimination in Employment Act
Introduction - The Age Discrimination in Employment Act (ADEA) was enacted in 1967 and protects certain applicants and employees 40 years of age and older from discrimination on the basis of age in hiring, promotion, discharge, compensation, or terms, conditions, or privileges of employment. Age discrimination involves treating an applicant or employee less favorably because of his or her age. The Act applies to all employers having 20 or more employees. The administration and enforcement of the ADEA falls under the jurisdiction of the EEOC.

Discrimination - The law prohibits discrimination in any aspect of employment, including hiring, firing, pay, job assignments, promotions, layoff, training, benefits, and any other term or condition of employment. Discrimination can occur when the victim and the person who inflicted the discrimination are both over 40.

Harassment - It is unlawful to harass a person because of their age. The harasser can be the victim's supervisor, a supervisor in another area, a co-worker, or someone who is not an employee of the employer, such as a client or customer. Simple teasing does not rise to the level of harassment, but the EEOC has stated:

> *Harassment is illegal when it is so frequent or severe that it creates a hostile or offensive work environment or when it results in an adverse employment decision (such as the victim being fired or demoted).*

Exclusions - The ADEA does not protect workers under the age of 40, although some states have laws to protect young workers from age discrimination. It is also not illegal for an employer or other covered entity to favor an older worker over a younger one, even if both are age 40 or older.

Americans with Disabilities Act
Introduction - The **Americans with Disabilities Act of 1990 (ADA)** is a federal statute prohibiting discrimination against the disabled in employment, public transportation, telecommunication services, and public accommodations and services. The review of the ADA related to *public accommodations* and the removal of barriers to disabled persons was provided in the chapter titled, *Funeral Establishment Laws*. The review here focuses on the ADA as it relates to *employment*.

The ADA prohibits funeral establishments with 15 or more employees from discriminating against qualified individuals with disabilities in job application procedures, hiring, firing, advancement, compensation, job training, and other terms, conditions, and privileges of employment.

Disability - An individual with a disability is a person who:

➢ has a physical or mental impairment that substantially limits one or more major life activities;

➢ has a record of such an impairment; or

➢ is regarded as having such an impairment.

Qualified employee - A qualified employee or applicant with a disability is an individual who, with or without reasonable accommodation, can perform the essential functions of the job in question.

Reasonable accommodations - Reasonable accommodations may include, but are not limited to:

Making existing facilities accessible	Job restructuring
Part-time or modified work schedules	Acquiring or modifying equipment
Changing tests, training materials, or policies	Reassignment to a vacant position
Providing qualified readers or interpreters	

An employer is required to make a reasonable accommodation to the known disability of a qualified applicant or employee if it would not impose an undue hardship on the operation of the employer's business. Reasonable accommodations are adjustments or modifications provided by an employer to enable people with disabilities to enjoy equal employment opportunities. Accommodations vary depending upon the needs of the individual applicant or employee, and not all people with disabilities, or even all people with the same disability, require the same accommodation.

Undue hardship - An employer does not have to provide a reasonable accommodation if it imposes an undue hardship, defined as an action requiring significant difficulty or expense when considered in light of factors such as:

➢ the nature and cost of the accommodation;

➢ an employer's size;

➢ financial resources; and

➢ the nature and structure of the employer operation.

Undue hardship is determined on a case-by-case basis. Where the facility making the accommodation is part of a larger entity, the structure and overall resources of the larger organization would be considered, as well as the financial and administrative relationship of the facility to the larger organization. In general, a larger employer with greater resources would be expected to make accommodations requiring greater effort or expense than would be required of a smaller employer with fewer resources.

If a particular accommodation would be an undue hardship, the employer must try to identify another accommodation that will not pose such a hardship. If the cost of an accommodation would impose an undue hardship on the employer, the individual with a disability must be given the option of paying that portion of the cost which would constitute an undue hardship for providing the accommodation.

An employer is not required to lower quality or production standards to make an accommodation; nor is an employer obligated to provide personal use items, such as glasses or hearing aids.

Medical exams and inquiries - Employers may not ask job applicants about the existence, nature, or severity of a disability; however, applicants may be asked about their ability to perform specific job functions. A job offer may be conditioned on the results of a medical examination, but only if the examination is required for all entering employees in similar jobs. Medical examinations of employees must be job related and consistent with the employer's business needs.

Medical records of employees are confidential under the Health Insurance Portability and Accountability Act (HIPPA), and an employee's request for a reasonable accommodation would be considered medical information subject to HIPPA privacy protection requirements.

Note: See the chapter titled, *Funeral Establishment Laws,* for more information on HIPPA.

Drug and alcohol abuse - Employees and applicants currently engaging in the illegal use of drugs are not covered by the ADA when an employer acts on the basis of such use, and tests for illegal drugs are not subject to the ADA's restrictions on medical examinations. Employers may hold illegal drug users and alcoholics to the same performance standards as other employees.

Retaliation - It is unlawful to retaliate against an individual for opposing employment practices that discriminate based on disability or for filing a discrimination charge, testifying, or participating in any way in an investigation, proceeding, or litigation under the ADA.

Chapter 20: Consumer Protection Laws

<u>Overview</u>
There are several federal laws and statutes that provide protections and rights to consumers that are applicable to the funeral service industry. Many address financial matters and have requirements for sellers to provide certain disclosures and statements, similar to the characteristics of the Funeral Rule. This chapter reviews these seven rules and acts:

FTC Credit Practices Rule	Truth-in-Lending Act
Gramm-Leach-Bliley Act	Fair Credit Reporting Act
Fair Debt Collection Practices Act	Magnuson-Moss Warranty Act
FTC Cooling-off Rule	

<u>FTC Credit Practices Rule</u>
Introduction - The Federal Trade Commission Credit Practices Rule went into effect in 1985 and has three major provisions. First, it prohibits creditors from using four specific contract provisions the FTC found to be unfair to consumers. Second, the rule requires creditors to advise consumers who cosign obligations about their potential liability if the other person fails to pay. And third, the rule prohibits late charges in some circumstances.

Definitions - A *creditor* is a person or entity to whom money is owed; a *debtor* is a person or entity that owes money; and a *judgment* is a court ruling against a debtor (defendant).

The rule applies to any **creditor** (person or company to whom money is owed) subject to the jurisdiction of the Federal Trade Commission. This of course includes funeral establishments, as they are a creditor and subject to the jurisdiction of the FTC.

Prohibited contract provisions - This is the first of the three major provisions in the Credit Practices Rule. There are four contract provisions prohibited by the rule.

1. Confessions of judgment. Prior to the rule, certain consumer credit contracts contained provisions taking away rights that consumers would otherwise ordinarily have when being sued. These included the rights to receive notice of the suit, to appear in court, and to raise any defenses that they may have. This provision, called a 'confession of judgment,' allowed **judgment** to be entered for the creditor automatically when they sued the **debtor** for breach of contract. The Credit Practices Rule prohibits creditors from including confession of judgment provisions in a contract agreement.

2. Waivers of exemption. Prior to the rule, some consumer credit contracts contained a 'waiver of exemption' provision that permitted creditors to seize (or threaten to seize) possessions or possessions of a specified value, even if state law treated them as exempt from seizure.

States have laws that define certain property as *necessities* that a debtor is allowed to keep, even if a creditor sues and obtains a judgment. By signing a waiver of exemption, a debtor makes that necessary property available to a creditor who obtains a judgment to satisfy a debt. The Credit Practices Rule prohibits creditors from including waiver of exemption provisions in a contract agreement.

3. Wage assignments. Prior to the rule, if a consumer did not pay as agreed, some credit contracts permitted creditors to go directly to the consumer's employers and have a portion of their wages paid to the creditors. Under the Credit Practices Rule prohibition against wage assignments, contracts may not provide for the advance assignment of wages if they do not pay the creditor as agreed. This includes irrevocable assignments to creditors of salaries, commissions, bonuses, pensions, and disability benefits, as well as wages due from the consumer's employment.

   The rule does permit provisions in an agreement to use payroll deduction plans where consumers choose and agree to pay with regular deductions from paychecks. And the prohibition against wage assignments does not prohibit the garnishment of wages. A wage garnishment is a *court order* authorizing the wages of the debtor to be seized to pay for a debt owed to a creditor. Wage garnishments are often a percentage of a debtor's wages paid directly to the creditor and subject to consumer protections provided by both federal and state laws.

4. Security interests in household goods. Prior to the rule, some consumer credit contracts contained provisions that allowed a creditor to repossess household goods in a debtor's home if they did not pay as agreed. The Credit Practices Rule prohibits provisions that provide for repossession of household goods, with some exclusions.

   The rule definition of household goods includes such household items as clothing, furniture, appliances, linens, china, kitchenware, pets, and personal effects. These items are protected from seizure.

   Excluded from the definition of household goods are works of art, electronic entertainment equipment (except one television and one radio), items acquired as antiques (more than 100 years old), and jewelry (except wedding rings). These items are subject to seizure if the consumer has offered these possessions as security to obtain credit, as well as pianos or other musical instruments, boats, snowmobiles, bicycles, cameras, and similar items.

Notice to cosigners - This is the second of the three major provisions in the Credit Practices Rule. If a funeral establishment requires a cosigner for a loan applicant who does not meet the standards of creditworthiness, the rule requires each cosigner be informed of the potential liability involved before the cosigner becomes obligated for the debt. This is the notice required by the rule:

Notice to Cosigner

You are being asked to guarantee this debt. Think carefully before you do. If the borrower doesn't pay the debt, you will have to. Be sure you can afford to pay if you have to, and that you want to accept this responsibility.

You may have to pay up to the full amount of the debt if the borrower does not pay. You may also have to pay late fees or collection costs, which increase this amount.

The creditor can collect this debt from you without first trying to collect from the borrower. *The creditor can use the same collection methods against you that can be used against the borrower, such as suing you, garnishing your wages, etc. If this debt is ever in default, that fact may become a part of your credit record.*

This notice is not the contract that makes you liable for debt. [**Bold** emphasis added.]

If a state statute or regulation requires a different notice to cosigners, it may be included on the same document if not inconsistent with the notice required by the federal rule. If a statement in the required FTC notice – such as the one shown in bold print above – is inaccurate under a state law, it may be omitted from the FTC notice as used in that state.

Late charges - This is the third of the three major provisions in the Credit Practices Rule. In the past, some creditors calculated late fees for delinquent payments using a practice called 'pyramiding' of late charges. When one payment was made after its due date and a late fee was assessed but not paid promptly, all future payments were considered delinquent even though they were, in fact, paid in full within the required time period. As a result, late fees were assessed on all future payments. In other words, each successive payment was considered 'short' by the amount of the previous late charge, with the result that another late charge was imposed. The rule prohibits this practice and provides a late fee cannot be assessed to a timely payment simply because a previous late fee has not been paid.

Federal Truth-in-Lending Act

The Truth in Lending Act (TILA) protects consumers against inaccurate and unfair credit billing and credit card practices. It requires creditors (lenders) to provide consumers with loan cost information so they can comparison shop for certain loans. For those funeral establishments that offer to finance the purchase of funeral goods and services, and meet the definition of a creditor, the Act requires them to provide standard disclosures about the terms of the financing.

Creditor - Not all funeral establishments will meet the definition of a creditor that triggers the requirement to comply with the Act. Creditor is defined as:

*... a person who **regularly** extends consumer credit that is subject to a finance charge or is payable by written agreement in more than four installments (not including a down payment), and to whom the obligation is initially payable, either on the face of the note or contract, or by agreement when there is no note or contract.* [**Bold** emphasis added.]

A 'person' in this definition includes any type of business.

When an establishment offers to extend credit subject to finance charges or payable in more than four installments, they are – for the purposes of the Act – extending consumer credit. However, an establishment *'regularly'* extends consumer credit only if it does so more than 25 times in a preceding calendar year, or more than 25 times in any current year if it did not exceed this number in the preceding year.

Consumer - For the purposes of TILA, a consumer is defined as a *natural person* to whom consumer credit is offered or extended. The requirements of the Act would not apply to a creditor (funeral establishment) when the obligator on the funeral contract is a not a natural person, such as a company, charity, corporation, executor, trustee, or fiduciary.

General disclosure requirements - If an establishment meets the definition of a creditor, they must provide consumers with mandatory disclosures and meet several requirements, including:

Format. A funeral establishment must provide the disclosures required by the Act clearly and conspicuously, in writing, and in a form that the consumer may keep. They may be provided to the consumer in electronic form, subject to compliance with the consumer's consent and federal regulations.

Acknowledgements - Disclosures may include an acknowledgment of receipt, the date of the transaction, and the consumer's name, address, and account number.

Time of Disclosures - The funeral establishment must make the required disclosures before concluding the transaction.

Basis of Disclosures and Use of Estimates - Disclosures must reflect the terms of the legal obligation between the parties. If any information necessary for an accurate disclosure is unknown to a funeral establishment at the time, they must make the disclosure based on the best information reasonably available at the time the disclosure is provided to the consumer and must clearly state the disclosure is an estimate.

Multiple Consumers - If a transaction involves more than one consumer, the disclosures may be made to any consumer who is primarily liable on the obligation.

Standard disclosures - The Act specifies the standard disclosures, when applicable, that must be provided to the consumer when extending consumer credit. These disclosures must be provided to the consumer on a separate document or form. They may not be included on the required FTC Statement, a funeral contract, or other similar funeral agreement, and must be provided to the consumer *before* the execution of the funeral agreement. The required disclosures are listed below.

Creditor. The name and identity of the creditor making the disclosures.

Amount Financed. This disclosure must be styled as 'Amount Financed' and include a brief description, such as the amount of credit provided to the consumer. The amount financed is calculated by:

- determining the principal loan amount or the cash price (subtracting any down payment);

- adding any other amounts that are financed by the creditor and are not part of the finance charge; and

- subtracting any prepaid finance charge.

Itemization of Amount Financed. There must be a separate disclosure with a written itemization of the amount financed, including:

- the amount of any proceeds distributed directly to the consumer;

- the amount credited to the consumer's account with the creditor; and

- any amounts paid to other persons by the creditor on the consumer's behalf. This section would require a funeral establishment to disclose all cash advances paid on behalf of the consumer, including the name of the person paid and the goods or services provided.

A creditor does not need to comply with the third section of this disclosure if they provide a statement that the consumer has the right to receive a written itemization of the amount financed, together with a space for the consumer to indicate whether it is desired, and the consumer elects not to request an itemization.

Finance Charge. This disclosure must be styled as 'Finance Charge' and include a brief description, such as 'the dollar amount the credit will cost you.'

Annual Percentage Rate. This disclosure must be styled as 'Annual Percentage Rate,' and include a brief description, such as 'the cost of your credit as a yearly rate.'

Payment Schedule. This schedule must include the number, amounts, and timing of payments scheduled to repay the obligation.

Total of Payments. This disclosure must be styled as 'Total of Payments,' and include a descriptive explanation, such as 'the amount you will have paid when you have made all scheduled payments.'

Total Sale Price. This disclosure must be styled as 'Total Sale Price' and include a descriptive explanation, such as 'the total price of your purchase on credit, including your down payment of $_____.' The total sale price is the sum of the cash price, any other amounts financed by the creditor and not part of the finance charge, and the finance charge disclosed under the finance charge section.

Prepayment. A consumer must be notified if there is a penalty if the obligation is prepaid in full; and conversely, if the funeral establishment offers a rebate for prepayment in full, the consumer must be notified in the disclosure.

Late Payment. Any charges imposed due to late payment must be included in the disclosures.

Security Interest. If the funeral establishment will acquire a security interest in the property purchased as a part of the transaction, or any other property, it must be disclosed and identified by item or type.

Note: See Form 5 to view a credit disclosure statement with the required disclosures and styling.

Prefunded preneeds - Preneed funeral arrangements are subject to the same provisions of TILA as at-need funeral arrangements. If a funeral establishment requires any type of finance charge or permits the consumer to pay for the preneed in more than four installments in accordance with a written agreement, they would be required to comply with the Act if they extend such credit more than 25 times in a year.

Late charges - Late charges are not considered to be 'finance charges' as defined under the Act. It is therefore very important funeral establishments do not label late charges on the FTC Statement – or any other written agreements for the purchase of funeral goods and services – as interest payments, finance charges, or other similarly worded phrases that might be considered a finance charge under the Act. They are simply 'late charges.'

Refinancing - A refinancing is a new transaction requiring new disclosures to the consumer, and the new finance charge must include any unearned portion of the old finance charge that is not credited to the existing obligation. The Act provides the following are not treated as a refinancing:

➢ a renewal of a single payment obligation with no change in the original terms;

➢ a reduction in the annual percentage rate with a corresponding change in the payment schedule;

➢ an agreement involving a court proceeding; and

➢ a change in the payment schedule or a change in collateral requirements (items pledged as security for prepayment, such as a car or home), as a result of the consumer's default or delinquency, unless the rate is increased.

Advertising - If an advertisement for credit states specific credit terms, it must state only those terms that actually are or will be arranged or offered by the creditor. They must be made clearly and conspicuously. If an advertisement states a rate of finance charge, it must state the rate as an 'annual percentage rate.' If the annual percentage rate may be increased after the credit agreement has been executed, the advertisement must also state this fact.

Record retention - A funeral establishment must retain evidence of compliance with TILA regulations for two years after the date disclosures are required to be made or action is required to be taken. They must also permit any agency responsible for enforcing the regulations to inspect relevant records for compliance.

Gramm-Leach-Bliley Act

The Gramm-Leach-Bliley Act requires *financial institutions* (companies that offer consumers financial products or services like loans, financial or investment advice, or insurance) to explain their information sharing practices to their customers and to safeguard sensitive data. The purpose of the act is to protect the private and personal information of consumers having any relationship with a financial institution.

In defining 'financial institution,' the FTC has stated entities that engage in financial activities but are not *significantly engaged* in those financial activities are not a financial institution. Therefore, a funeral establishment may be regarded as a financial institution by the FTC if they are:

- ➤ significantly involved in offering consumer credit to the purchaser of funeral goods and services;

- ➤ arranging or assisting consumers in obtaining a loan to pay for a funeral; or

- ➤ serving as agents for insurance companies offering preneed insurance.

Compliance areas - There are two important areas of compliance for any funeral establishment that meets the definition of a financial institution. First, they must comply with the FTC Safeguarding Rule that provides for the safeguarding of financial information and requires companies to develop a written information security plan that describes their program to protect customer information. The plan must be appropriate to the company's size and complexity, the nature and scope of its activities, and the sensitivity of the customer information it handles.

Second, funeral establishments must provide the consumer with a privacy notice that explains what information the company is gathering; where and with whom it is shared; and how the company is safeguarding the information. In addition, these notices must provide an option for the consumer to control the sharing of this information with others.

Fair Credit Reporting Act

The Fair Credit Reporting Act (FCRA) promotes the accuracy, fairness, and privacy of information in the files of consumer reporting agencies. There are many types of consumer reporting agencies, including credit bureaus and agencies that sell information about check writing histories, medical records, and rental history records. The three major consumer credit reporting agencies in the United States are Equifax, Experian, and TransUnion.

Businesses, such as a funeral establishment, that provide information to consumer reporting agencies have requirements under the Act. Known as 'information furnishers,' they are responsible for:

- ➤ reporting accurate financial information to consumer reporting agencies;

- ➤ promptly correcting any inaccurate information previously provided;

- ➤ advising consumers within 30 days of any negative information being reported; and

> having procedures for responding to identity theft notices sent by consumer reporting agencies.

Fair Debt Collection Practices Act

Introduction - The Fair Debt Collection Practices Act is a federal law that provides limitations on what debt collectors can do when collecting certain types of debt from debtors. It prohibits debt collection companies from using abusive, unfair, or deceptive practices to collect debts.

Debt collectors can include any individual or business, collection agencies, debt buyers, and lawyers who collect debts. Debt buyers are companies that buy past-due debts from creditors or other businesses and then try to collect on them. The Act describes numerous restrictions and prohibitions on debt collectors when attempting to collect a debt.

Communications - In 2021, new rules were adopted allowing debt collectors to give notices and make attempts to collect debts by using *electronic* communications. For example, debt collectors may *email, fax, and text* debtors, as well as communicate with them via any *social media* accounts they may own. When a collector is going to use electronic communications, debtors must be given the option to opt out of being contacted electronically. Collectors are prohibited from posting anything on a social media page if it can be viewed by either the debtors contacts or the public.

Prior action required - A debt collector – such as funeral establishment – cannot give a consumer reporting agency information about a debt before the debt collector:

> speaks to the consumer about the debt in person or by telephone; or

> places a letter in the mail or sends an electronic message to the consumer about the debt and waits a reasonable period of time to receive any notice of undeliverability. The 'reasonable' period of time has been clarified to mean at least 14 consecutive days.

Speaking to a debtor - After speaking to a debtor, the debt collector must wait one week before again contacting the same debtor about the same debt; however, the collector can make up to seven attempted calls to consumers and contact the consumer's family or friends to obtain contact information.

Time and place - Generally, debt collectors may not contact a consumer at an unusual time or place, or at a time or place known to be inconvenient for the consumer, and are prohibited from contacting debtors before 8 a.m. or after 9 p.m. In addition, if a debt collector knows a debtor is not allowed to receive debt communications at work, the collector is not allowed to contact the debtor at work.

Harassment - Debt collectors may not harass debtors or anyone else over the phone or through any other form of contact.

Representation by attorney. If a debt collector knows an attorney is representing a debtor about the debt, the collector generally must stop contacting the debtor and instead contact the attorney.

This is only true if the debt collector knows, or can easily determine, the name and contact information of the attorney.

Written notification to stop making contact - If a debt collector is notified in writing to stop contacting a debtor, the collector cannot contact the debtor again except to say there will be no further contact or to notify the debtor the creditor may take certain specific action it is legally allowed to take, such as filing a lawsuit.

Required information disclosure - A debt collector must provide a debtor with a number of items on a required disclosure, including but not limited to:

 ➢ a debt collector communication disclosure;

 ➢ the name, mailing information, and telephone contact information of the debit collector;

 ➢ the name of the creditor;

 ➢ an itemization of the current amount of debt, including interest, fees, payments, and credits;

 ➢ information about consumer protections;

 ➢ a consumer's right to dispute a debt;

 ➢ information regarding the Consumer Protections Bureau's website for more information on consumer debt;

 ➢ information on how to dispute a debt electronically;

 ➢ electronic communication information; and

 ➢ Spanish-language disclosures.

If a collector does not provide this information when first making contact, they are required to send a written notice including that information to the debtor within five days of the initial contact.

Note: This is a summary only of the Act, and the author recommends consultation with legal counsel before hiring a collection agency or furnishing any data to a consumer reporting agency. Further, most states have similar statutes that may expand on the rights of a debtor with respect to collection practices. Establishments must be in compliance with *both* federal and state laws.

Magnuson-Moss Warranty Act
Introduction - This Act directed the Federal Trade Commission to:

 ➢ develop regulations for written warranties;

 ➢ establish disclosure standards for written warranties;

> limit disclaimer of implied warranties; and

> establish consumer remedies for breach of warranty or service contract obligations.

Implied warranties - An implied *warranty of merchantability* is presumed to exist when a product is sold. The product must:

> conform to the standards of the trade;

> be fit for the purpose the goods are ordinarily used;

> uniform as to quality and quantity; and

> meet the specifications on any package labels.

If a product has an implied warranty of merchantability and it does not meet its intended purpose, there are legal remedies available to the consumer.

An implied *warranty of fitness* is presumed to exist when a seller, at the time of sale, has reason to know any particular purpose for which the goods are required, and the buyer is relying on the seller's skill or judgment to select or furnish suitable goods. The warranty usually is implied through the salesperson's assurance or recommendation of an item for a specific purpose. For example, if a funeral director assures a consumer an urn will hold up to 200 cubic inches of cremated remains and it turns out the maximum capacity is less than 200 cubic inches, the urn could be returned to the seller under the implied warranty of fitness.

To avoid complications with implied warranties, funeral establishments should rely on and refer to the manufacturer descriptions, information, and warranty when speaking with consumers. In the urn example above, the funeral director could tell the buyer that, *according to the manufacturer of the urn*, it will hold a minimum of 200 cubic inches of cremated remains, rather than assuring the buyer it will hold that amount and thereby implying the funeral director, not the manufacturer, is making the representation.

Disclaimer - A warranty disclaimer is a statement that informs a buyer the seller is not bound by any warranty guarantees or promises regarding the product. Funeral establishments may disclaim warranties by means of a statement that uses specific language and is presented to the consumer in a clear and conspicuous manner. The Uniform Commercial Code (UCC) provides a warranty disclaimer must mention merchantability and must be conspicuous.

The UCC also provides:

> *All implied warranties are excluded by expressions like 'as is' 'with all faults' or other language which in common understanding calls the buyer's attention to the exclusion of warranties and makes plain that there is no implied warranty.*

A typical disclaimer of warranties statement that may be used by a funeral establishment is provided here. However, funeral establishment owners and operators should always consult with an attorney in developing a disclaimer that complies with both the Magnuson-Moss Warranty Act and any applicable laws in those states where they offer funeral goods to the public.

Disclaimer of Warranties

XYZ Funeral Home makes no representations or warranties regarding the caskets, vaults, urns, or other goods and merchandise we offer. We do not warrant or claim that any casket or vault we offer is airtight and/or watertight. We do not claim that any casket or vault we offer has preservative qualities. Our funeral establishment hereby expressly disclaims all warranties, expressed or implied, relating to the merchandise we offer, including but not limited to, the implied warranties of merchantability and fitness for a particular purpose. The only warranties, expressed or implied, granted in connection with the merchandise we offer are the express written warranties, if any, granted by the manufacturer of the goods and merchandise.

Display of manufacturer warranty - The Act also provides the seller of a consumer product with a written manufacturer warranty must make the text of the warranty readily available for examination by a prospective buyer. This may be accomplished in either of two ways:

1. Displaying it in close proximity to the warranted product. This includes through electronic or other means if the manufacturer has elected to use an accessible digital format on the manufacturer's website.

2. Furnishing it upon request prior to the sale (including through electronic or other means) and placing signs in prominent locations reasonably calculated to elicit the prospective buyer's attention and advise them of the availability of warranties upon request.

To avoid any sense of offering or sharing responsibility for a warranty with a manufacturer, funeral establishments should refrain from making any claims as to the qualities, abilities, or capabilities of a product without expressly stating product attributes and guarantees are warranted by the manufacturer, *not* the funeral director or the funeral establishment.

FTC Cooling-Off Rule

This FTC rule was written to provide consumer protections for sales made at homes or certain other locations. It gives consumers a three-day right to cancel a sale made at their home, workplace, or a seller's temporary location, like a hotel or motel room, convention center, fairground, or restaurant. It also applies when a salesperson is *invited* to make a presentation in a person's home.

At the time of a sale, a seller, such as a funeral establishment, must inform a consumer of the right to cancel the sale. They must provide the consumer with two copies of a cancellation form, one to keep and one to send in if they decide to cancel the sale. They must also provide a copy of the contract or receipt, which must be dated; identify the name and address of the seller; and explain the right to cancel. The contract or receipt must be in the same language used in the sales presentation. The right to cancel for a full refund extends until midnight of the third business day after the sale.

Exceptions - Certain types of sales cannot be canceled, even if they take place in locations normally covered by the rule. The rule does not cover sales that are:

- ➤ under $25 for sales made at a person's home;

- ➤ under $130 for sales made at temporary locations;

- ➤ for goods or services not primarily intended for personal, family or household purposes;

- ➤ made entirely online, or by mail or telephone;

- ➤ the result of prior negotiations at the seller's permanent place of business where the goods are sold regularly;

- ➤ needed to meet an emergency; or

- ➤ made as part of a request for the seller to do repairs or maintenance on personal property (purchases made beyond the maintenance or repair request are covered).

How to cancel - Consumers have a right to change their mind and do not have to give a reason for canceling a purchase. To cancel a sale, all the consumer has to do is sign and date one copy of the cancellation form, and then mail it to the address given for cancellations, making sure the envelope is post-marked before midnight of the third business day after the contract date.

For the purposes of the rule, Saturday is considered a business day, while Sundays and federal holidays are not. Because proof of the mailing date and receipt are important, the FTC recommends sending the cancellation form by certified mail and requesting a return receipt. If the seller does not provide cancellation forms as required, a consumer may write a cancellation letter and mail it to the seller. Any such cancellation letter must be post-marked within three business days of the sale.

Seller responsibilities - When a seller receives a notice of cancellation, within 10 days they must cancel and return any check signed by the consumer (purchaser); refund any money paid by the purchaser; and advise the purchaser whether any goods they possess will be picked up.

Within 20 days, a seller must either pick up any items left with a consumer, or reimburse them for mailing expenses if the purchaser agrees to send the items back to them.

Form 1: General Price List

The FTC required disclosures on this sample General Price List have been *italicized* for instructional purposes, but the Funeral Rule does not require them to be italicized on an actual GPL. Author notes are also provided to communicate important information about a particular item or disclosure and are identified with gray shading.

For a full description and explanation of the items and disclosures that must be on a General Price List, see the chapter titled, *FTC Funeral Rule - General Price Lists*.

Smith and Sons Funeral Home
123 Main Street
Brookdale, NK 12345

GENERAL PRICE LIST

These prices are effective January 1, 2022.

The goods and services shown below are those we can provide to our customers. You may choose only the items you desire. However, any funeral arrangements you select will include a charge for our basic services and overhead. If legal or other requirements mean you must buy any items you did not specifically ask for, we will explain the reason in writing on the statement we provide describing the funeral goods and services you selected.

Basic Services of Funeral Director and Staff and Overhead...................... $ _____
Our services include: conducting the arrangements conference; planning the funeral; consulting with family and clergy; shelter of remains; preparing and filing of necessary notices; obtaining necessary authorizations and permits; and coordinating with the cemetery, crematory, or other third parties. In addition, this fee includes a proportionate share of our basic overhead costs.

This fee for our basic services and overhead will be added to the total cost of the funeral arrangements you select. (This fee is already included in our charges for direct cremations, immediate burials, and forwarding or receiving remains.)

Forwarding of Remains to Another Funeral Home.................................... $ _____
Our charge includes: basic services of funeral director and staff; a proportionate share of overhead costs; removal of remains; preparation of remains, including embalming; and local transportation.

Note: The words 'including embalming' is usually included here if required by a state law or common carrier. For states that have no such requirement, an embalming charge will most often be recorded in the Embalming item.

Receiving Remains from Another Funeral Home.................................... $ _____
Our charge includes: basic services of funeral director and staff; a proportionate share of overhead costs; care of remains; transportation of remains to the funeral establishment, and to a cemetery or crematory.

Direct Cremation - Price range: $_____ to $_____

Our charge for a direct cremation (without ceremony) includes: basic services of funeral director and staff; a proportionate share of overhead costs; removal of remains; transportation to crematory; necessary authorizations; and cremation.

Note: The words 'and cremation' would not be included here if cremation charges are being listed as a cash advance item.

If you want to arrange a direct cremation, you can use an alternative container. Alternative containers encase the body and can be made of materials like fiberboard or composition materials (with or without an outside covering). The containers we provide are a fiberboard container or an unfinished wood box.

A. Direct cremation with container provided by the purchaser......................... $ _____

B. Direct cremation with a fiberboard container.. $ _____

C. Direct cremation with an unfinished wood box.. $ _____

Immediate Burial - Price range: $_____ to $_____

Our charge for an immediate burial (without ceremony) includes: basic services of funeral director and staff; a proportionate share of overhead costs; removal of remains; and local transportation to cemetery.

A. Immediate burial with casket provided by the purchaser............................ $ _____

B. Immediate burial with an alternative container... $ _____

C. Immediate burial with an unfinished wood box... $ _____

Transfer of the Remains to the Funeral Home (within a 30 mile radius).......... $ _____

    Beyond this radius we charge _____ per mile

Note: While a flat fee and a mileage charge have been used here as an example, the rule also allows the use of an hourly rate.

Embalming.. $ _____

[Except in certain special cases] [E]mbalming is not required by law. Embalming may be necessary, however, if you select certain funeral arrangements, such as a funeral with viewing. If you do not want embalming, you usually have the right to choose an arrangement, such as direct cremation or immediate burial, that does not require you to pay for it.

Note: The phrase [Except in certain special cases] would not be used if a state has no law that requires embalming, and the paragraph would start with *Embalming is not required by law.*

Other Preparation of the Body

    Cosmetology.. $ _____

    Dressing and casketing... $ _____

    Topical disinfection... $ _____

Restoration work.. $ _____

Note: The items listed above are representative of those that typically found on a GPL, but they are not specifically required items under the Funeral Rule.

Use of the Facilities and Staff for Viewing at the Funeral Home.................. $ _____

    Staff for viewing at a location other than the funeral home.......................... $ _____

Use of Facilities and Staff for a Funeral Ceremony at the Funeral Home....... $ _____

    Staff for a funeral ceremony at a location other than the funeral home............ $ _____

Use of Facilities and Staff for a Memorial Service at the Funeral Home....... $ _____

    Staff for a memorial service at a location other than the funeral home............ $ _____

Use of Equipment and Staff for a Graveside Service................................ $ _____

Use of Hearse (within a 30 mile radius)... $ _____

    Beyond this radius we charge _____ per mile

Use of Limousine (within a 30 mile radius).. $ _____

    Beyond this radius we charge _____ per mile

Use of other livery (within a 30 mile radius)... $ _____
    Specify the vehicle _____

    Beyond this radius we charge _____ per mile

Note[1]: While a flat fee for 30 miles and a mileage charge have been used here as examples, the rule also allows the use of an hourly rate.

Note[2]: The rule only requires a hearse and limousine be listed; however, in practice, most states require all livery options be listed.

Caskets.. $ _____
A complete price list will be provided at the funeral establishment.   to
                                                       $ _____

Outer Burial Containers.. $ _____
A complete price list will be provided at the funeral establishment.   to
                                                       $ _____

Note: The Casket and Outer Burial Container items have two options in the rule. Option 1 is shown here with the required disclosure. Option 2, not shown here, is to list all casket and outer burial container prices directly on the GPL.

This concludes the listing of items and disclosures required by the Funeral Rule for inclusion on a General Price List (GPL). There are however many states that have adopted laws requiring cash advances also be included on the GPL. In those states, the most common practice is to list the cash advances here, immediately following the 16 items required by the rule.

Form 2: Casket Price List

While this document is called a casket price list, the Funeral Rule requires it include the prices for both caskets *and* alternative containers. It is not acceptable to have caskets on one price list and alternative containers on a separate list. See the chapter titled, *FTC Funeral Rule - Other Price Lists and a Required Statement,* for additional information about casket price lists.

Smith and Sons Funeral Home
CASKET PRICE LIST

These prices are effective January 1, 2022.

Alternative Containers

1. Presidio corrugated cardboard with reinforced base......................................	$550
2. Presidio fiberboard box...	$800
3. Presidio unfinished wooden box (Pine)..	$1200

Caskets (wood)

4. Americana cloth-covered Eastern White Pine, blue, embossed.......................	$900
Also available in beige color, embossed	
5. Americana Ponderosa Pine w/summit white crepe interior.............................	$1500
Also available with light beige, light blue, or pink crepe interior	
6. Americana Poplar, gloss dark finish w/rose color crushed interior....................	$1900
7. Borderland Dark Walnut w/pink velvet interior...	$2400
Also available in light blue or off-white velvet interior	
8. Borderland Maple w/white satin interior and matching tufted pillow...................	$2900
Also available in velvet interior w/matching tufted pillow	
9. Borderland Oak Veneer w/shaded tan satin interior.......................................	$3200
10. Borderland Solid Oak w/medium gold velvet interior....................................	$4900

Caskets (metal)

11. Lincoln Thunder, 20 gauge, gray, hammertone finish, and crepe interior...........	$1400
12. Lincoln Skyline, 18 gauge, light blue, brushed finish, and white satin interior.....	$2100
Also available in dark blue, black, or Canadian blue exterior	
13. Lincoln Night, stainless-steel, black, polished finish, and white interior.............	$2800
14. Lincoln Cloud, solid bronze, 32 oz., polished finish, and beige tailored interior...	$3500
15. Lincoln Gold, copper plated, 32 oz., brushed finish, and blue tailored interior ...	$4500

Form 3: Outer Burial Container Price List

For additional information on using an outer burial container price list, see the chapter titled, *FTC Funeral Rule - Other Price Lists and a Required Statement.*

Smith and Sons Funeral Home
OUTER BURIAL CONTAINER PRICE LIST

These prices are effective January 1, 2022.

In most areas of the country, state or local law does not require that you buy a container to surround the casket in the grave. However, many cemeteries require that you have such a container so that the grave will not sink in. Either a grave liner or a burial vault will satisfy these requirements.

Outer Burial Containers (concrete)

1. Springfield concrete sectionals..	$750
2. Springfield concrete grave box liner...	$1200
3. Springfield reinforced concrete burial vault..	$1600
4. Springfield reinforced concrete burial vault w/single carbon steel liner	$2100
5. Springfield reinforced concrete burial vault w/double carbon steel liner.............	$2600
6. Springfield reinforced concrete burial vault w/stainless steel liner....................	$3200

Outer Burial Containers (metal)

7. Winchester carbon steel dome burial vault...	$1900
8. Winchester 304-stainless steel dome burial vault.......................................	$2400
9. Winchester solid copper, 12-gauge, dome burial vault..................................	$2900
10. Winchester solid aluminum, 1/8" thick, dome burial vault	$3200

Outer Burial Container (polymer)

11. Martin top seal, polypropylene burial vault, non-porous..............................	$1800
12. Martin bottom seal, polypropylene burial vault, non-porous..........................	$1850
13. Martin double seal, polypropylene burial vault, non-porous..........................	$2100

Note: If no state or local law requires an outer burial container surround a casket in the grave, the Funeral Rule allows a funeral establishment to delete the phrase, 'In most areas of the country,' from the disclosure shown above. In addition, if the option of having these prices on the GPL were chosen instead of using a separate price list, as shown here, the disclosure would need to be located with the Outer Burial Container items listed on the GPL.

Form 4: Statement of Funeral Goods and Services Selected

The sample shown here is provided for instructional purposes only. Readers are reminded the Funeral Rule requires no specific form, heading or caption on the statement, nor does it require any specific order to the items listed. It is however recommended the order follow the same order as the GPL from which the items and prices were selected by the consumer. This sample lists the items following the same order as the GPL sample shown in Form 1. The three FTC required disclosures on this sample Statement have been *italicized* for instructional purposes, but the Funeral Rule does not require them to be italicized on an actual Statement.

Smith and Sons Funeral Home
STATEMENT OF FUNERAL GOODS AND SERVICES SELECTED

Charges are only for those items that you selected or that are required. If we are required by law or by a cemetery or crematory to use any items, we will explain the reasons in writing below.

Decedent: _____ Date of death: _____

Purchaser: _____ Phone No. _____

Purchaser address: _____

— FUNERAL HOME CHARGES —

Basic Services of Funeral Director and Staff and Overhead............................ $ _____

Forwarding of Remains to Another Funeral Home..................................... $ _____

Receiving Remains from Another Funeral Home...................................... $ _____

Direct Cremation.. $ _____

Immediate Burial.. $ _____

Transfer of the Remains to the Funeral Home... $ _____

    Additional mileage for _____ miles at _____ per mile............................. $ _____

Embalming.. $ _____
> *If you selected a funeral that may require embalming, such as a funeral with viewing, you may have to pay for embalming. You do not have to pay for embalming you did not approve if you selected arrangements such as a direct cremation or immediate burial. If we charged for embalming, we will explain why below.*

Other Preparation of the Body

    Cosmetology.. $ _____

    Dressing and casketing... $ _____

    Topical disinfection... $ _____

    Restoration work... $ _____

Note: Items listed are representative of those that may be found on a Statement.

Use of the Facilities and Staff for Viewing at the Funeral Home..................... $ _____

    Staff for viewing at a location other than the funeral establishment............... $ _____

Use of Facilities and Staff for a Funeral Ceremony at the Funeral Home............ $ _____

    Staff for funeral ceremony at location other than funeral home.................... $ _____

Use of Facilities and Staff for a Memorial Service at the Funeral Home............ $ _____

    Staff for memorial service at location other than the funeral home............... $ _____

Use of Equipment and Staff for a Graveside Service................................... $ _____

Use of Hearse... $ _____

    Additional mileage for _____ miles at _____ per mile............................. $ _____

Use of Limousine.. $ _____

    Additional mileage for _____ miles at _____ per mile............................. $ _____

Use of Other Livery (specify) _____........... $ _____

    Additional mileage for _____ miles at _____ per mile............................. $ _____

Note: The rule only requires a hearse and limousine be listed as livery items; however, in practice, most states require all livery options be listed.

Casket... $ _____

Outer Burial Container.. $ _____

TOTAL OF FUNERAL HOME CHARGES $_____.

— CASH ADVANCE CHARGES —

We charge you for our services in obtaining: (specify cash advance items).
Cemetery/crematory charges... $ _____

Common carrier charges... $ _____

Newspaper notice.. $ _____

Death certificates: _____ at $ _____ per certificate................................. $ _____

Flowers.. $ _____

Other: _____.................. $ _____

TOTAL OF CASH ADVANCE CHARGES $_____.

TOTAL COST OF FUNERAL ARRANGEMENTS $_____.
Including all services, merchandise, and cash advance items

Explanation for any legal, cemetery, crematory, or other goods or services that required the purchase of any of the items listed above:

_____

_____

_____

_____

Reason for embalming: _____

Form 5: Credit Disclosure Statement

This is a sample credit disclosure statement a funeral establishment might use when providing financing to a consumer to pay for funeral expenses.

Date: _____

Creditor: _____

Consumer/Applicant: _____

ANNUAL PERCENTAGE RATE The cost of your credit as a yearly rate.	FINANCE CHARGE The dollar amount the credit will cost you.	Amount Financed The amount of credit provided to you or on your behalf.	Total of Payments The amount you will have paid after you have made all payments as scheduled.
%	$	$	$

You have the right to receive at this time an Itemization of the Amount Financed.

❑ I want an itemization.   ❑ I do not want an itemization.

Your payment schedule will be:

Number of Payments	Amount of Payments	When Payments Are Due

Insurance
Credit life insurance and credit disability insurance are not required to obtain credit, and will not be provided unless you sign and agree to pay the additional cost.

Type	Premium	Signature	
Credit Life		I want credit life insurance.	_____ Signature
Credit Disability		I want credit disability insurance.	_____ Signature
Credit Life and Disability		I want credit life and disability insurance.	_____ Signature

You may obtain property insurance from anyone you want that is acceptable to _____ (creditor) _____ . If you get

the insurance from _____ (creditor) _____ , you will pay $ _____ .

Security: You are giving a security interest in:

❑ The goods or property being purchased.

❑ _____ (brief description of other property) _____ .

Filing fees $ _____   **Non-filing insurance** $ _____

Late Charge: If payment is late, you will be charged $ _____ / _____ % of the payment.

Prepayment: If you pay off early, you:

❑ may   ❑ may not   have to pay a penalty.

❑ may   ❑ may not   be entitled to a refund of part of the finance charge.

See your contract documents for any additional information about nonpayment, default, any required repayment in full before the scheduled date, and prepayment refunds and penalties.

_____
'e' means an estimate

Guide 1: OSHA - Formaldehyde Exposure Standard

Source: OSHA Formaldehyde Fact Sheet - 2011.

Introduction - Formaldehyde is a colorless, strong-smelling gas often found in aqueous (water-based) solutions. Commonly used as a preservative in medical laboratories and mortuaries, formaldehyde is also found in many products such as chemicals, particle board, household products, glues, permanent press fabrics, paper product coatings, fiberboard, and plywood. It is also widely used as an industrial fungicide, germicide, and disinfectant.

Although the term formaldehyde describes various mixtures of formaldehyde, water, and alcohol, the term 'formalin' is used to describe a saturated solution of formaldehyde dissolved in water, typically with another agent, most commonly methanol, added to stabilize the solution. Formalin is typically 37% formaldehyde by weight (40% by volume) and 6-13% methanol by volume in water. The formaldehyde component provides the disinfectant effects of formalin.

Exposure levels - The OSHA Formaldehyde standard and equivalent regulations in states with OSHA-approved state plans protects workers exposed to formaldehyde and apply to all occupational exposures to formaldehyde from formaldehyde gas, its solutions, and materials that release formaldehyde.

> The permissible exposure limit (PEL) for formaldehyde in the workplace is 0.75 parts formaldehyde per million parts of air (0.75 ppm) measured as an 8-hour time-weighted average (TWA).

> The standard includes a second PEL in the form of a short-term exposure limit (STEL) of 2 ppm which is the maximum exposure allowed during a 15-minute period.

> The action level, which is the standard's trigger for increased industrial hygiene monitoring and initiation of worker medical surveillance, is 0.5 ppm when calculated as an 8-hour TWA.

Harmful effects - Formaldehyde is a sensitizing agent that can cause an immune system response upon initial exposure. It is also a cancer hazard. Acute exposure is highly irritating to the eyes, nose, and throat and can make anyone exposed cough and wheeze. Subsequent exposure may cause severe allergic reactions of the skin, eyes, and respiratory tract. Ingestion of formaldehyde can be fatal, and long-term exposure to low levels in the air or on the skin can cause asthma-like respiratory problems and skin irritation such as dermatitis and itching. Concentrations of 100 ppm are immediately dangerous to life and health (IDLH), and the National Institute for Occupational Safety and Health considers 20 ppm of formaldehyde to be IDLH.

Airborne concentrations of formaldehyde above 0.1 ppm can cause irritation of the respiratory tract. The severity of irritation intensifies as concentrations increase.

Exposure routes - Workers can inhale formaldehyde as a gas or vapor or absorb it through the skin as a liquid. They can be exposed during the treatment of textiles and the production of resins. In addition to healthcare professionals and medical lab technicians, groups at potentially high risk include mortuary workers as well as teachers and students who handle biological specimens preserved with formaldehyde or formalin.

Requirements for employers - Provisions of the standard require employers to do the following:

➢ Identify all workers who may be exposed to formaldehyde at or above the action level or STEL through initial monitoring and determine their exposure.

➢ Reassign workers who suffer significant adverse effects from formaldehyde exposure to jobs with significantly less or no exposure until their condition improves. Reassignment may continue for up to 6 months until the worker is determined to be able to return to the original job or to be unable to return to work, whichever comes first.

➢ Implement feasible engineering and work practice controls to reduce and maintain worker exposure to formaldehyde at or below the 8-hour TWA and the STEL. If these controls cannot reduce exposure to or below the PELs, employers must provide workers with respirators.

➢ Label all mixtures or solutions composed of greater than 0.1 percent formaldehyde and materials capable of releasing formaldehyde into the air at concentrations reaching or exceeding 0.1 ppm. For all materials capable of releasing formaldehyde at levels above 0.5 ppm during normal use, the label must contain the words "potential cancer hazard."

➢ Train all workers exposed to formaldehyde concentrations of 0.1 ppm or greater at the time of initial job assignment and whenever a new exposure to formaldehyde is introduced into the work area. Repeat training annually.

➢ Select, provide, and maintain appropriate personal protective equipment (PPE). Ensure that workers use PPE such as impervious clothing, gloves, aprons, and chemical splash goggles to prevent skin and eye contact with formaldehyde.

➢ Provide showers and eyewash stations if splashing is likely.

➢ Provide medical surveillance for all workers exposed to formaldehyde at concentrations at or above the action level or exceeding the STEL, for those who develop signs and symptoms of overexposure, and for all workers exposed to formaldehyde in emergencies.

Recordkeeping requirements - Employers are required to do the following regarding worker exposure records:

➢ Retain exposure records for 30 years.

➢ Retain medical records for 30 years after employment ends.

➢ Allow access to medical and exposure records to current and former workers or their designated representatives upon request.

Guide 2: OSHA - Hazard Communication Standard

Sources: OSHA Hazard Communication Guidelines for Compliance (Pub. 3111) - Revised 2000; and Chemical Hazard Communication (Pub. 3084) - Revised 1998.

Introduction - OSHA's Hazard Communication Standard (HCS) is based on the concept that employees have both a need and a right to know the hazards and identities of the chemicals they are exposed to when working. They also need to know what protective measures are available to prevent adverse effects from occurring. OSHA designed the HCS to provide employees with the information they need to know.

Under the provisions of the Hazard Communication Standard, employers are responsible for informing employees of the hazards and the identities of workplace chemicals to which they are exposed.

Exposure hazards - Chemical exposure may cause or contribute to many serious health effects, such as heart ailments, central nervous system, kidney and lung damage, sterility, cancer, burns, and rashes. Some chemicals may also be safety hazards and have the potential to cause fires and explosions and other serious accidents.

The Hazard Communication Standard establishes uniform requirements to make sure that the hazards of all chemicals imported into, produced, or used in U.S. workplaces are evaluated, and that this hazard information is transmitted to affected employers and exposed employees.

Downstream flow of information - The hazard communication standard is different from other OSHA health rules because it covers all hazardous chemicals. The rule also incorporates a 'downstream flow of information,' which means that producers of chemicals have the primary responsibility for generating and disseminating information, whereas users of chemicals must obtain the information and transmit it to their own employees.

Chemical Manufacturer's and Importers
- Determine the hazards of each product.

Chemical Manufacturer's, Importers, and Distributors
- Communicate the hazard information and associated protective measures downstream to customers through labels and SDSs.

Employers
- Identify and list hazardous chemicals in their workplaces.
- Obtain SDSs and labels for each hazardous chemical, if not provided by the manufacturer, importer, or distributor.
- Develop and implement a written hazard communication program, including labels, SDSs, and employee training.
- Communicate hazard information to their employees through labels, SDSs, and formal training programs.

Hazard communication program - A written hazard communication program ensures that all employers receive the information they need to inform and train their employees properly and to design and put in place employee protection programs. It also provides necessary hazard information to employees, so they can participate in, and support, the protective measures in place at their workplaces.

Employers therefore must develop, implement, and maintain at the workplace a written, comprehensive hazard communication program that includes provisions for container labeling, collection and availability of safety data sheets, and an employee training program.

Use of labels - Chemical manufacturers and importers must convey the hazard information they learn from their evaluations to downstream employers by means of labels on containers and safety data sheets (SDSs).

Chemical manufacturers, importers, and distributors must be sure that containers of hazardous chemicals leaving the workplace are labeled, tagged, or marked with the identity of the chemical, appropriate hazard warnings, and the name and address of the manufacturer or other responsible party.

In the workplace, each container must be labeled, tagged, or marked with the identity of hazardous chemicals contained therein, and must show hazard warnings appropriate for employee protection. The hazard warning can be any type of message, words, pictures, or symbols that provide at least general information regarding the hazards of the chemical(s) in the container and the targeted organs affected, if applicable. Labels must be legible, in English (plus other languages, if desired), and prominently displayed.

Safety data sheets (SDSs) - The SDS is a detailed information bulletin prepared by the manufacturer or importer of a chemical that describes the physical and chemical properties, physical and health hazards, routes of exposure, precautions for safe handling and use, emergency and first-aid procedures, and control measures. Chemical manufacturers and importers must develop an SDS for each hazardous chemical they produce or import, and must provide the SDS automatically at the time of the initial shipment of a hazardous chemical to a downstream distributor or user. Distributors also must ensure that downstream employers are similarly provided an SDS.

Each SDS must be in English and include information regarding the specific chemical identity of the hazardous chemical(s) involved and the common names. In addition, information must be provided on:

➢ the physical and chemical characteristics of the hazardous chemical;

➢ known acute and chronic health effects and related health information;

➢ exposure limits;

➢ whether the chemical is considered to be a carcinogen;

> precautionary measures;

> emergency and first-aid procedures; and

> the identification (name, address, and telephone number) of the organization responsible for preparing the sheet.

Copies of the SDS for hazardous chemicals in a given worksite are to be readily accessible to employees in that area. As a source of detailed information on hazards, they must be readily available to workers during each work shift. SDSs have no prescribed format.

Employers must prepare a list of all hazardous chemicals in the workplace. When the list is complete, it should be checked against the collected SDSs that the employer has been sent. If there are hazardous chemicals used for which no SDS has been received, the employer must contact the supplier, manufacturer, or importer to obtain the missing SDS. A record of the contact must be maintained.

GHS system - GHS is an acronym for the Globally Harmonized System of Classification and Labeling of Chemicals. The GHS is a system for standardizing and harmonizing the classification and labeling of chemicals and a comprehensive and logical and approach to:

> defining health, physical and environmental hazards of chemicals;

> creating classification processes that use available data on chemicals for comparison with the defined hazard criteria; and

> communicating hazard information, as well as protective measures, on labels and Safety Data Sheets (SDS).

GHS provides standardized hazard testing criteria, universal warning pictograms, and harmonized safety data sheets to provide a wealth of information on hazardous materials.

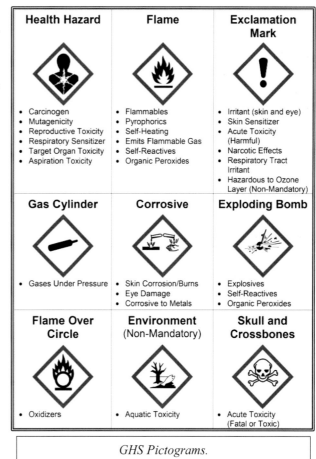

GHS Pictograms.

Training requirements - Employers must establish a training and information program for employees who are exposed to hazardous chemicals in their work area at the time of initial assignment and whenever a new hazard is introduced into their work area.

At a minimum, the discussion topics must include the following:

➢ The hazard communication standard and its requirements.

➢ The components of the hazard communication program in the employees' workplaces.

➢ Operations in work areas where hazardous chemicals are present.

➢ Where the employer will keep the written hazard evaluation procedures, communications program, lists of hazardous chemicals, and the required SDS forms.

The employee training plan must consist of the following elements:

➢ How the hazard communication program is implemented in that workplace, how to read and interpret information on labels and the SDS, and how employees can obtain and use the available hazard information.

➢ The hazards of the chemicals in the work area. (The hazards may be discussed by individual chemical or by hazard categories such as flammability.)

➢ Measures employees can take to protect themselves from the hazards.

➢ Specific procedures put into effect by the employer to provide protection such as engineering controls, work practices, and the use of personal protective equipment (PPE).

➢ Methods and observations, such as visual appearance or smell workers can use to detect the presence of a hazardous chemical to which they may be exposed.

Guide 3: OSHA - Bloodborne Pathogens Standard

Source: OSHA Bloodborne Pathogens Standard Fact Sheet - 2011.

Introduction - Bloodborne pathogens are infectious microorganisms present in blood that can cause disease in humans. These pathogens include, but are not limited to, hepatitis B virus, hepatitis C virus, and human immunodeficiency virus, the virus that causes AIDS. Workers exposed to bloodborne pathogens are at risk for serious or life-threatening illnesses.

The standard has requirements for what employers must do to protect workers who are occupationally exposed to blood or other potentially infectious materials (OPIM), as defined by the standard. The standard protects workers who can reasonably be anticipated to come into contact with blood or OPIM as a result of doing their job duties. The standard requires employers:

Establish an exposure control plan. This is a written plan to eliminate or minimize occupational exposures. The employer must prepare an exposure determination that contains a list of job classifications in which all workers have occupational exposure and a list of job classifications in which some workers have occupational exposure, along with a list of the tasks and procedures performed by those workers that result in their exposure.

Employers must update the plan annually to reflect changes in tasks, procedures, and positions that affect occupational exposure, and also technological changes that eliminate or reduce occupational exposure. In addition, employers must annually document in the plan that they have considered and begun using appropriate, commercially-available effective safer medical devices designed to eliminate or minimize occupational exposure. Employers must also document that they have solicited input from frontline workers in identifying, evaluating, and selecting effective engineering and work practice controls.

Implement the use of universal precautions. Treat all human blood and OPIM as if known to be infectious for bloodborne pathogens.

Identify and use engineering controls. These are devices that isolate or remove the bloodborne pathogens hazard from the workplace. They include sharps disposal containers, self-sheathing needles, and safer medical devices, such as sharps with engineered sharps-injury protection and needleless systems.

Provide personal protective equipment (PPE). This includes such items as gloves, gowns, eye protection, and masks. Employers must clean, repair, and replace this equipment as needed. The provision, maintenance, repair, and replacement of these items must be at no cost to the worker.

Make available hepatitis B vaccinations to all workers with occupational exposure. This vaccination must be offered after the worker has received the required bloodborne pathogens training and within 10 days of initial assignment to a job with occupational exposure.

Identify and ensure the use of work practice controls. These are practices that reduce the possibility of exposure by changing the way a task is performed, such as appropriate practices for handling and disposing of contaminated sharps, handling specimens, handling laundry, and cleaning contaminated surfaces and items.

Make available post-exposure evaluation and follow-up to any occupationally exposed worker who experiences an exposure incident. An exposure incident is a specific eye, mouth, other mucous membrane, non-intact skin, or parenteral contact with blood or OPIM. This evaluation and follow-up must be at no cost to the worker and include:

> ➢ documenting route(s) of exposure and circumstances of how the incident occurred;
>
> ➢ identifying and testing the source individual for HBV and HIV infectivity, if the source individual consents or the law does not require consent;
>
> ➢ collecting and testing the exposed worker's blood, if the worker consents;
>
> ➢ offering post exposure treatment and counseling; and
>
> ➢ evaluating reported illnesses.

Use labels and signs to communicate hazards. Warning labels must be affixed to:

> ➢ containers of regulated waste and contaminated reusable sharps;
>
> ➢ refrigerators and freezers containing blood or OPIM;
>
> ➢ other containers used to store, transport, or ship blood or OPIM;
>
> ➢ contaminated equipment that is being shipped or serviced; and
>
> ➢ bags or containers of contaminated laundry, except as provided in the standard.

Provide information and training to workers. Employers must ensure their workers receive regular training that covers all elements of the standard including, but not limited to information on:

> ➢ bloodborne pathogens and diseases;
>
> ➢ methods used to control occupational exposure;
>
> ➢ hepatitis B vaccine; and
>
> ➢ medical evaluation and post-exposure follow-up procedures.

Employers must offer this training on initial assignment, at least annually thereafter, and when new or modified tasks or procedures affect a worker's occupational exposure. Workers must have the opportunity to ask the trainer questions. Also, training must be presented at an educational level and in a language that workers understand.

Maintain worker medical and training records.
The employer also must maintain a sharps injury log.

Guide 4: Environmental Protection Agency (EPA) Burial at Sea Instructions

Source: Environmental Protection Agency website; retrieved online August 2019.

Instructions for Burial at Sea

The EPA has issued a general permit under the Marine Protection, Research and Sanctuaries Act (MPRSA) to authorize the burial of human remains at sea. The general permit is published in the federal regulations at 40 CFR 229.1.

The following activity is not allowed under the MPRSA general permit for burial at sea:

- Placement of human remains in ocean waters within three nautical miles from shore, i.e., the ordinary low water mark or a closing line drawn on nautical charts across the openings of bays and rivers.

- Placement of non-human remains (such as pet remains).

- Placement of materials which are not readily decomposable in the marine environment, such as plastic or metal flowers and wreaths, tombs, tombstones, gravestones, monuments, mausoleums, artificial reefs, etc.

Preparation for Burial at Sea

Human remains shall be prepared for burial at sea and buried in accordance with accepted practices and requirements as may be deemed appropriate and desirable by the United States Navy, United States Coast Guard or civil authority charged with the responsibility for making such arrangements. In addition, state and/or local requirements may apply to the transportation of human remains on land, for example, to locations other than cemeteries.

Non-cremated, non-casketed remains

If no casket is used, EPA recommends wrapping a natural fiber shroud or sail cloth around the body and adding additional weight, such as a steel chain, to aid in rapid sinking.

Non-cremated casketed remains

If using a casket, plastic materials should be removed from the casket before burial at sea because plastic materials do not degrade and may create unacceptable marine debris. A metal casket, as used by the United States Navy, should be considered. EPA recommends that:

- a minimum of twenty 2-inch (5 cm) holes be drilled into the casket to facilitate rapid flooding and venting of air. The holes should be evenly spaced on the top (8 holes), bottom (8 holes) and head and foot ends (2 holes each) of the casket. The holes may be covered with a porous material like cloth or paper so that the remains are not visible, as long as plastic-containing adhesives like tape are not used;

- to aid rapid sinking, additional weight, such as sand or concrete (but not lead), be added to the casket to achieve a total weight of at least 300 pounds (136 kg)

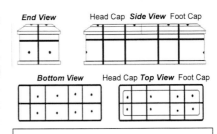

Recommended casket preparations to aid rapid, permanent, and intact sinking: twenty 2-inch holes, six bands and a total weight of at least 300 pounds. Diagram from the United States Navy Burial at Sea Program, *Guidelines for Casket Preparation* (2010).

to offset the buoyancy of both the body and the casket. Weighing the foot end of the casket facilitates feet-first sinking; and

- the casket should be banded with at least six durable stainless-steel bands, chains, or natural fiber ropes in order to ensure rapid and permanent sinking of the intact casket. One band should be placed over each of the two lengthwise axes of the casket (top-to-bottom and head-to-foot), as well as four bands at evenly spaced intervals along the narrow axis of the casket. The latter is important for caskets with separate head and foot caps. Commercial shipping straps are likely to deteriorate rapidly in the marine environment and should not be used.

Disposal Location and Measures

Non-cremated remains

The MPRSA general permit authorizes burial at sea of non-cremated human remains at locations at least three nautical miles from land and in ocean waters at least 600 feet deep. In certain areas, specifically east central Florida, the Dry Tortugas, Florida and west of Pensacola, Florida to the Mississippi River Delta, such at sea burials are only authorized in ocean waters at least 1,800 feet deep. Refer to 40 CFR 229.1(a)(2) for details. All necessary measures must be taken to ensure that the remains sink to the bottom rapidly and permanently.

Cremated remains

Cremated remains shall be buried in or on ocean waters of any depth provided that such burial takes place at least three nautical miles from land.

Decomposable flowers and wreaths

Flowers and wreaths consisting of materials that are readily decomposable in the marine environment may be placed at the burial site. Plastic flowers or synthetic wreaths would not be expected to decompose rapidly.

Notice to EPA within 30 days

You must notify EPA of the burial at sea within 30 days following the event. All burials at sea conducted under the MPRSA general permit must be reported to the EPA Region from which the vessel carrying the remains departed.

A burial at sea of non-cremated and cremated human remains may be reported to EPA using the Burial at Sea Reporting Tool. The Burial at Sea Reporting Tool enables individuals or companies that have conducted a burial at sea to enter information into a simple online form and report the burial directly to EPA. For information about the Burial at Sea Reporting Tool including instructions for reporting, please see the Burial at Sea Reporting Tool Fact Sheet. Please note that you do not need to submit documentation, such as a Certificate of Death, to EPA when reporting a burial at sea.

To report a burial of human remains by other means, please contact the EPA Region where the vessel carrying the remains departed. To identify the appropriate EPA Regional contact, please see EPA's Regional Offices Contact List.

Guide 5: United States Navy Burial at Sea Program

Source: United State Navy Mortuary Affairs website; retrieved online August 2019.

UNITED STATES NAVY MORTUARY AFFAIRS
BURIAL AT SEA PROGRAM

Burial at Sea is a means of final disposition of remains that is performed on United States Navy vessels. The committal ceremony is performed while the ship is deployed. Therefore, family members are not allowed to be present. The commanding officer of the ship assigned to perform the ceremony will notify the family of the date, time, and longitude and latitude once the committal service has been completed.

Eligibility: Individuals eligible for this program are: (1) active-duty members of the uniformed services; (2) retirees and veterans who were honorably discharged; (3) U.S. civilian marine personnel of the Military Sealift Command; and (4) dependent family members of active-duty personnel, retirees, and veterans of the uniformed services.

How to get started: After the death of the individual for whom the request for Burial at Sea is being made, the Person Authorized to Direct Disposition (PADD) should contact the Navy and Marine Corps Mortuary Affairs office at 1-866-787-0081 to request a packet and for additional information.

Supporting documents which must accompany this request are:

(1) a photocopy of the death certificate

(2) the burial transit permit or the cremation certificate

(3) a copy of the DD Form 214, discharge certificate, or retirement order.

The Burial at Sea Request Form and the three supporting documents listed above make up the Burial at Sea Request package.

Burial Flag: A Burial Flag is required for all committal services performed aboard United States Naval vessels, except family members, who are not authorized a burial flag. Following the services at sea, the flag that accompanied the cremains/remains will be returned to the PADD. If the PADD does not wish to send a burial flag for the service, a flag will be provided by the Navy for the committal service, but will not be sent to the PADD.

Cremated Remains (Cremains): Cremated Remains (Cremains): Cremains must be in an urn or temporary container (preferably Bio-degradable) to prevent spillage in shipping. Recent changes in law prohibit the discharge of plastics at sea. Families are encouraged to have the cremains inurned directly, or transferred to a sturdy biodegradable urn at their local funeral establishment to facilitate burial at sea. Burial at Sea Coordinators at the ports of embarkation are available to field any questions regarding the urns. The cremains, along with the completed Burial at Sea Request package should be forwarded to the Burial at Sea Coordinator at the desired port of embarkation (listed below). Prior to shipment, it is recommended that a phone call be made informing the coordinator of the pending request. Only Priority Mail Express Service is authorized when shipping cremains and it is recommended that Tracking and Signature on

Delivery is used to ensure the package is delivered to the correct individual in a timely manner.

Intact Remains (Casketed): Specific guidelines are required for the preparation of casketed remains. All expenses incurred in this process are the responsibility of the PADD, who will select a funeral establishment in the area of the port of embarkation. After this selection has been made and notification has been provided to the coordinator, the casketed remains, the request form, supporting documents, and the burial flag are to be forwarded to the receiving funeral establishment. The coordinator will make the inspection and complete the checklist for the preparation of casketed remains. It is recommended that funeral establishments responsible for preparing and shipping intact remains contact the Mortuary Services office at Navy Casualty in Millington, TN to receive the preparation requirements.

PORTS OF EMBARKATION / COORDINATORS

Norfolk, Virginia
Commander, Naval Medical Center
ATTN: Code 0210C
620 John Paul Jones Cir.
Portsmouth, VA 23708-5100
Phone: (757) 953-2617\2618

Jacksonville, Florida
Officer in Charge
Naval Hospital Branch Clinic
P. O. Box 280148
Naval Station
Mayport, FL 32228-0148
Phone: (904) 270-4285

Honolulu, Hawaii
Navy Liaison Unit
Tripler Army Medical Center
Tripler AMC, HI 96859-5000
Phone: (808) 433-4709
(808) 577-7590

San Diego, California
Commanding Officer
Naval Medical Center
Decedent Affairs Code: 09O4
34800 Bob Wilson Drive
San Diego, CA 92134-5000
Phone: (800) 290-7410

Bremerton, Washington
Commanding Officer
Naval Hospital Bremerton
Code: 015-BAS/HP01 Boone Road
Bremerton, WA 98312-1898
Phone: (360) 475-4313

Questions concerning Burial-at-Sea?
Please call Monday - Friday, 0730-1600 Central Time
Toll Free - 1-866-787-0081
DSN - 882-8576

Reviewed: 27 MAY 2016

Guide 6: USPS Publication 139 - September 2019

How to Package and Ship Cremated Remains

The United States Postal Service® offers Priority Mail Express® and Priority Mail Express International® service for shipping human or animal cremated remains domestically and internationally. Whether you are shipping the remains of a loved one or a pet to or between family members or to an artisan to incorporate the remains into blown glass or other works of art, this publication is designed to provide the necessary preparation and packaging requirements that will aid in protecting this special mailing during transit.

General Instructions

Cremated remains are permitted to be mailed to any domestic address when the package is prepared as described below and in the referenced postal manuals.

Cremated remains are permitted to be mailed to an international address when the designating country does not prohibit the contents and when Priority Mail Express International service is available to that country. You can verify this by checking the Individual Country Listing in the *Mailing Standards of the United States Postal Service, International Mail Manual* (IMM®).

Packaging

You will need a primary inner sift-proof container, cushioning material, and an outer shipping package.

Note: A sift-proof container is any vessel that does not allow loose powder to leak or sift out. There are many options available to store cremated remains - from simple wooden boxes to decorative urns. USPS® recommends consulting with a licensed funeral director to help you select the best container.

Inner Primary Container

- **Domestic Shipping:** The inner primary container must be strong, durable, and constructed in such a manner as to protect and securely contain the contents inside. It must be properly sealed and sift-proof.

- **International Shipping:** A funeral urn is required as the inner primary container. It must be properly sealed and sift-proof.

Seal and Address the Inner Primary Container

In the event the shipping label becomes detached from the outer container, the Postal Service™ recommends that you put the sift-proof container in a sealed plastic bag. Then, attach a label with the complete return address and delivery address on the sealed plastic bag and the wording "Cremated Remains."

Cushioning Material

For both domestic and international shipping, place sufficient cushioning all around the inner primary sift-proof container to prevent it shifting inside the outer shipping package during transit and to absorb any shock to prevent breakage.

Outer Shipping Package

For both domestic and international shipping, cremated remains must be shipped by USPS Priority Mail Express or Priority Mail Express International Service utilizing either a USPS-produced or customer-supplied shipping package. If using a customer-supplied shipping package, it must be strong and durable to withstand transportation handling.

For convenience, the Postal Service has a Priority Mail Express Cremated Remains box that may be used for domestic or international shipments using the applicable Priority Mail Express service. The Priority Mail Express Cremated Remains box can be ordered online at the Postal Store on USPS.com® and is available as part of a kit.

Before closing and sealing the shipping package, the Postal Service recommends adding a slip of paper with both the sender's and recipient's address and contact information inside the package. This extra step will help to identify the sender and receiver in the event the shipping label becomes detached.

Labeling and Markings

To increase the visibility of mail pieces containing cremated remains, the outer shipping box (USPS- produced or customer-supplied) containing cremated remains must be marked with Label 139, *Cremated Remains,* affixed to each side (including top and bottom). Label 139 is available at the Postal Store on USPS.com or can be obtained at a retail Post Office™ location.

Address Your Package

Domestic Shipping:

- A complete return address and delivery address must be used. The address format for a package is the same as for an envelope. Write or print address labels clearly. Use ink that does not smear and include the addresses and ZIP Codes™ for you and your recipient.

- Double check the mailing address, especially the ZIP Code. You can use Look Up a ZIP Code™ on USPS.com.

- Mailers may generate single-ply Priority Mail Express labels through Click-N-Ship® or other USPS-approved methods.

International Shipping:

A complete return address and delivery address must be used. The mailer must indicate the identity of the contents (Cremated Remains) on the required applicable customs declaration form. To determine the applicable customs form, see IMM Section 123.61.

Note: If available, the cremation certificate should be attached to the outer box or made easily accessible. The sender is responsible for adherence to any restrictions or observances noted by the designating country.

Guide 7: International Shipping of Human Remains

Source: *Funeral Directing in the United States: A Guide for Funeral Service Students*, 2nd ed. June 2022.

International Shipping

Government embassies - The U.S. Department of State has government representatives working in almost 400 embassies, consulate offices, and diplomatic missions all over the world. Embassy buildings serve as the headquarters and work place for U.S. government employees and are usually located in the capital city of the foreign country.

An ambassador, also known as the chief of mission, is the highest-ranking diplomat to the host country and a personal representative of the President. Branches of an embassy within the same country are known as consulates and often located in larger cities of the foreign country. One of the primary purposes of a U.S. embassy (or consulate) is to assist American citizens who travel to or live in the host country. This includes assisting families when a U.S. citizen dies in a foreign country.

Foreign countries also have facilities and personnel stationed all over the world for the same reasons the United States does. As of this writing, 178 foreign countries have an embassy office in Washington, D.C., with many maintaining additional consulate offices in large metropolitan areas of the United States. For example, Great Britain has consulate offices in Atlanta, Boston, Chicago, Houston, Los Angeles, Miami, New York, and San Francisco. When human remains must be shipped internationally, these world-wide embassy and consulate offices play a major role in facilitating the process.

Time considerations - Time delays when shipping internationally are very common. These may be due to a number of factors, including:

> legal mandates;

> conflicting time zones;

> number of parties involved;

> documentation authentication requirements;

> flight schedules and availability; and

> language barriers.

Care should therefore be taken by a funeral establishment to inform families to expect the process to take up to a week or more.

On the same token, many countries have strict parameters limiting the length of time that may pass before a final disposition must – by law – take place. It is therefore very important when handling international cases that decisions be made as soon as possible to avoid any delay that might result in failure to comply with the laws or customs of a foreign country.

Shipments to a foreign country - When human remains must be shipped from the United States to a foreign country, the funeral director should contact the embassy or consulate office located in the United States that represents the foreign country for assistance. They are familiar with regulatory compliance issues that must be met for their country to receive an international shipment of human remains from the United States. The requirements and documentation vary from one country to the next but may include any or all of the following:

➢ certified copy of a death certificate;

➢ government issued burial, transit, or disposition permit;

➢ a 'Letter of Non-Contagious Disease,' stating the decedent did not have a contagious disease or illness at the time of death;

➢ an affidavit, sworn statement, letter, or other written documentation from a licensed or certified embalmer, or other authorized funeral service practitioner, that the body has been embalmed;

➢ foreign passport or visa of the decedent (if they had one);

➢ copy of the flight or other mode of transportation itinerary;

➢ letter from the funeral establishment attesting to the contents of the transportation container(s);

➢ letter from the funeral establishment or a shipping company acting on behalf of the funeral establishment that international shipping container requirements in the destination country have been complied with fully;

➢ translation of U.S. documents to the language of the destination country; and

➢ compliance with customs requirements of the destination country.

Documentation may need to be endorsed by **apostille**, defined as the certification or legalization of a document for international use in accordance with the 1961 Hague Convention. An apostille endorsement is affixed to a document by designated authorities, such as embassies, ministries, courts, and state or local governments. In the United States, each of the Departments of State in the 50 states are designated authorities.

Funeral directors must ensure strict compliance with the foreign country requirements and any related fees. If human remains arrive without the required documentation or fees, or the documents are not authenticated as required, human remains may be refused and returned to the United States.

Shipments from a foreign country - When a United States citizen dies abroad, notification of the death is usually received by the family via cable from the U.S. embassy (or consulate office) located in the foreign country where the person died. This same office will coordinate with a funeral establishment in the United States to assist in getting the remains returned as soon as possible. They also provide assistance and guidance for any family members in the host country at the time.

When working with a foreign country, funeral directors should be aware of the following:

➤ The U.S. Embassy located in the foreign country will provide information on the available disposition options in the country of death and the associated costs.

➤ The preparation, handling, and disposition of human remains must comply with the laws and customs of the host country, not the United States.

➤ Many foreign countries do not offer or include embalming as an option in caring for the dead and, in those countries that do, embalming and cosmetics may not meet standards commonly accepted in the United States. Families should be made aware the remains may not be suitable for viewing.

➤ International air freight charges are very expensive.

➤ All of the expenses related to a death in a foreign country are the responsibility of the immediate family. The United States government does not provide any financial support to pay for funeral expenses or to repatriate (return) human remains to the United States.

➤ The U.S. Embassy in the foreign country will assist with transmitting funds; disbursing those funds on behalf of the family; providing an account of the disbursements; and refunding any surplus funds.

➤ If no one assumes financial responsibility for a final disposition, the U.S. consulate office is required to request local authorities to provide for the disposition in accordance with the laws of the host country.

➤ Cremation is an option in most countries, but there are locations where local laws or customs may forbid the cremation of human remains. In addition, cremation facilities may not be located in close proximity to where the death occurred, and the cost for transportation may be excessive when compared to standards in the United States.

➤ Burial in the foreign country where the death took place may also be an option for final disposition and potentially far less expensive than transporting the remains back to the United States. There are however some countries that do not allow for the burial of foreign nationals on their soil.

Shipping by Airline Carriers

While different modes of transportation are available, airline service is the predominate means to move human remains long distances, both domestically and internationally. Funeral establishments must comply with the shipping requirements for the airline they have chosen. These requirements vary from one carrier to the next; however, all of the major carriers usually have requirements for shipping human remains posted on their websites.

In addition to the airline requirements, funeral establishments must apply to each airline they wish to use to be registered as a *known shipper*. The known shipper program – administered by the federal Transportation Security Administration (TSA) – is designed to:

> *… impose significant barriers to terrorists seeking to use the air cargo transportation system for malicious purposes.*

By requiring airlines to only accept shipments from known shippers, the TSA has significantly reduced this potential threat.

As an alternative to the known shipper program, establishments may contract with private entities to provide for the shipment of human remains. These companies register as a known shipper with each of the major airlines and are then in position to schedule flights with any carrier; coordinate with the sending and receiving funeral establishments; pay cash advance expenses; and ensure compliance with airline regulations.

Glossary

Abatement - a proportional reduction of a devise when estate assets are not sufficient to pay it in full. (Chapter 11)

Actual custody - the physical possession of the dead human body or other property. (Chapter 3)

Ademption - the extinction or withdrawal of a devise because decedent did not own the named property at the time of death. (Chapter 11)

Administrative agency - a governmental body created by legislation empowered to make and enforce rules and regulations. (Chapters 2 and 14)

Administrative law - the rules and regulations created by Federal and State administrative agencies (e.g., OSHA, FTC, state board rules and regulations). (Chapters 2 and 14)

Aftercare - those appropriate and helpful acts of counseling, personal and/or written contact that come after the funeral. (Chapter 4)

Agent driver - those drivers under the directions and control of the funeral establishment which is liable for the driver's negligent actions. (Chapter 5)

Alkaline hydrolysis - a process that uses water, alkaline chemicals, heat and sometimes pressure and agitation to accelerate natural decomposition, leaving bone fragments. (Chapter 10)

Alternative container - an unfinished wood box or other non-metal receptacle or enclosure, without ornamentation or a fixed interior lining, which is designed for the encasement of human remains and which is made of fiberboard, pressed-wood, composition materials (with or without an outside covering) or like materials [CFR 16 §453.1(a)]. (Chapters 10, 16, 17 and 18)

Alternative price lists - price lists which may be prepared for use in certain limited situations such as children/infants, for government agencies to provide for indigent persons, for agreements with religious groups, burial, or memorial societies for members of their group [FTC Guide, pg. 11]. (Chapter 18)

Americans with Disabilities Act (ADA) - a federal statute prohibiting discrimination against the disabled in employment, public transportation, telecommunication services, and public accommodations and services. (Chapters 6 and 19)

Apostille - certification/legalization of a document for international use (under terms of the 1961 Hague Convention) [FD term]. (Guide 7)

Apprenticeship (internship/resident training) - the process a person engages in to learn the practice of funeral directing and/or embalming under the instruction, direction, or personal supervision of a duly licensed funeral director and/or embalmer. (Chapter 13)

At-need cases - funeral service cases where funeral arrangements are made immediately after a death has occurred; as contrasted with preneed cases, where funeral arrangements are made prior to a death occurring, in preparation for use in the future [by Author]. (Chapters 7, 8 and 15)

Authorizing agent - the person(s) with the paramount right to authorize cremation and disposition [CRM term]. (Chapter 18)

Autopsy (post-mortem examination) - An examination of a human body, organ, or other body part following death to determine the cause and manner of death [by Author]. (Chapter 4)

Bailee - a person who receives personal property from another as a bailment. (Chapter 5)

Bailment - a delivery of personal property by one person (the bailor) to another (the bailee) who holds the property for a certain purpose under an express or implied-in-fact contract. (Chapter 5)

Bailor - a person who delivers personal property to another as a bailment. (Chapter 5)

Beneficiary - means the named individual for whom a preneed agreement is purchased. The beneficiary may also be the purchaser [by Author]. (Chapters 7 and 8)

Body parts - organs, tissues, eyes, bones, arteries, blood, other fluids, and other portions of a human body. (Chapter 10)

Brain death - total and irreversible cessation of brain function as indicated by a flat EEG reading. (Chapter 3)

Building code - laws, ordinances, and government regulations setting forth requirements for construction, maintenance, operation, occupancy, use or appearance of buildings. (Chapter 5)

Burial - (see interment.) (Chapter 9)

Cadaver - a dead human body intended solely for scientific study and dissection. (Chapters 3 and 10)

Case law - appellate court decisions based on custom and usage and prior decisions. (Chapter 2)

Cash advance items - any item of service or merchandise described to a purchaser as a "cash advance," "accommodation," "cash disbursement," or similar term. A cash advance item is also any item obtained from a third party and paid for by the funeral provider on the purchaser's behalf. Cash advance items may include, but are not limited to: cemetery or crematory services; pallbearers; public transportation; clergy honoraria; flowers; musicians or singers; nurses; obituary notices; gratuities and death certificates [CFR 16 §453.1(b)]. (Chapter 17)

Casket - a rigid container which is designed for the encasement of human remains and which is usually constructed of wood, metal, fiberglass, plastic, or like material, and ornamented and lined with fabric which is usually constructed of wood, metal, fiberglass, plastic, or like material, and ornamented and lined with fabric [CFR 16 §453.1(c)]. (Chapter 17)

Casket handling fees - a fee charged to a consumer who exercises the right to purchase a casket from another seller; these fees are prohibited under the Funeral Rule [FTC Guide, pg. 20]. (Chapter 18)

Casket price list (CPL) - a printed or typewritten list containing at least the retail prices of all caskets and alternative containers offered by a funeral establishment which do not require special ordering, enough information to identify each, and the effective date for the price list [CFR 16 §453.2(b)(2)]. (Chapter 17)

Cause of death - diseases, injuries, or complications that resulted in death [by Author]. (Chapter 4)

Cemetery - an area of ground set aside and dedicated for the final disposition of human bodies. (Chapters 5 and 9)

Codicil - an addition or amendment of a last will and testament executed with the same formality of the will. (Chapter 11)

Columbarium - a structure, room or space in a mausoleum or other building containing niches or recesses used to hold cremated remains. (Chapter 10)

Commission - refers to the Federal Trade Commission [CFR 16 §453.1(d)]. (Chapter 15)

Common carrier - any carrier required by law to convey passengers or freight, without refusal, if the approved fare or charge is paid (e.g., airline, train, etc.). (Chapter 13)

Constitution - the fundamental law that establishes the government; limits what government can and cannot do; and states the underlying principles to which the government will conform. (Chapter 2)

Constructive custody - the situation whereby one party has a right to acquire actual custody and possession of the dead body although another party has actual physical possession. (Chapter 3)

Contract - a legally enforceable agreement. (Chapters 2, 3 and 8)

Contract carrier - provides transportation for compensation only to those with whom it desires to do business (e.g., livery service). (Chapter 13)

Coroner - a public officer whose duty it is to investigate the cause of death when a question of accident, suicide, or homicide may be evident or where there was no doctor in attendance (see also medical examiner). (Chapter 4)

Corpse (dead human body) - the body of a dead human being, deprived of life, but not yet entirely disintegrated. (Chapter 3)

Cremated remains - the final product remaining after completion of the entire cremation and pulverization process. (Chapter 10)

Cremation - the reduction of a dead human body to inorganic bone fragments by intense heat in a specifically designed retort or chamber. (Chapter 10)

Crematory - the location of the retort/cremation chamber which will perform a cremation process. (Chapters 5 and 10)

Crime - an action against society as a whole in violation of a constitution, statues, or ordinances, e.g., treason, felony, misdemeanor. (Chapter 14)

Crypt - a chamber in a mausoleum, of sufficient size, generally used to contain the casketed remains of a deceased person. (Chapter 9)

Custodian - status associated with the funeral service practitioner and funeral establishment who become the legal protector of human remains from the time of removal until final disposition. (Chapter 3)

Dead human body - (see corpse). (Chapter 3)

Death - the cessation of life; permanent cessations of all vital functions and signs. (Chapter 3)

Degree of kindred - relationship of decedent to blood relatives. (Chapter 3)

Devise - a gift of real or personal property by will. (Chapters 11 and 12)

Devisee - the person who receives a devise. (Chapters 11 and 12)

Direct cremation - disposition of human remains by cremation without formal viewing, visitation, or ceremony with the body present [CFR 16 §453.1(g)]. (Chapters 16 and 18)

Disclosures - required statements on Funeral Rule price lists that must be placed exactly as provided in the rule; use the identical wording provided in the rule; cannot be edited or paraphrased; and must be presented in a clear, conspicuous, and legible manner (FTC Guide, pgs. 4 and 22). (Chapter 18)

Disinterment (exhumation) - the removal of human remains from a previous location of final disposition. (Chapter 9)

Due diligence - the attention reasonably expected from, and ordinarily exercised by, a person who seeks to satisfy a legal requirement or to discharge an obligation. (Chapters 4, 5, 10, 13 and 18)

Durable power of attorney - a power of attorney that remains in effect after the disability or incapacity of the principal (see also power of attorney). (Chapter 12)

Embalmer - a person, properly licensed, who disinfects, preserves, and/or restores a dead human body. (Chapters 13 and 14)

Eminent domain - the inherent power of a government to take private property for public use. In the U.S. just compensation to the property owner(s) is required. (Chapter 9)

Entombment - the placing of a human remains in a crypt in a mausoleum. (Chapter 9)

Environmental Protection Agency (EPA) - a governmental agency with environmental protection regulatory and enforcement authority. (Chapters 6 and 9)

Escheat - forfeiture of a decedent's property to the state in the absence of heirs. (Chapter 11)

Escrow account - in funeral service, a vehicle used to hold monies on prefunded contracts and beyond the control of the funeral director. (Chapter 7)

Estate - the property and debts of a deceased person, both real and/or personal. (Chapter 3)

Estrangement - the physical and/or emotional separation for a period of time showing the lack of affection, trust, and regard. (Chapter 3)

Exhumation - (see disinterment). (Chapter 9)

Federal Trade Commission (FTC) - an agency of federal government created in 1914 to promote free and fair competition by prevention of trade restraints, price fixing, false advertising, and other unfair methods of competition. (Chapter 15)

Fiduciary - means an individual in whom another has placed the utmost trust and confidence to manage and protect property or money. The relationship wherein one person has an obligation to act for another's benefit. (Chapter 7)   West's Encyclopedia of American Law, edition 2. ©2008 The Gale Group, Inc.

Final disposition - the conclusive performance of services with respect to the dead human body by one of the legally recognized methods. (Chapters 9 and 10)

Forwarding of remains - one of the 16 items required on a GPL (if the funeral provider offers this service). This involves services of the funeral provider in the locale where death occurs and preparation for transfer to another funeral provider as selected by the family (consumer). Funeral Rule requires package pricing of this service with a description of the components included. (Chapter 16)

Free items - none of the 16 specified items required to be separately itemized on the GPL can be listed as free or no charge. Items not required by the rule can be listed as free (FTC Guide, pg. 20). (Chapter 18)

Funeral ceremony - service commemorating the deceased with the body present [CFR 16 §453.1(m)]. (Chapter 16)

Funeral director (funeral service practitioner) - a person properly licensed, engaged in, or conducting, or holding himself/herself out as being engaged in preparing, other than by embalming, for the burial or disposition of dead human bodies. (Chapters 3, 13, 14 and 15)

Funeral establishment - a facility used in the care and preparation for the funeral and/or final disposition of dead human bodies. (Chapters 5 and 14)

Funeral goods - the goods which are sold or offered for sale directly to the public for use in connection with funeral services [CFR 16 §453.1(h)]. (Chapter 15)

Funeral provider - any person, partnership or corporation that sells or offers to sell funeral goods and funeral services to the public [CFR 16 §453.1(i)]. (Chapter 15)

Funeral pyre - an outdoor wooden structure upon which human remains rest and are cremated when the pyre is set on fire [by Author]. (Chapter 10)

Funeral service law (mortuary law/mortuary jurisprudence) - that branch of law which relates to matters concerned with the disposal of the dead and regulation of funeral directors, embalmers, and funeral establishments. (Chapter 2)

Funeral service practitioner - (see funeral director). (Chapters 3, 13, 14 and 15)

Funeral services - any services used to: (1) care for and prepare deceased human bodies for burial, cremation, or other final disposition; and (2) arrange, supervise, or conduct the funeral ceremony or the final disposition of deceased human bodies [CFR 16 §453.1(j)]. (Chapter 15)

General power of attorney - a written instrument granting the agent broad powers to act for the principal. (Chapter 12)

General price list (GPL) - a printed or typewritten list that must be given for retention to all persons who inquire in person about the funeral goods, funeral services, or prices of funeral goods or services offered by a funeral establishment [CFR 16 §453.2(b)(4)]. (Chapter 16)

Graveside service - for the purposes of Funeral Rule pricing, a service intended for those situations where there is no funeral ceremony at the funeral establishment or elsewhere. (Chapter 16)

Green burial - (see natural burial). (Chapter 9)

Gross negligent act - the intentional failure or the reckless disregard of the consequences with respect to conduct affecting the life or property of another. (Chapter 4)

Guaranteed contract - an agreement whereby the funeral establishment promises that the services and merchandise will be provided at the time of need (in the future) for a sum not exceeding the original amount of the aforementioned contract plus any accruals, regardless of the current prices associated with providing the services and merchandise at the time of the funeral. (Chapter 7)

Guardian - person appointed by the court to administer the affairs of another person who is incompetent by virtue of age or legal disability. (Chapter 3)

Heir - one who inherits, or is entitled to receive property by laws of intestacy. (Chapters 11 and 12)

Holographic will - a will written entirely by the hand of the testator. (Chapter 11)

Immediate burial - a disposition of human remains by burial, without formal viewing, visitation, or ceremony with the body present, except for a graveside service [CFR 16 §453.1(k)]. (Chapter 16)

Inheritance - the estate assets which pass from the decedent to his/her heirs. (Chapter 12)

Inhumement - (see interment). (Chapter 9)

Insolvent estate - the condition of the estate of a deceased person which is unable to pay the debts of the decedent and/or the estate. (Chapter 12)

Inter - to bury in the ground. (Chapter 9)

Interment (burial/inhumement) - the act of placing a dead human body in the ground. (Chapter 9)

Internship - (see apprenticeship). (Chapter 13)

Interstate - between two or more states. (Chapter 13)

Intestate - the state or condition of dying without having made a will; intestacy. (Chapter 11)

Intestate succession - the method used to distribute property owned by a person who dies without a valid will. (Chapters 9 and 11)

Intrastate - within a state. (Chapter 13)

Inurnment - placing cremated remains in an urn or placing cremated remains in a niche or grave. (Chapter 10)

Inventory - listing and valuation of a decedent's assets by personal representative of the estate. (Chapter 12)

Invitee - one who has been invited on the property by the landowner; persons coming to a funeral establishment for the purpose of attending funerals, viewing remains, or engaging the funeral director's services are some examples. (Chapter 5)

Irrevocable contract - an agreement for future funeral services which cannot be terminated or canceled prior to the death of the beneficiary. (Chapter 7)

Itemization - a method of listing goods and services on a General Price List that treats each individual good or service being offered as a separate line item that includes the price for the item [by Author]. (Chapters 16, 17 and 18)

Kin - one's relatives collectively; referring to blood relationship (legally, the surviving spouse is not a kin). (Chapter 3)

Law - those rules of conduct commanding what is right and prohibiting what is wrong. (Chapter 2)

Layperson - an ordinary person; one without special training in a profession or occupation [by Author]. (Chapter 4)

Liability - responsibility for actions and/or other debts; the quality or state of being legally obligated or accountable. (Chapter 3)

Lien - a claim or charge against real or personal property for payment of some debt (there can be no lien against a dead human body for it is not property). (Chapter 4)

Livery - automotive equipment made available for hire. (Chapter 5)

Living will - a document which governs the withholding or withdrawal of life-sustaining treatment from an individual in the event of an incurable or irreversible condition that will cause death within a relatively short time, and which becomes effective when such person is no longer able to make decisions regarding his/her medical treatment. (Chapter 12)

Malpractice - failure to perform a professional service with the ability and care generally exercised by others in the profession. (Chapter 4)

Manner of death - the mode of death, such as accident, homicide, natural, or suicide [by Author]. (Chapter 4)

Mausoleum - a building containing crypts or vaults for entombment. (Chapter 9)

Medical examiner - a forensically-trained physician whose duty it is to investigate questionable or unattended deaths (has replaced the coroner in many states); (see also coroner). (Chapter 4)

Memorial service - a ceremony commemorating the deceased without the body present [CFR 16 §453.1(l)]. (Chapter 16)

Mental anguish - a condition which may result from an outrageous intentional or grossly negligent act and may be accompanied by physical injury. (Chapter 4)

Moral turpitude - an act showing inherent baseness or vileness of principle or action; shameful wickedness; depravity. (Chapter 14)

Morgue - a place where dead human bodies are kept until identified and/or released for final disposition. (Chapter 6)

Mortgage - a secured loan on a parcel of real property. (Chapter 12)

Mortuary jurisprudence - (see funeral service law). (Chapter 2)

Mortuary law - (see funeral service law). (Chapter 2)

Mutilation - any altering or change made to a dead human body from the time of death, other than by natural causes. (Chapter 4)

Natural (green) burial - and eco-friendly method of final disposition that utilizes products, services, and merchandise free of toxic/hazardous materials, are biodegradable or that minimize use of energy. (Chapter 9)

Natural (green) cemetery - a place of interment that bans the use of metal caskets, toxic embalming, and concrete vaults and may also require the use of aesthetically natural monuments. (Chapter 9)

Negligence - failure to exercise care. (Chapter 4)

Niche - a recess or space in a columbarium used for the permanent placing of cremated remains. (Chapter 10)

Non-declinable service fee - with respect to a GPL Basic Services Fee, the only fee for services, facilities or unallocated overhead permitted in the Funeral Rule that may be non-declinable, unless otherwise required by law [CFR 16 §453.2(b)(4)(iv]. (Chapter 16)

Non-guaranteed contract - agreement in which the funeral establishment promises to apply the amount prepaid plus any accruals to the balance due. However, the cost of the funeral will be based upon the current price for the services and merchandise at the time services are provided. (Chapter 7)

Nuisance - a landowner's use of property which interferes with the public or another landowner's use of their property. (Chapter 5)

Nuisance in fact - acts, occupations or structures which are not nuisances per se, but may become nuisances by reason of the location or manner in which it is operated. (Chapter 5)

Nuisance per se - acts, occupations or structures which are nuisances at all times and under all circumstances; it may be prejudicial to public morals, dangerous to life, or injurious to public rights. (Chapters 5 and 9)

Nuncupative will - oral will declared or dictated by testator during last illness before appropriate witnesses to dispose of personal property and afterwards reduced to writing (not valid in all states). (Chapter 11)

Occupational Safety and Health Administration (OSHA) - a governmental agency with the responsibility for regulation and enforcement of safety and health matters for most employees. (Chapter 6)

Ordinance - a law passed by a local municipal governing body (e.g., zoning, building, safety, etc.). (Chapters 2 and 5)

Outer burial container - any container which is designed for placement in the grave around the casket including, but not limited to, container commonly known as burial vaults, grave boxes, and grave liners [CFR 16 §453.1(n)]. (Chapters 9 and 17)

Outer burial container price list (OBC Price List) - a printed or typewritten list containing at least the retail prices of all outer burial containers offered by a funeral establishment which do not require special ordering, enough information to identify each container, and the effective date for the prices listed [CFR 16 §453.2(b)(3)]. (Chapter 17)

Outrageous act - an act with complete disregard for proper conduct which transcends the bounds of common decency. (Chapter 4)

Package pricing - a pricing method whereby several items of goods and/or services are bundled together and offered for one price for all the included items [by Author]. (Chapters 16 and 17)

Per capita - the method of dividing an estate by which an equal share is given to each of a number of persons, all of whom stand in equal degree of kindred to the decedent. (Chapter 11)

Per stirpes - the method of proportionately dividing an estate between beneficiaries according to their deceased ancestor's share. (Chapter 11)

Personal representative - person who is appointed by the court to represent and administer the estate of a deceased person. (Chapter 12)

Police power - the inherent power of a government to make reasonable laws to protect the safety, health, morals, and general welfare of its citizens. (Chapters 2 and 3)

Power of attorney - an instrument granting someone authority to act as agent or attorney-in-fact for the principal; an ordinary power of attorney is revocable and automatically terminates upon the death or incapacity of the principal. (Chapter 12)

Preferred claim - a claim which is accorded a priority, advantage, or privilege. (Chapters 3 and 12)

Prefunded funeral arrangements - funeral arrangements made in advance of need that include provisions for funding or prepayment. (Chapters 3, 7, 8, and 15)

Preneed cases - funeral service cases where funeral arrangements are made prior to a death occurring, in preparation for use in the future; as contrasted with at-need cases, where funeral arrangements are made immediately following a death [by Author]. (Chapters 7, 8 and 15)

Preparation room - that portion or location in a funeral establishment specifically designed and equipped for embalming and otherwise preparing dead human bodies. (Chapter 6)

Pre-planned funeral arrangements - funeral arrangements made in advance of need that do not include provisions for funding or prepayment. (Chapters 3 and 7)

Priority - the order in which claims will be paid when there are insufficient assets to pay all of the claims, or the order in which certain classes of people have the right to make decisions concerning the disposition of the dead body. (Chapter 3)

Private carrier - those who transport only in particular instances and only for those they choose to contract with (e.g., funeral establishment vehicles and livery). (Chapter 13)

Private cemetery - a cemetery owned by a private enterprise such as a corporation for profit, a non-profit corporation, partnership, sole owners, religious orders, etc. (Chapter 9)

Probate - the process of administering the estate and determining the validity of a will. (Chapter 12)

Probate court - a court having jurisdiction over estates. (Chapter 12)

Probate estate - the property and debts of a decedent that is subject to administration by the personal representative of an estate. (Chapters 12)

Public cemetery - a cemetery owned by a governmental unit (federal, state, or municipal). (Chapter 9)

Purchaser - means the named individual paying for and purchasing a preneed account. The purchaser may also be the beneficiary [by Author]. (Chapters 7 and 8)

Quasi contract - a fictional contract created or implied by a court for a person who is unable to contract for himself (e.g., medical care, death); an obligation which law creates in the absence of agreement; is invoked by courts where there is unjust enrichment. (Chapter 3)

Quasi-property theory - the accepted theory of the legal status of a dead human body; rights associated with the body are as if it were property for the purpose of disposition only. (Chapter 3)

Receiving remains - one of the categories required to be itemized on the GPL (if the funeral provider offers the service). This involves services of the funeral provider after initial services have been provided by another firm at the locale of death. Funeral Rule requires package pricing of this service with a description of the components included. (Chapter 16)

Receiving vault - a structure designed for the temporary storage of bodies not to be immediately interred. (Chapter 9)

Reciprocity - the relationship existing between two states whereby each extends some privileges of licensure to licensees of the other state. (Chapter 13)

Replevin - an action to recover possession of wrongfully withheld personal property. (Chapter 4)

Resident training - (see apprenticeship). (Chapter 13)

Restrictive covenant - provision in a deed limiting the use of real property and prohibiting certain uses. (Chapter 5)

Revocable contract - agreement which may be terminated by the purchaser at any time prior to the death of the beneficiary with a refund of the monies paid on the contract as prescribed by state law. (Chapter 7)

Revocation - the omission or cancellation of an instrument, act, license, or promise. (Chapter 11)

Rules and regulations - laws created by an administrative agency within its jurisdiction. (Chapter 2)

Secured claim - a debt which is supported by a pledge, mortgage, or lien on assets belonging to the debtor. (Chapters 3 and 12)

Services of Funeral Director and Staff - basic services, not to be included in prices of other categories on a General Price List, that are furnished by a funeral provider in arranging any funeral, such as conducting the arrangements conference, planning the funeral, obtaining necessary permits, and placing obituary notices [CFR 16 §453.1p]. (Chapter 16)

Solvent estate - an estate in which the assets exceed the liabilities. (Chapter 12)

Springing power of attorney - a written instrument authorizing one person to act as an agent for another effective only upon a certain event occurring. (Chapter 12)

Stare decisis - a policy of courts to stand by a decision and apply it to future cases where the facts are substantially the same. (Chapter 2)

Statement of Funeral Goods and Services Selected - an itemized list of goods and services that a consumer has selected during an arrangement conference that allows them to evaluate the selections and make any desired changes [FTC Guide, pg. 15]. (Chapter 17)

Statute - a law enacted by a legislative body. (Chapter 2)

Telephone price disclosures - a mandate in the FTC Funeral Rule that requires funeral establishments to provide consumers who inquire about prices or offerings any available information from required price lists [FTC Guide, pg. 17]. (Chapter 18)

Temporary container - a receptacle for cremated remains, usually made of cardboard, plastic, or similar materials designed to hold cremated remains until an urn, other permanent container is acquired, or other disposition is made. (Chapter 10)

Testate - the condition of leaving a will at death. (Chapter 11)

Testator - a person who makes a valid will. (Chapter 11)

Third party contracts - agreements which are incident to providing services and merchandise other than by the funeral establishment, e.g., caskets, vaults, urns, cremation services, etc. (Chapter 8)

Third party merchandise - funeral goods a consumer purchases from a source other than the funeral establishment with whom the consumer is making funeral arrangements [by Author]. (Chapter 18)

Tort - a private or civil wrong against a person or his or her property, other than by breach of contract, for which there may be action for damages. (Chapters 4, 5, 10 and 14)

Transfer (removal) of remains - The transportation of human remains from a place of death or other location from where the remains are released by legal authority [by Author]. (Chapter 16)

Trespasser - one who intentionally and without consent or privilege enters another's property. (Chapter 5)

Triggering event - the event (discussion) that occurs requiring a GPL be given to a consumer for retention. The triggering event for giving out the GPL is a face-to-face meeting to discuss funeral goods, services, and prices [CFR 16 §453.2(i)(B)]. (Chapter 16)

Trust account - account established by one individual to be held for the benefit of another (as a method of payment of funeral expenses); creates a fiduciary responsibility. Money paid to a funeral establishment for future services is placed in an account with the funeral establishment as trustee for the benefit of another. (Chapter 7)

Trustee - one who holds title to property or another position of trust to a beneficiary. (Chapter 7)

Tying arrangements - a condition that exists when a consumer is required to purchase funeral goods or funeral services they do not want, to be able to acquire or receive funeral goods or funeral services they do want [by Author]. (Chapter 18)

Uniform Anatomical Gift Act (UAGA) - a law permitting competent persons or others to give gifts of all or any part of the body, to take effect upon death. (Chapter 10)

Uniform Probate Code - a model law intended to achieve uniformity in probate proceedings throughout the U.S. (Chapter 12)

Unsecured claim - a claim which is not supported by a pledge, mortgage, or lien on other assets. (Chapters 3 and 12)

Urn - permanent container for cremated remains meant for decorative or inurnment purposes. (Chapter 10)

Viewing - (calling hours, visitation, visiting hours, wake) time set aside for friends and relatives to pay respect for the deceased prior to the funeral service. (Chapter 5)

Vital statistics - the registration, preparation, transcription, collection, compilation, and preservation of data pertaining to births, adoptions, deaths, stillbirths, marital status, etc. (Chapter 13)

Volunteer driver - those drivers not under the control of the funeral director. (Chapter 5)

Will - an instrument executed with required formality, by persons making disposition of their property to take effect upon their death. (Chapters 3 and 11)

Zoning ordinance - a law passed by a local unit of government which regulates and prescribes land use planning. (Chapters 5 and 9)

Sources Consulted

American Board of Funeral Service Education. "Federal Trade Commission." Curriculum outline as approved in 2012.

---, "Funeral Service Law." Curriculum outline as approved in April 2019.

Banton, Caroline. "Escrow." Investopedia, Dotdash Publishing, New York, NY, April 19, 2019; retrieved online September 2019.
URL: https://www.investopedia.com/terms/e/escrow.asp

BBC News. "Mississippi Man Found Alive in Body Bag at Funeral establishment." London, England, February 28, 2014; retrieved online June 2019.
URL: https://www.bbc.com/news/world-us-canada-26388426

Bio-Response Solutions. "Aquamation." Danville, IN, retrieved online June 2020.
URL: https://aquamationinfo.com/

Black's Law Dictionary. "Indemnify." The Law Dictionary, featuring Black's Law Dictionary Free Online Legal Dictionary 2nd Ed, retrieved online February 2020.
URL: https://thelawdictionary.org/indemnify/

Bromwich, Jonah Engel. "An Alternative to Burial and Cremation Gains Popularity." *The New York Times*, October 19, 2017; retrieved online August 2019.
URL: https://www.nytimes.com/2017/10/19/business/flameless-cremation.html

Burnham, Scott J. *Contract Law for Dummies*. John Wiley & Sons Inc., 2012.

Cleveland, Larry J. *Cremation in the United States: A Guide for Funeral Service Students*. Hudson Valley Funeral Services, 2021.

---, *Funeral Directing in the United States: A Guide for Funeral Service Students*. Hudson Valley Professional Services, 2019.

---, *Funeral Service Law in New York: A Guide for Funeral Service Students*. Hudson Valley Professional Services, 2021

---, *Funeral Service Marketing and Merchandise: A Guide for Practitioners and Mortuary Science Students*. Hudson Valley Professional Services, 2018.

---, *Funeral Service Rites and Customs: A Guide for Funeral Service Students*. Hudson Valley Professional Services, 2019.

Cremation Association of North America. "2019 Annual Statistics Report." Wheeling, Illinois; retrieved online September 2019.
URL: https://www.cremationassociation.org/page/IndustryStatistics

Crestone End of Life Project. "Informed Final Choices." Crestone, Colorado, October 2020.
URL: http://informedfinalchoices.org/crestone/

DeSmith, Kristy. "What Makes a Contract Invalid?" Law Depot, June 17, 2015; retrieved online August 2019.
URL: https://www.lawdepot.com/blog/what-makes-a-contract-invalid/

Gilligan, T. Scott and Thomas F.H. Stueve. *Mortuary Law, 10th ed.* The Cincinnati Foundation for Mortuary Education, 2003.

Habenstein, Robert Wesley, and William M. Lamers. *The History of American Funeral Directing, 9th ed.* National Funeral Directors Association, 2018.

Kirby, Brendan. "Funeral Director Arrested on 2 Counts of Abuse of Corpse Following Excavation of Graves." FOX10 News, a Meredith Corporations Station, Mobile, Alabama, June 26, 2019; retrieved online July 2019.
URL: https://www.fox10tv.com/news/funeral-director-arrested-on-counts-of-abuse-of-corpse-following/article_21b61256-9805-11e9-a193-1b4a2dabe46d.html

LegalMatch. "Difference Between Traditional and Military Will." South San Francisco, California, established 1999, article last modified June 6, 2018; retrieved online September 2019.
URL: https://www.legalmatch.com/law-library/article/military-will.html

Legal Dictionary by Farlex. "Reality of Consent." The Free Dictionary, Farlex, Inc., Huntingdon Valley, Pennsylvania, 2018; retrieved online August 2019.
URL: https://legal-dictionary.thefreedictionary.com/Reality+of+Consent

Legal Information Institute. "Contract." Cornell Law School; Cornell, New York; retrieved online September 2019.
URL: https://www.law.cornell.edu/wex/contract

---, "Testamentary Capacity." Cornell Law School; Cornell, New York; retrieved online August 2019.
URL: https://www.law.cornell.edu/wex/testamentary_capacity

---, "Tort." Cornell Law School; Cornell, New York; retrieved online August 2019.
URL: https://www.law.cornell.edu/wex/tort

National Conference of Commissioners on Uniform State Laws. "Anatomical Gift Act (2006)". Uniform Law Commission, Chicago, Illinois, 2017; retrieved online September 2019.
URL: http://www.uniformlaws.org/act.aspx?title=Anatomical%20Gift%20Act%20%282006%29

---, "Uniform Probate Code (2010)". Uniform Law Commission, Chicago, Illinois, 2017; retrieved online September 2019.
URL: https://www.uniformlaws.org/

National Funeral Directors Association. "2017 Consumer Awareness and Preferences Study." Brookfield, Illinois; press release dated June 22, 2017; retrieved online July 2018.
URL: http://www.nfda.org/news/media-center/nfda-news-releases/id/2419/nfda-consumer-survey-funeral-planning-not-apriority-for-americans

---, "Music and Webcasting Licenses." Brookfield, Illinois; retrieved online October 2019.
URL: http://www.nfda.org/resources/compliance-legal/music-and-webcasting-licenses

Nemeth, Peter F. "Legal Rights and Obligations to a Corpse." Notre Dame Law Review; Volume 19, Issue 1, 1943; retrieved online July 2019.
URL: http://scholarship.law.nd.edu/ndlr/vol19/iss1/6

Order of Christian Funerals. Appendix on Cremation Rites; Catholic Book Publishing Co, 1998.

Resomation. "Natural Water Cremation." Glasgow, Scotland, retrieved online June 2020.
URL: https://resomation.com/about/

Sisario, Ben and Steve Friess. "Aretha Franklin's Sons Debate Whether New Will Is Valid." The New York Times, New York, New York, May 24, 2019; retrieved online September 2019.
URL: https://www.nytimes.com/2019/05/24/arts/music/aretha-franklin-will.html

U.S. Centers for Disease Control and Prevention: National Center for Health Statistics. "Deaths and Mortality." U.S. Government, Washington, DC, 2019; retrieved online August 2019.
URL: https://www.cdc.gov/nchs/fastats/deaths.htm

U.S. Centers for Medicare & Medicaid Services. "Estate Recovery and Liens." U.S. Government, Baltimore, Maryland, 2019; retrieved online August 2019.
URL: https://www.medicaid.gov/medicaid/eligibility/estate-recovery/index.html

U.S. Department of Labor, Occupational Safety and Health Administration. "Chemical Hazard Communication, OSHA 3084." Washington, DC, 2004; retrieved online August 2019.
URL: https://www.osha.gov/Publications/osha3151.pdf

---, "Fact Sheet: Formaldehyde." Washington, DC, April 2011, retrieved online October 2020.
URL: https://www.osha.gov/OshDoc/data_General_Facts/formaldehyde-factsheet.pdf

---, "Hazard Communication Guidelines for Compliance, OSHA 3111." Washington, reprinted in 2000, retrieved online October 2020.
URL: https://www.osha.gov/Publications/osha3111.pdf

---, "Personal Protective Equipment, OSHA 3151." Washington, DC, 2004; retrieved online August 2019.
URL: https://www.osha.gov/Publications/osha3151.pdf

U.S. Department of Labor, Wage and Hour Division. "Handy Reference Guide to the Fair Labor Standards Act." Washington, DC, revised September 2016; retrieved online September 2019.
URL: https://www.dol.gov/whd/regs/compliance/hrg.htm#12

U.S. Environmental Protection Agency. "Burial at Sea." Washington, DC, 2019; retrieved online August 2019.
URL: https://www.epa.gov/ocean-dumping/burial-sea

U.S. Federal Trade Commission. "Buyer's Remorse: When the FTC's Cooling-Off Rule May Help." Washington, DC, August 2015; retrieved online August 2019
URL: https://www.ftc.gov/tips-advice/business-center/guidance/complying-funeral-rule

---, "Complying with the Funeral Rule." Washington, DC, April 2015; retrieved online August 2019
URL: https://www.ftc.gov/tips-advice/business-center/guidance/complying-funeral-rule

U.S. Navy Mortuary Affairs. "Burial at Sea Program." Washington, DC, May 27, 2015; retrieved online August 2019.
URL: https://www.navy.mil/navydata/nav_legacy.asp?id=204

West's Encyclopedia of American Law, 2nd ed. "Bailment." Thomas/Gale Publishers, Detroit, Michigan, Vol. 1, pg. 444, 2005.

---, "Corpse: Property and Possession Rights." Thomas/Gale Publishers, Detroit, Michigan, Vol. 3, pg. 227, 2005.

---, "Escheat." Thomas/Gale Publishers, Detroit, Michigan, Vol. 4, pg. 206, 2005.

---, "Holographic Will." Thomas/Gale Publishers, Detroit, Michigan, Vol. 5 pg. 276, 2005.

---, "Nuncupative Will." Thomas/Gale Publishers, Detroit, Michigan, Vol. 7, pg. 285, 2005.

---, "Operation of Law." Thomas/Gale Publishers, Detroit, Michigan, Vol. 7, pg. 320, 2005.

---, "Public Policy." Thomas/Gale Publishers, Detroit, Michigan, Vol. 8, pg. 173, 2005.

---, "Uniform Acts." Thomas/Gale Publishers, Detroit, Michigan, Vol. 10, pg. 154, 2005.

Index

Hudson Valley Professional Services
~ Educating the Funeral Service Industry ~